RELIGION, REVOLUTION AND THE
RUSSIAN INTELLIGENTSIA, 1900-1912

Religion, Revolution and the Russian Intelligentsia 1900–1912

The *Vekhi* Debate and its Intellectual Background

Christopher Read
Lecturer in History
University of Warwick

BOOKS
10 East 53d St., New York 10022
(a division of Harper & Row Publishers, Inc.)

First published 1979 by
THE MACMILLAN PRESS LTD
London and Basingstoke

Published in the U.S.A. 1980 by
HARPER & ROW PUBLISHERS, INC.
BARNES & NOBLE IMPORT DIVISION

Library of Congress Cataloging in Publication Data

Read, Christopher, 1946–
 Religion, revolution, and the Russian intelligentsia, 1900–1912.

 Includes index.
  1. Russia—Religion. 2. Russia—Intellectual life—1801–1917. 3. Revolutionists—Russia.
4. Vekhi. I. Title.
BL980.R8R4   947.08   79-13453′
ISBN 0-06-495822-1

Printed in Great Britain

TO MY MOTHER AND FATHER

Contents

Acknowledgements

I would like to record my thanks to some of the many people who gave me advice, encouragement, support and assistance at vital stages in my work. I am indebted to Professor D. Nicholl and Professor E. Lampert who diverted my initial enthusiasm for Russian studies into realistic channels; to Professor A. Nove, Mr J. D. White and Mr M. Dewhirst for invaluable assistance in the early stages; to Professor L. Schapiro and Dr N. Andreev for generous help, encouragement and criticism as my work took on a fuller shape, and to the personnel of the exchanges branch of the British Council, without whose assistance the accumulation of material for this book would have been impossible. I would also like to thank Ms Annabel Yarrow for turning my hieroglyphics into a high-quality typescript, and Mrs Y. Slater who typed the final version. Even such excellent help will not have been enough to eliminate all the mistakes arising from my own fallibility, and, of course, I assume full responsibility for all errors of fact and of judgement in the pages which follow.

Christopher Read
Warwick
December 1978

Introduction

Of the major European powers only Russia had an 'intelligentsia question'. Elsewhere, wrote the literary critic and historian of the intelligentsia D. Ovsyaniko-Kulikovsky in 1908 there was discussion of science, politics, philosophy and art; in Russia there was only discussion of the nature of the intelligentsia.[1] The purpose of this study is to examine the parameters of this discussion in one of its last and most intense phases, that which occurred at the time of the attempted revolution of 1905. In view of the unfamiliarity of, first, the concept of an 'intelligentsia' as it was understood in Russia and, second, the context of this last outburst of the debate, it is necessary to make a few preliminary remarks, though this in itself is difficult in that the answers to the preliminary questions about the intelligentsia are the stuff of the debate itself and to give a full answer would pre-empt all that follows.

The complex questions of pinpointing the origin and defining the essential characteristics of the intelligentsia have never been answered to everyone's satisfaction. There are almost as many solutions as there are discussants of the question. However, certain elements are fundamental to any definition. The first of these is that all *intelligenty* possessed a deep concern for the social question and some degree of identification with the poor and oppressed of Russia. Since it would be wrong to assume that only liberals and radicals felt this way – Tsar Nicholas II, for example, often expressed in his letters a sympathy for and a naive belief in the innate benevolence of the peasantry – this criterion has to be modified by a second. The *intelligent* invariably had a critical and, to some extent, hostile attitude towards the government and in particular to its handling of the social question. The degree of hostility could vary from mild to violent and the opposition could be partial or total, but a feeling that the political and social structure as it then existed was fundamentally unjust and indefensible was shared by all *intelligenty*. In order to differentiate intelligentsia opposition from other more spontaneous outbursts which were occurring regularly in villages

I

and cities, it is necessary to add a third criterion: self-consciousness or articulation of the feeling of hostility. In most cases this quality pre-supposed an advanced formal education but this in itself was not essential. Many commentators emphasised that an unlettered peasant could be an *intelligent* if he possessed a reflective turn of mind and was able to express himself verbally. The best known examples of this type are various peasants whom Tolstoy knew and communicated with who became models for his philosopher-peasant Platon Karataev in *War and Peace*. Thus one cannot assume that all *intelligenty* were university graduates or former students any more than one can use the opposite definition, that all graduates were *intelligenty*. This last sociological definition has been taken up in the Soviet Union but was not in the minds of any *intelligent* in the late nineteenth century. It is essentially a western European Marxist definition of the class of mental labourers and was imported into Russia in the early twentieth century. Since the revolution this definition has become the only one used in Soviet discussions and the earlier sense of the word has been officially obliterated.

In essence, these criteria give a picture which the Russian intelligentsia liked to have of itself as the voice of the inchoate, oppressed masses. It will be noted that even the most rigorous critics of the intelligentsia from within its own ranks did not question this role, but argued that the intelligentsia as it was then constituted was incapable of fulfilling it. Thus, to all *intelligenty*, this self-ascribed role was the decisive element, though it could be fulfilled in very different ways. One can find, to a greater or lesser degree, signs of the role in the works of individuals as diverse as Radishchev, Turgenev, Dostoevsky and Lenin, not all of whom would have felt comfortable being called *intelligenty*. For this reason, even a definition that an *intelligent* was someone who considered himself to be an *intelligent* has its limitations. For instance, Lenin is by all objective criteria a good example of one particular strand of the intelligentsia, but no one was more contemptuous than he of the intelligentsia as a whole.

No simple formula has proved acceptable as a general definition of the Russian intelligentsia. Lavrov's 'critically thinking people' is loose enough to include, without too much strain, some of the relatively enlightened government ministers such as Witte and even the arch-reactionary Pobedonostsev was nothing if not a critically thinking person, even though the object of his criticism was democracy. The later populist definition of the intelligentsia as the mind, honour and conscience of the people is perhaps the closest, though as an unqualified statement it is unduly presumptuous as well as being vague. What is clear, however, is that an *intelligent* was primarily concerned with creating and testing values and ideas with particular reference to the material and spiritual (or intellectual) liberation of the population from the yoke imposed on it by the wealthy and the powerful.

It would be a very poor society which completely lacked individuals having such moral and ethical impulses. Russian history certainly provides examples of this type from the time of the Middle Ages. One historian of the intelligentsia, Ivanov-Razumnik, considered Prince Kurbsky, Ivan the Terrible and Peter the Great, among others, to be isolated *intelligenty*.[2] However, one could not, he said, talk about the existence of an intelligentsia class. No one has been more successful in pinpointing the precise origin of the intelligentsia than they have been in giving it a succinct definition. It is fairly common to recognise the late eighteenth century writers Radishchev and Novikov as forerunners of the intelligentsia. By the second quarter of the nineteenth century these isolated voices had, at least in the major cities, coalesced into small discussion groups self-consciously modelled on the French salons of the *Ancien Regime*. These groups, known as *kruzhki* (circles) had become well established by the mid-1840s and the undoubtedly pre-eminent performer at them was Vissarion Belinsky (1810–48). One can perhaps get the feel of the intellectual intensity of Belinsky from the reminiscences of another participant, the novelist Turgenev. On one occasion Turgenev was in animated discussion with Belinsky when his energy began to wane and his thoughts turned away from philosophy to more mundane matters. Belinsky reproached Turgenev bitterly. 'We haven't decided the question of the existence of God yet and you want to eat!'[3]

Despite this, it was only in the third quarter of the century that the number of *intelligenty* had extended sufficiently for it to be considered as a class. Conventionally the word itself came into use at this time through the novelist Boborykin[4] though it may have had connotations of white-collar workers as well as of the opposition intellectual.

From that time onwards the word came to be used more and more to mean the politically conscious opposition to the government and indeed this opposition became more widespread. Its development is intimately connected with the fundamental problem of modernisation faced by Russia after the trauma of the Crimean war had brought home the extent to which she had fallen behind the European powers. A half-century of stagnation had allowed her rivals to build up a lead in military strength, based on their industrial power. In response, the Russian autocracy embarked on a series of reforms designed, among other things, to make Russia a more powerful state by strengthening the morale of its citizens, its strategic communications, the efficiency of its bureaucracy and increasing its natural wealth. At the same time as the state was to be strengthened by these changes, the autocracy should also preserve its political position and retain full authority in its own hands. As a result of this the government was caught in a complex trap. The jaws of the trap were that many of the measures designed to strengthen the state through making it more up to date were in themselves potentially harmful to the state. The need for a higher level of culture and education, for purposes of improving the bureaucratic, managerial and professional skills of the country, without which modernisation was impossible, is a particularly good example, because the expansion of higher education produced, in addition to a class of skilled mental labourers, a group of articulate critics of the regime, the intelligentsia, which provided the backbone of all the opposition, liberal and radical, which the government had to face. Had it been decided, as was almost the case in Alexander II's reign, to widen participation in the political life of the country through a restricted constitution, then pressure from the educated opposition might have been dissipated. As it was, however, the creaking mechanism of the traditional political structure, from 1881 increasingly dependent on the police and the army, contrasted ill with the attempt to reorganise the economic and social structure of Imperial Russia.

In this atmosphere of attempted transformation and ensuing tension the intelligentsia grew to maturity, ceasing to be a scattering of individuals and becoming a recognisable, distinct social group. It would, however, be wrong to equate the intelligentsia with the revolutionaries. There has been a tendency to do this because the revolutionaries were, almost without exception, members of the intelligentsia and, by their nature, are much easier to define. This overlooks the fact that many who shared the revolutionaries' antipathy to the *status quo* were equally opposed to the revolutionaries' prescriptions for solving the visible shortcomings. The intelligentsia of all types, as was said above, united around the demand for greater social justice but split over tactics to achieve it. Three main divisions existed – non-revolutionaries, violent revolutionaries and non-violent (or reluctantly violent) revolutionaries – each of which could be broken down into further subdivisions.

The roots of the divisions lay in the fundamental dilemma facing the intelligentsia. Having analysed the shortcomings of the political, social and economic system, how were they, a tiny minority, a fraction of one per cent of the population, ruthlessly excluded from political power, to effect the changes they believed necessary? The development of the intelligentsia from 1860–1914 was largely determined by its successes and failures in trying to solve this dilemma. By 1900 three distinct groups had matured to the extent of crystallising into Russia's first recognisable political parties. The oldest of the three was made up of those who believed that the Russian peasant was a potential revolutionary, an idea based first on the history of frequent, scattered and unsuccessful peasant disturbances which had occurred throughout modern Russian history, and secondly on the belief that the communal landholding pattern of the Russian village could form an adequate foundation for the future socialist society. Those who belonged to this current of thought, known as populists, had been divided, since at least the mid-1870s, into those who believed that education and propaganda among the peasantry would raise their political awareness sufficiently for them to carry out the hoped for transformation of society and others who believed that the militant example of the terrorist onslaught on the functionaries of the state was an essential additional element. Despite energetic application of both these theories for more than a quarter of a century, neither seemed to have made much impact on the peasantry themselves by 1901 when the Party of Socialist Revolutionaries, comprising an uneasy alliance between both points of view, was founded.

It had been preceded in 1898 by other socialist intellectuals who had come to doubt that there was any revolutionary potential in the peasantry at all. They placed their hopes on the small, but militant and expanding, industrial working-class. This party, the Russian Social Democratic Labour Party, despite being firmly grounded in the theories of Marx, was also divided, particularly after 1903, over critical issues such as the attitude which the party should have towards the liberal democrats. These differences were exploited by a young activist, Vladimir Lenin, who built up a personal faction within the party and eventually split the party irrevocably. As will be seen below, philosophy was one of the battlefields in this war.

A third grouping of intellectuals, roughly corresponding to the middle-class liberals and radicals of England and France, to whom they looked for inspiration and assistance, formed, in 1903, the Liberation group which was, in its turn, the nucleus of the Constitutional Democratic (Kadet) Party in 1905. As their name implies, the desire for a democracy, by which they meant a parliamentary, constitutional form of government, was their unifying strand. By and large, they were the descendants of those critics of tsarism who believed that a combination of continuing reforms and constant use of such institutions as already existed, such as the local councils (*zemstva*) could provide enough impetus to overcome Russia's backwardness and improve the condition of the poorer sections of society.

Despite their differences these groups shared at least two features – they were all led by intellectuals and they were all influenced by Western ideas, though only to a very limited extent in the case of the populists. There was, in addition, a completely distinct group of conservative intellectuals who looked back to the Slavophiles. They thought that Russia was a unique entity which had nothing to learn from industrial Europe which was rent by political factions, strikes, revolution and urban misery resulting from, as the Slavophiles saw it, the loosening of traditional forms of government, the removal of the restraints of established religion and the desertion of the village and the land in favour of the city and the factory. As a result, the moral soundness of these countries declined as their wealth increased. These conservatives fall outside our definition of the intelligentsia primarily because their solution to Russia's problems, the return to a hierarchical golden age in the past, was not a reflection of the real ambitions of the peasants, whom they claimed to understand, but the projection of historical fantasies upon them. Even so, certain elements of their ideas could be found in unexpected quarters, particularly the religious concept of *sobornost'* which will be discussed frequently in the following chapters.

The exact size of the intelligentsia cannot be calculated with any accuracy. The 1897 census gives the total number of professional people including senior state administrators, teaching, the arts, medicine, law and engineering as about 325,000 rising to three-quarters of a million if dependants are included.[5] A Soviet scholar has calculated that in 1900 there were 85,000 people in Russia with higher education qualifications and that the total number of university graduates in the period 1859–1900 was about 60,000.[6] However, the intelligentsia proper is only a fraction of these figures. Circulation figures for the major journals would give some indication of the proportion who had an interest in politics and ideas but such figures as are available are unsystematic. Soviet sources usually only quote the circulation figures of journals which supported Lenin and even then only the peak figures achieved. These might reach 13,000 to 15,000 in the case of the Social-Democratic journal *Mir Bozhii* in the period before 1905 but since no subsequent figures are given in Soviet sources one can only assume that its circulation fell dramatically after 1905.[7] Purely artistic journals had a smaller readership. *Zolotoe runo*, for instance, had 934 subscribers in 1906 and *Vesy* 845 in the same year.[8] The central book of the period, *Vekhi*, which seems to have been read by every *intelligent*, was published in several editions, the total number of copies reaching 23,000 in about a year.[9] As a rough estimate it seems likely that the intelligentsia comprised no more than 50,000 people. Certainly, this would be the right order of magnitude. This represents a minute proportion of Russia's population. Its influence, like that of other minorities, such as Grand Dukes, army officers and officials, cannot be gauged purely from numbers. Their influence in opposition parties was paramount and after the February revolution of 1917 they emerged as the political leaders of Russia. After October, they provided a hardcore of activists who helped Lenin to retain power. But by the 1930s the intelligentsia tradition was in cold storage. The fascinating story of its apparent triumph and demise is not the subject of this study, though the final chapter indicates that in recent years in Russia there has been an attempt to pick up the threads of the intellectual tradition of the immediate pre-revolutionary period, so that it can be seen that the influence of the period has not been entirely lost. The divisions within the intelligentsia which came out into the open in these later years were inherent in the period discussed in this study, which was thus an important one in shaping the intellectual future of the country. In the event, within Russia one section of the intelligentsia throttled the others, but the great products of the intelligentsia in this period – Stravinsky, Scriabin, Chagall, Kandinsky, the Russian Ballet, Blok and Mayakovsky – have enriched the culture of the world. Indeed, for the first time, Russian culture was reaching parity with western

Europe in the sense that it was contributing as well as receiving. In a sense, the dispute over Russia and Europe was becoming less relevant. Russia was being firmly integrated into European politics, international relations, financial system and culture.

The object of this study is to produce a plan of Russia's intellectual framework in the early twentieth century. Themes rather than personalities are under discussion and attention will be paid more to relating the ideas of a particular individual to the other ideas of the period than to the works of that person as a whole. In following this guideline the major themes of religion and revolution have been chosen as the basis of the study because these were the two great poles around which the debates of the period revolved. In Western thought these themes might be said to belong to different spheres, the abstract and the practical, but in Russia pure thought had not been as divorced from real life as had been the case elsewhere. Thought in Russia was still close to what had long been called 'the cursed questions' of love, death, God and immortality rather than to abstract concepts and logical reasoning. Philosophy, psychology and theology remained much less distinct than in western Europe. In this way Russian thought remained much closer to life, and, like existentialism which shared this characteristic, found its expression in literature, literary criticism and political, social and economic analyses rather than in philosophical treatises. In this atmosphere religion and revolution shared certain characteristics. They were both complete systems giving meaning to life and defining goals and actions for the individual. For some thinkers the two became fused in that religion might be thought to be revolutionary or revolution might be a kind of religion. How, then, can they be defined?

In a sense both terms are used here only as shorthand for a more complex mixture of ideas. The two great philosophical axes at the heart of the debates were collectivism and individualism, idealism and materialism. A religious thinker was one who based his outlook on individualism and idealism, while at the other end of the scale the revolutionary was a collectivist and materialist. All combinations of these categories existed, such as the individualist materialists among the anarchists, or collectivist idealists like the God-builders who will be discussed below. In addition there were political axes, reform or revolution and acceptance or rejection of the intelligentsia tradition. There was a similar variety of combinations in this sphere too. The most common opinion was one in favour of both the revolution and the intelligentsia tradition, while the liberal intelligentsia opposed both. Again there were anomalous non-conforming groups, for instance, supporters of the intelligentsia who had come to oppose revolution and even a small group of ardent revolutionaries who attacked the intelligentsia for using the revolutionary ideal as a cover for its own material interests. Each of these positions will be examined in turn, though a disproportionate amount of attention will be paid to smaller, less well-known groups (sometimes composed of only a handful of people like the so-called mystical anarchists) which cut across these axes than to the larger, better known groups which cluster at each end. The first half of the study is devoted to more theoretical, philosophical issues, while the second half is devoted to more practical questions of political thought. The groupings which emerge in the first part do not exactly coincide with those of the second. Nor are the dividing lines between groups clear and precise, and a certain amount of repetition and overlap cannot be avoided in describing them.

It should also be added that attention is restricted to 'intelligentsia' thought, which means the exclusion of important areas – academic philosophy and the Orthodox seminaries – with the result that this is by no means an attempt at a comprehensive history of Russian thought in this period.

The overwhelming impression created by this period is one of variety, even of confusion. The vital question for the intelligentsia of what had gone wrong in 1905, why the attempted revolution had failed, had to be answered. Vehement disagreements about answers, even about the terms of the debate, came rushing to the surface. The whole period was dominated by this spirit of enquiry, of a search for solutions. The common thread running through the diversities of the period was the belief that a creative leap was being made. For the advocates of new ideas, even people as diverse as Rozanov and Bogdanov, this was an exciting prospect. For the guardians of the old dogmatic orthodoxies of Right and Left, of autocracy and positivist socialism, it was a cause for alarm. The new younger generation of innovators thought of themselves as the real revolutionaries and they dismissed the old style revolutionaries as the autocracy turned inside out. Struve, amongst others, wrote about 'the conservatism of intelligentsia thought'. True, these new movements were fragile but they have proved tenacious. The questions posed remain valid, replies are still being published by the Soviet press. Lenin's views on *Vekhi* have been enshrined as the basis of official Soviet responses to many forms of modern and abstract art and as a warning against the seductions of 'bourgeois' ideology. This is the only period in which Russia has achieved such wide-ranging intellectual pluralism. The divisions revealed remained long after. In a letter to his former patroness Zinaida Gippius, the poet Aleksandr Blok said that the split between them over poetry, aesthetics and politics had originated in 1905 not in 1917.[10] This remark could be applied to the intelligentsia as a whole.

Part I

The Intelligentsia and Religion

1 Religious belief among the intelligentsia

If the Russian intelligentsia after 1860 had a unifying factor, it was probably militant atheism. This common idea was shaken in the minds of some of its holders after the 'going to the people' of the 1870s when members of the intelligentsia were converted to religious belief by the example of the peasantry.[1] A similar process occurred in the development of the hero of the intelligentsia, Tolstoy, who was converted to peasant simplicity. His example was followed by numerous disciples from the intelligentsia who formed a kind of sect based on Tolstoy's outlook. But despite these cracks in the monolith of militant atheism, the effects were not far-reaching and were fully accepted by only a small part of the intelligentsia. The major impulse to religious and philosophical values came from quite another direction and it is this which will be the object of attention in this chapter.

It should be made clear from the outset that these religious thinkers cannot be classified together as a school even in the loosest possible sense of the term. Most historians of the period tend to bracket the various phenomena they describe under the general heading of 'the new religious consciousness'. If one has to talk in terms of schools, then there were actually two separate ones existing at this time. On the one hand there were the people whose means of expression was through scholarly articles and on the other the creative writers. Among the former there were the Trubetskoi brothers, Struve, Frank, Askol'dov and other people who contributed in 1903 to *Problemy idealizma*. At the head of the second group there were Merezhkovsky, Filosofov, Gippius, Rozanov and Belyi. The difference between these two groups was substantial and went further than simply a difference in modes of expression. For example, Struve's outlook had very little in common with that of Merezhkovsky, who was one of the more moderate members of 'the new religious consciousness' and nothing at all with the extremists of that movement such as Vyacheslav Ivanov, Chulkov and Gorodetsky.

Two things have obscured these differences. The more important one was a very significant indebtedness on the part of both groups to Vladimir Solov'ev, but even this was not as significant as might have been expected. The Solov'ev admired by the philosophers was not the same one as the Solov'ev admired by the poets. The latter were attracted above all by his mystical side, the visions of Sophia, the final apocalyptic and prophetic writings. The former were impressed less by his literary work than by his more strictly philosophical writing.[2] These two influences were not mutually exclusive but in the hands of the disciples the forms they took would hardly lead one to suspect a common source. The second confusing factor has been the prominence in the picture of Berdyaev and Bulgakov, through whose eyes several of the historians have looked at this period. This would not, in itself, be of any great significance were it not for the fact that Berdyaev and Bulgakov were anomalies who themselves stood in a median position between these two groups so that their views do not show the divisions but in fact obliterate them. They did not fit into either of the two 'schools' which existed and were very much on the borderline to the extent that they will not be treated in detail in this section at all, but will be considered in the third chapter where they can be seen in the context of yet another 'religious' group, the God-builders.

The people dealt with in this chapter have in common the fact that they are idealist and individualist in one way or another. The only general title which might cover *all* the thinkers in this chapter would be 'God-seekers' but this term is almost devoid of specific meaning and it is possible to substitute the word 'religious' without loss. The disadvantage of calling them 'God-seekers' is that it tends to hide the divisions which existed between the various thinkers and possibly leads to the mistake made by other historians, who see a unified movement. In the very broadest sense perhaps they do form a movement but this would not help one to understand the period any more than calling the whole intelligentsia a 'social reform movement' helps one to understand the various branches of that movement. This chapter is intended to show that there was a variety of approaches to the problem of religion.

PHILOSOPHICAL LIBERALISM

It is very fortunate that, in this area, there is a natural starting point from which to begin an exploration. Struve's introduction to Berdyaev's first book *Sub"ektivizm i individualizm*, written in 1901, and the collection of essays under the title *Problemy idealizma* published in 1902, were the final signs of the maturity of an idealist school in Russian thought of this period. The ideas on which this school was based were continued in *Vekhi* in 1909, *Iz glubiny* in 1918 and into the emigration, and exist even today among those still in Russia who reject the official Marxist-Leninist ideology.

This last fact is hardly surprising since one of the most important impulses in the movement was revulsion from Marxism and Bolshevism in its nascent form, and the idealists were at their most united when criticising the Marxist world view. A list of people who had been attracted by Marxism in their early years but who had rejected it would include such apparently thorough-going idealists as Solov'ev himself and Sergei Trubetskoi. Others whose Marxism was more enduring and even left noticeable, significant traces in their outlook throughout their lives, included Struve, Berdyaev, Bulgakov and Izgoev. There can be no doubt that the impulse to move from Marxism to idealism was a strong one in the minds of almost all the 'philosophical liberals'. In fact, in several cases, such as Berdyaev and even Struve, it was partly through study of Marx that idealism was reached. But it would be a distortion of the truth to look at idealism simply as a reaction against prevailing positivist and socialist ways of thought. It was rather that the idealists found positivism and nihilism utterly inimical to their own view of man and were distressed above all at the vulgar and philistine presuppositions often associated with it.[3]

The basis of the outlook of the idealists was the defence of the individual as the sole source of creativity, as the originator and preserver of all that was valuable in civilisation. This came out clearly in *Problemy idealizma (Problems of Idealism)*. In the preface Novgorodtsev pointed out that the idealist movement was above all a search for a new morality of which the cornerstone was to be the principle of 'the unconditional significance of the individual'.[4] Askol'dov took up the theme. For him the task of philosophy was the opening up of new goals and the suggestion of ways to reach these goals, the presentation of choice to people. 'At the basis of all these alternatives will be the concept of individuality' which had to be understood in the context of the requirements needed for its spiritual development.[5] This remained a constant feature of idealist thought.

For all the idealists the importance of individualism and its necessary connection with idealism arose from the fact that only the individual could be the creator, conveyor and evaluator of the ideas and ideals in which they believed. In a remarkable essay Prince Sergei Trubetskoi (1862–1905) established the relativity of all philosophies and the abiding value only of the *sum* of competing schools rather than of any one alone. For him the fullness of truth was beyond the scope of any one philosophical system, only the ideal of truth, as the objective of all philosophical activity, was valid.[6] He demolished the idea of philosophy, however defined, as an aspiration, 'an integral conception of the world'. No philosophical teaching could provide this: 'in each philosophical teaching we find only a particular human conception of the world, bearing the imprint of its time, of that environment in which it arose, of that individual genius who worked it out; and this human representation stands in the place of integral, whole (*vseedinyi*) truth.'[7] Consequently, it should be remembered, he continued later, that philosophy in the exact sense of the word, was not 'wisdom' that is an ideal, perfect authority, but only 'love of wisdom'.[8] Philosophical development, therefore, was not a dialectical process of contending systems as Hegel said but of 'the concrete reason of man, in the totality of its cognitive function and of the creative activity of separate individual minds'.[9]

The connection between idealism and religion was seen by these thinkers to be as necessary as that between idealism and individualism. The fullness of the idea was attainable not in the completely relative condition of human existence but only in the absolute. 'We seek absolute commandments and principles' proclaimed Novgorodtsev in the introduction to *Problemy idealizma*, 'in this consists the essence of the moral quest – but the reply given to us is that everything in the world is relative, everything is conditional.'[10] For Askol'dov the connection was best made by Kant who provided the highest example of moral duty deriving its right to existence from free will, the existence of God and the immortality of the soul.[11] 'The organic link between ethics and metaphysics must be recognised as unconditionally necessary.'[12] It was for his establishment of this link that Kant was esteemed by almost all of the religious philosophers of this time.

Thus ethical, religious individualism, in one form or another, was at the core of the thought of the idealists. These principles brought them into a head-on collision with the prevailing intellectual atmosphere of the time, and they did not shirk the challenge. The earliest works of the idealists at this time were devoted to refuting the intelligentsia's intellectual mentors, of whom Marx, Comte and Mikhailovsky were the first targets. To some extent this was an expression of the struggle within the minds of certain of the leading idealists, in particular Struve, Berdyaev and Bulgakov, who were still in the process of shaking off the Marxist outlook and naturally tended to define their new position in relation to their old one. Struve protected the idealists from the charge of being largely negative in their views by pointing out in his introduction to Berdyaev's first book, which was concerned to refute Mikhailovsky, that Marxism itself grew out of opposition to idealist philosophy in general and that of Hegel in particular.[13] Although they found their natural enemies in each other, one cannot accuse materialism and idealism of each being negative in relation to the other: symbiosis is perhaps a more accurate way of explaining their interrelationship. Novgorodtsev was aware of this in his assessment of idealism in Russia in 1902.

> Setting out from a critical attitude to the recent history of our thought, this is connected with the reign of positivism, they [the idealists] look to the future in expectation of new perspectives not included in the programme of 'positive philosophy'. Their point of departure is the opinion that the contemporary critical movement calls not only for the affirmation of science on durable and truly positive foundations, but also for the defence of the necessary miscellaneous requirements and tasks of the human spirit, for which science is only one of the spheres of manifestation.[14]

The assault on positivism was at the heart of the idealist movement. Their conception of individualism did not allow them to accept the fundamental assertions of positivism as they appeared in the writings of Mikhailovsky, other positivists and the Marxists. The notions that societies were governed by scientific laws analogous to those governing physical objects, and that social phenomena, including ideas, were determined (*zakonomernyi*) in the strictest possible sense, were completely opposed to the views of the idealists and they set out to attack them at the foundations. 'There can be no sharper antithesis than that between Marx and Kant and idealist philosophy in general', wrote Struve in 1900.[15] From many angles and at many points the idealists set to work to demolish the totempole of positivism around which most of the intelligentsia had gathered.

A young, as yet little known writer, who had himself been an active 'legal Marxist' opened up the attack on positivism with characteristic audacity by aiming straight at the leading theorist of the intelligentsia. In this struggle Berdyaev was David to Mikhailovsky's Goliath. As a former social democrat Berdyaev (1874–1948) would in any case have been critical of Mikhailovsky's view of Marx but this volume went far beyond criticism of the populist version of Marxism and was an attack on the fundamentals of Marxist materialism itself. As yet the contradiction between the views of Berdyaev and Struve and Marxism was not fully realised. 'Berdyaev's book makes an important step towards the critical reconstruction of Marxism on idealist foundations' wrote Struve.[16] At this stage the influence of Marx was still strong.

The main object of Berdyaev's attack was Mikhailovsky's so-called 'subjective method' in sociology which Berdyaev summarised on the first page as 'Russian utopianism' because the basic problem of subjectivism was not solved by Mikhailovsky. The difficulty lay in the conflict between 'logical criteria', that is, those which were valid for all people in all circumstances, and 'psychological criteria', that is, the idiosyncratic element in perception. Mikhailovsky reached objectivism by suggesting that in the event of a conflict between the former and the latter, the former should be regarded as correct. For Berdyaev this was a 'theoretical illusion' and a 'fig leaf' covering 'the lowest sort of subjectivism'.[17] Berdyaev could not accept that objective perception was possible, at least in relation to social conflict and social science in general which was very close to life and was therefore more liable to subjective influences than the natural sciences.[18] In his words, every person came to his investigation 'not only with logical norms, the same for all, but with the whole content of his psychic life, historically formed under the influence of various conditions of life, of different experiences, which strongly distinguish people from one another'.[19] That every enquiry and every perception should be made up of logical presuppositions which were objective plus psychological ones which gave the former a subjective colouring was, he said, 'a completely unavoidable and insuperable fact'.[20] In this way Berdyaev proclaimed the impossibility not only of Mikhailovsky's position, but that of positivism in general. Social laws, claiming total objectivity could not exist in the same way that physical laws existed because in human affairs, no matter how hard one tried, the individual element could not be eliminated.

Berdyaev underlined his differences in other spheres particularly in relation to the concept of progress and its relationship to truth. Like Sergei Trubetskoi, Berdyaev followed Solov'ev's view that the objective of intellectual progress was the attainment of absolute truth, which was a gradual process in which each step represented a slight gain over the previous one. Truth was not, therefore, the monopoly of any one class, the Marxists said, but was universal and equally binding on all. 'Thus we may view intellectual development as a gradual approach to objective absolute truth by the path of elimination of subjectivism.'[21] Berdyaev saw the same process at work in the sphere of morals.

> Absolute morality stands at the end of progress as the goal which is eternally being realised (*osushchestvlyayushchyasa*). . . . Every historical epoch creates in its progressive class a paradigm of morality higher than that of the preceding one.[22]

Berdyaev's final word, distinguishing his position from that of positivists and evolutionists in general, was that social processes occurred in the mind and were not mechanical.[23]

Implicit in much of Berdyaev's work, but not actually dealt with by him at this time, was the question of the relationship between the mind and the environment. Did the latter determine the former? This question was central to the idealist interpretation of life and their affirmation of the responsibility of the individual for his actions and of the significance of the human individual. The most extreme deterministic view was not widespread in Russia at any time, and had been attacked by Marx and by Marxists wherever it had appeared. But even so the crucial point remained. Did matter have priority over mind or mind over matter? The idealist point of view was that mind had an independent existence and was more important than the environment in which it existed. The materialists, on the other hand, set out to prove that matter preceded consciousness. The topic became important at this time largely through idealist criticism of Marx's view on this question, and the apparent contradiction between Marxism and liberty. One of the first idealists to pose these problems was Evgenii Trubetskoi (1863–1920) and it is to his article 'Towards a characterisation of the teaching of Marx and Engels on the significance of ideas in history', published in *Problemy idealizma*, that we now turn.

One of the most surprising and perhaps even one of the most significant aspects of the article was that Trubetskoi's ideas on Marx were couched in almost revisionist, rather than outright condemnatory, terms. He was appreciative of the contribution to the development of thought made by Marx and Engels, but at the same time he pointed out deficiencies in their theories. He began by quoting Kautsky with approval. Marx's theory of historical materialism was not, said Kautsky and Trubetskoi, fully worked out by him but was left inconclusive at many points. One of these points was Marx's statement that 'consciousness does not determine being but being determines consciousness'.[24] The main point of the problem was left unsolved. 'Are we,' asked Trubetskoi, 'to understand economic factors as the *producing cause* of ideas or only as the *necessary condition* for their growth?' He developed this in a metaphor. Did Marx see economic factors as the soil in which ideas grew? If so it could be said that it was not only the soil which was the producing cause of growth but also the seed must be taken into account and it was within the seed that the ultimate cause of growth was to be found.[25] This metaphor illustrated the balance which Trubetskoi maintained in considering the views of Marx and Engels. For him their ideas were correct – up to a point. Economic factors, he continued, did play a primary role in social revolutions, and people did prefer legal and political principles which corresponded most closely with their own interests, but this did not justify Marx and Engels in their claim that these were the *only* causes.[26] Similarly, on the question of base and superstructure, said Trubetskoi, Marx was not giving a philosophical definition of their interrelationship but simply a comparison with architecture. Trubetskoi continued Marx's comparison: 'In architecture it is not the foundations which define the structure which will be erected upon it.' It was equally true to say that the shape of the superstructure determined the foundations, and one had to search elsewhere for the ultimate explanation of the shape of the building.[27] Trubetskoi followed up his comments with a lengthy examination of the specific question of the origin and development of legal ideas, and found the Marxist explanation of them totally inadequate because legal ideas – utopian and scientific, false and true – all equally resulted from complex mental processes not dependent on specific economic interest. His conclusion was that the human mind, whether its findings were progressive or obscurantist, was 'one of the primary driving forces of history', an independent factor free of economic or other causation.[28]

For Sergei Bulgakov too the confines of orthodox Marxism had proved too constricting and he proceeded to a view of the world based on the freedom of the individual rather than on his limitations. 'For men, man must be an absolute value'.[29] He saw liberty as the necessary prerequisite for a just social ideal. 'The building (*zdanie*) of social politics is based on two foundations – on the economic and the social ideal, and on the pediment of this building is inscribed one word, expressing the whole content of both these ideals and, consequently, the whole task of social politics: this magic word is freedom.'[30] The uniqueness of the individual was matched by the uniqueness of events. 'History does not repeat itself',[31] he said, and with these words launched another salvo at determinism. Idealism, in Bulgakov's hands, could even penetrate the inner sanctum of Marxism – political economy. 'The very subject of political economy is not defined objectively but by the subject's own values and need of freedom rather than knowledge.'[32]

Such were the major arguments used by the liberal thinkers to define their specific conceptions of idealism and of religion as the guarantor and culmination of the value of the individual. Their position was not an original one in Russian thought, nor was it even the only idealist view. In most cases liberal idealism was indissolubly linked with religion and it was on this point that Berdyaev and Bulgakov broke with the liberals of the Kadet party which was, they said, 'atheist'. Indeed, Milyukov, Kizevetter and many of the thinkers of the Kadets, with the exception of Struve, would be better described as 'liberal materialists', although for the most part it is hard to discern any consistent philosophical outlook on the part of most of these men who in general confined their attention to the routine of everyday political and economic activity and, like the businessmen that many of them were, looked askance at any metaphysical explanation whatsoever. But Milyukov was certainly much closer to the revolutionary tradition, to militant atheism and to positivism than any of the people who have been mentioned so far.

However, the people considered above were not the only ones propagating idealist views. Another *Champion of Idealism*, as his book was called, was Akim L'vovich Flekser (1863–1926) who wrote under the name 'Volynsky'. His views, which were derived from an older generation of neo-Kantian idealists, were hostile to decadents – amongst whom he included Struve and Berdyaev – and symbolists. Writing in 1902 he stated that his view of Russian intellectual development was that it would graduate from the naive simplicity of Tolstoy to the – in the best sense – madness (*bezumie*) of Dostoevsky.[33] His views created a storm of criticism in the press and he was attacked by many sections of public opinion, a reaction which seemed to delight him. Today this man, who called *Mir iskusstva* a little conservatory in which an artificial atmosphere and glass walls protected the exotic flower from damage by wind and storm,[34] is labelled by the Soviet Encyclopaedia as a decadent himself because he also had the temerity to attack the revolutionary democrats for transgressing his Kantian ideals. His meteoric rise to notoriety was not repeated later in his life and he never again caused the same furore, but this episode did provide a minor parallel with the *Vekhi* debate and a very interesting contrast with *Problemy idealizma*, the publication of which provoked nothing like the same reaction as Volynsky had done one year previously. The reason is probably that Volynsky was using a more provocative style, more easily accessible to the intelligentsia as a whole than the abstruse philosophical articles in *Problemy idealizma* which could be grasped only with effort by the *intelligenty*, even though it provoked a response among the philosophically inclined such as the writers of *Ocherki realisticheskogo mirovozzreniya*, the first collective work of the God-builders. But despite this Volynsky himself stood outside the categories under examination and his views had practically no influence after their immediate impact.

Apart from an anomaly like Volynsky the main current of idealism was on the lines described above. These were the years of growth and maturation of idealism and the basic theoretical foundations, laid at this time, were to persist throughout the life of the movement. After 1905 the mode of expression changed from the philosophical article or monograph to journalism which dealt with more immediate problems, and to more provocative articles such as those in *Vekhi*. The tradition of liberal idealist journalism centred round the career of Struve and it was his journalistic activity in *Osvobozhdenie*, *Polyarnaya zvezda*, *Voprosy kultury* and *Russkaya mysl'* which together with *Novyi put'* and *Voprosy zhizni* formed the core of liberal intellectual activity in the years after *Problemy idealizma*.

Because of the more practical nature of journalism many of the issues discussed in these publications can be more appropriately considered in the second part of this survey, together with the other large political issues of the day, but there were some important theoretical discussions as well.

The most important development of these basic principles was to be found in Frank and Struve's article on the nature of culture. The article stood at the mid-point between purely theoretical and purely practical discussions. In it Struve and Frank attempted to give their general principles a degree of social significance. The transmission belt between the ideal and the real world was, for them, the individual.[35] The creation and preservation of absolute values was the objective of cultural activity. Culture, said Struve and Frank, was the sum of the absolute values created by man and established in his spiritual—social existence and there was no creator of such values other than the individual.[36] The idea of culture was threatened from two sides, the utilitarian and the ascetic. Utilitarianism, they said, denied culture because it would not recognise any values other than those arising from practical usefulness, from 'low subjective needs'. Asceticism denied culture because it recognised only one absolute value—the moral one—and considered all remaining values to be spectres created by the devil. On one hand utilitarianism denied the divine spirit of man in the name of his earthly aspirations and needs, while on the other asceticism denied the earthly activity of man in the name of his divine being. Both were alien to the idea of Godmanhood, the idea of the incarnation of the absolute values of the spirit in the terrestrial environment, the idea which lay at the heart of the philosophical conception of culture.[37] In practice Russian social thought had, they said, been under the influence of both of these and had indeed been created by people embodying both aspects so that their first target was culture, as Pisarev showed in his preference of a kitchen utensil to all the works of Pushkin, and also Tolstoy who condemned all art to oblivion because it distracted man from living the simple, pure, moral life.[38]

Apart from this one example, the discussions after 1905 became much more closely tied to particular political questions arising from the immediate circumstances of the Russian situation and wide ranging philosophical issues became less talked about than in the period up to 1905. The liberals had made their stand on the platform of preservation of absolute values, of individualism, idealism and religion and were concerned to apply their critical outlook to the conservative 'establishments' of both the state and the revolutionaries, each of which posed a serious threat to absolute values. At this point they will be left for the time being. There was another group which could also claim to be individualist, idealist and religious defenders of absolute values, detesting positivism and vulgar materialism as much as the people who have been considered so far. Though the similarities seem to be great, closer examination reveals that this group, the possessors of 'the new religious consciousness', was in essence a very different movement from the politically-oriented – one might also say realistic – figures of the liberal idealist movement. The new religious consciousness had more in common with Dionysus than with Christ, with Nietzsche than with Kant.

THE NEW RELIGIOUS CONSCIOUSNESS

For the members of the 'Universal Order of Infant Prodigies' life was a 'golden caravelle' sailing to 'the shining heavens'. A liturgy was recited at the meetings – 'God is Spirit; his apparel-beauty; Prayer is creativity; The Temple is art; the art of arts is ritual; the prayers of prayers is the service; our homeland is the shining Heavens; radiant life is in beauty.' The members then made vows of renunciation of the world: the first was a renunciation of weak-willed omnivorousness; the second of politeness; the third of all passionate relations with the female sex; and the last was of all the vanities of this-worldly culture including medicine, the police, advocates, solicitors, art exhibitions and concert halls and recognising only the ritual of their own order, they especially renounced worldly rituals.

This was one of the 'little religions' which existed in St Petersburg in 1909 as it was described from first hand by Botsyanovskii and reprinted in his book *Bogoiskateli (The Godseekers).*[39] Many groups of this nature are believed to have existed in the capital at this period. This example illustrates several of the features running through the new religious consciousness: first of all mysticism and irrationality; secondly worship of absolute ideals; thirdly the use of religious forms as the ultimate in symbolist art; and fourthly a revulsion from the philistinism of everyday life. To this could be added from other sources irrational egoism and orgiastic paganism to complete a list of the movement's main characteristics. Not all manifestations shared all the characteristics but the majority could usually be found, especially the worship of beauty for its own sake and extreme individualism.

One of the difficulties of giving a coherent account of this vague body of ideas is the illogicality, sometimes deliberate, of many pronouncements by its spokesmen. Contradictions are to be found at every turn, in particular between its hostility to Christianity and to God on the one hand and its religious form and impulses on the other. It was both materialist and idealist in a sense, rejecting this world and denying the existence of any other. It was individualist but also proclaimed the collective. It was pagan and rejected reason but revered Vladimir Solov'ev.

All the characteristics and contradictions within the movement were at their most extreme in mystical anarchism, one of the smallest and shortest lived intellectual movements in history which boasted two members, Vyacheslav Ivanov (1866–1949) and G. I. Chulkov (1879–1939), and lasted for only a few months in the summer of 1906 after which, said one commentator, no one ever heard it mentioned again.[40] It did, however, make a brief re-appearance in 1907 when Chulkov, and others who could only loosely be described as 'mystical anarchists' such as Shestov, produced a three-volume collection of belles-lettres and articles on themes of mysticism and anarchism. Despite the lack of acceptance of his movement, Vyacheslav Ivanov was a central figure in the symbolist movement at this time and many of the ideas which were present in mystical anarchism had wide currency. In looking first of all at the most extreme form of the new religious consciousness it is possible to see its characteristics magnified so that they are easily discernible and present a complete contrast with the philosophical liberals whom, according to some, they resembled.

Mystical anarchism attempted to produce a consistent world view based on the self-sufficiency of the individual and the belief that infinite experience was available to each living individual. Like the more conventional version of anarchism it aimed at the overthrow of all externally or internally imposed restrictions on individual freedom. It rejected the world (*nepriyatie mira*) and denied the validity of social and physical laws. In their view the world was incomprehensible and any attempt which claimed to explain the world would have to be dismissed as false. This divided them most obviously from the positivists and socialists, whose views they considered to be enslaving; and, less obviously, from the decadents who asserted what Chulkov called 'the empirical personality'[41] as an end in itself. They differed from the anarchists in that they believed that political anarchism, in the tradition of Bakunin, was mistaken in attaching a social programme to its striving for individual freedom. The final and most objectionable restrictions on freedom, however, were the Church, Christianity and the idea of God. Their final struggle was against God (*bogoborchestvo*).

As with the liberals the corner stone of their outlook was individualism. Chulkov's main article in the second volume of the symposium *Fakely* was entitled 'On the assertion of individuality' and the manifesto he wrote to introduce the first volume stated that the torches (*fakely*) of the title were raised in the name of the self-expression of the individual and 'in the name of the free union of people, based on love, in the future transfigured world'. To this extent mystical anarchism shared common ground with liberals and anarchists, but its beliefs diverged from them considerably.[42] The foundation of the difference was that their ideas were founded on 'a mystical understanding of world' and that despite differences among its sympathisers they at least had this point in common, plus extreme individualism.[43] Their mysticism was a natural corollary to their individualism and was an attempt to make the experience of the individual self-sufficient by expanding the barriers of consciousness to embrace the irrational and the inexplicable and to assert the very incomprehensibility of the world. At the same time they rebelled against the restrictions placed on individuality by reason and by society. In Vyacheslav Ivanov's words, true anarchists need not fear for their conception because 'only such a union [as that of mysticism and anarchism] is able to justify and affirm anarchism to its conclusion'.[44] Only the true mystic is *eo ipso* an unconditionally autonomous individual,[45] the attainment of which state was the ultimate goal of the anarchists. The pursuit of this autonomy made a clash with Christianity inevitable because they thought that the Church had enslaved man most thoroughly in that area where his individuality should be most asserted. The root of this enslavement was the idea of God and the claim that God had revealed truths not available to man by his own imaginative intellectual effort. For Vyacheslav Ivanov only that which was in accordance with such effort was binding on man and revelation had to be rejected. Man must act only in accordance with his inner authority, not in response to truth impressed from without.[46] The dictates of that inner authority directed him to love, particularly sexual love which could lead man to the highest state of his being, to ectasy. In this way man could attain to his divine station and become God-man. For them, this was the true religion, because all religion had its origin in mystical experience, in particular the orgiastic frenzy of the classical world, and ecstasy was its fulfillment.[47] Chulkov's views were more related to social aspirations than Vyacheslav Ivanov's, but all the same they were aspirations beyond the horizon of most social activists. For Chulkov the 'perfected individual' would 'seek his expression in society' but the only society capable of fulfilling the individual was one based

> on principles of a free anarchist union of love. A society constructed on principles of law and coercion does not express but kills individuality. From this arises our rejection of, and our revolutionary attitude toward, all states and toward the institution of property. We set no limitations on ourselves and recognise no authority . . . Our relation to the historical process is always an active one . . . We are there where there is revolution. But we not only destroy but also create – but our creation is completely hostile to mechanical principle. Our creativity is the creativity of love.[48]

Their views were deliberately based on contradictions. Its predecessors included Bakunin, Dostoevsky and Jesus Christ as early examples of mystical anarchists, as well as Kant, Solov'ev and Ibsen as possessors of part of its ideas, and Nietzsche as its greatest prophet. This motley selection of sources is itself revealing as is the fact that accepted interpretations of almost all these persons were stood upside down by the mystical anarchists.

According to Chulkov, the main predecessors of mystical anarchism were Bakunin, who was a mystic Hegelian turned revolutionary, and Dostoevsky, a revolutionary turned mystic. Their shortcoming was that neither of them found the means to unite the principles of love and freedom.[49] Bakunin was admired for his atheist humanism, particularly his maxim 'man is free therefore there is no God',[50] but he and anarchists in general were mistaken in so far as they were 'dreamers' in attaching a social programme to their desires for liberation. This, continued Chulkov, was particularly strange in the case of Bakunin who was formerly a mystic, but even after his conversion he still thought in terms of emancipation from social forms. The defect of all anarchist social programmes was, in the eyes of the mystical anarchists, their failure to propose a satisfactory bond or cement linking individual to commune, and commune to federation. Only love, as understood by Chulkov, was able to achieve this. The problems of property, of the family, of sex, needed 'new experience' and a 'new psychology' for their solution.[51] The revision of Dostoevsky proposed by the mystical anarchists was even more radical. They suggested that the figure of Ivan Karamazov, the prototype of the struggler against God, was his most important character. It was from Ivan that Vyacheslav Ivanov derived his central idea – rejection of the world – which was, he claimed, one of the ancient forms of *bogoborchestva*. 'Without opposition to the Divinity there can be no mystical life in man, no inner drama, no acts or events, which distinguish religious creativity and dynamic religiousness (its name is mysticism) from the static devotion to an enclosed dogma, tables of moral commandments and rules of ritual.'[52] Despite the fact that Dostoevsky did not develop his ideas 'along the true path of the final expression of the individual' and instead 'bowed his head before the empirical state and the dead image of the Orthodox Church, he nonetheless revealed the mystical—anarchic idea of 'rejection of the world'.[53] In this way Bakunin and Dostoevsky, who were in Chulkov's words 'arch-enemies',[54] were both made to serve the mystical anarchist cause.

This synthetic approach was very reminiscent of that of Solov'ev who was also of the opinion that each philosophical school contained a certain amount of truth and a certain amount of error. It is quite possible that the mystical anarchists took this directly from Solov'ev because he was regarded as another prototype of mystical anarchism. Solov'ev, they claimed, marked nothing less than the end of the old religion and the birth of the new. In its concepts of Godmanhood, the Eternal Feminine and World Spirit, particularly in *Smysl lyubvi* (The Meaning of Love), Solov'ev's thought 'stands on that path where the funeral procession of *historic* Christianity comes to an end and where the further movement ahead of the religion of emancipation and renewal sets out'.[55] Chulkov then went on to illustrate from Solov'ev's poetry that rejection of the world lay at the heart of his mystical concepts. In this way Solov'ev, who was concerned to justify good, was turned into a preacher of misrule. From Solov'ev they also took the idea of *sobornost'*, not, as Ivanov pointed out, in the sense in which it was used by Bulgakov, who connected it to an external religious—social organisation, but as a means of creating a direct relationship of love between people.[56] It was, said Chulkov, specifically designed to by-pass the dogmatic Church and establish a direct union with Jesus Christ.[57] Exactly how Jesus Christ could have been a struggler against God was not clarified. According to Vyacheslav Ivanov his contribution was that he preached rejection of the world and warned against immersion in it.[58]

The most wholeheartedly accepted predecessors were the ancient Greeks and Nietzsche, whom Chulkov and Vyacheslav Ivanov did not criticise. The assertive paganism of Nietzsche, added to what they saw as the origins of religion in sexual ecstasy as practised by Bacchanalians and Dionysians, provided the fullest example of the attitude to life which they proposed. The importance of ecstasy was that it 'liberated the Psyche from the power and tutelage of our conscious principles as though it were plunged into self-oblivion or death, and allowed it to wander in search of Eros, like Maenads, at the command of Dionysus'.[59]

Such were the main features of mystical anarchism. Its importance for this study is greater than its significance as a philosophical system because it highlighted certain of the themes contained in other religious outlooks. The synthetic nature of mystical anarchism made it the most comprehensive body of ideas in the new religious consciousness, touching on anarchism, liberalism, revolution and decadence at important points and yet diverging substantially from each of them. From anarchism it borrowed struggle for individualism but rejected social programmes. In the case of revolution, mystical anarchism borrowed the revolutionary idea and developed it to new levels while at the same time joining with the liberals in a vigorous denunciation of positivism which they rejected because according to its outlook the individual could not liberate himself from the laws governing him, which was the whole object of anarchism. The struggle for liberation through positivism, said Chulkov, must therefore be an illusory one because 'in positivism there is not even the theme of the assertion of individuality: the individual is only a link in the mechanical evolution of the world'.[60] In common with practically all the revolutionary and reform movements in Russia, the mystical anarchists saw the Church as an arch-enemy, its dogmatism being considered as enslaving as the dogma of the positivists.[61] In this respect too the mystical anarchists resembled Struve and others of the liberals who opposed revolutionaries and reactionaries alike. From Nietzsche they borrowed their concept of anarchism as the freeing of the individual from all inner and outer inhibitions,[62] but their use of mysticism as a means to this end was completely contrary to Nietzsche. They used Solov'ev in the reverse way, in order to justify their mysticism, while rejecting Solov'ev's complete antipathy to the unbridled egoism they preached. The decadents, such as Merezhkovsky, Rozanov and Filosofov, whose aestheticism, mysticism and egoism the mystical anarchists apparently shared, were rejected because they were not free of what Chulkov liked to call 'empirical' characteristics – meaning that the decadents still inhabited the real world which it was the business of the mystical anarchists to reject totally.[63] In this way, although they bore some resemblance to and borrowed from almost every intellectual group in Russia at that time, they were thoroughly rejected by all.

The other part of the new religious consciousness, which the mystical anarchists most resembled, was the most forthright in its denunciations. Ellis, the critic and historian of the symbolist movement, called the second volume of *Fakely* 'a pantheon of contemporary banality'.[64] Zinaida Gippius (1869–1945) called the movement 'mystical Chulkovism' which had only one follower – Chulkov himself. For her, *O misticheskom anarkhizme* was 'a book – in its essence and for the most part merely useless and unnecessary but for the rest harmful, plunged into pessimism and despair'.[65] Another reviewer said that Ivanov's central idea – 'rejection of the world' – was at the root of all religions.[66] Andrei Belyi (1880–1934) writing in *Zolotoe runo* saw three shortcomings in Chulkov's anarchism. First it was not clear how his individualism related itself to society; second his views on the relationship between religion and mysticism were questionable; and third any anarchist theory ought to take into account the existence of social democracy and define its relations to social democracy, otherwise it was in danger of being reactionary and bourgeois.[67]

D. V. Filosofov (b. 1872) wrote in a completely different vein. For him the interesting feature of mystical anarchism was that Chulkov did attempt to find a satisfactory link between the individual and society in his use of the concept of *sobornost'* borrowed from Solov'ev. Their individualism was, he said, bought at the extremely high price of their own solitude, a solitude heightened by their rejection of the world. The problem was that they sought to escape from this solitude and, consequently, to relate themselves to the world. They attempted to overcome this difficulty through *sobornost'* – the idea that a mystical individual could only express himself in relation to others. Like the decadents, continued Filosofov, the mystical anarchist considered the assertion of individuality to be an end in itself (if Vyacheslav Ivanov's words that 'the true mystic is *eo ipso* an unconditionally autonomous individual' are to be believed), but unlike the decadent the mystical anarchist refused to accept this and felt that his duty was to save society as well. This, concluded Filosofov, was because Chulkov was, at heart, nothing less than a social democrat and because of this inclination he could not face society as it was without a chance of liberation. In Filosofov's eyes the solution failed because, as was the case with all anarchists, the mystical anarchists' assertion of individuality could only be achieved at the expense of society and entering society could only result in a loss of individuality.[68]

In this way the more orthodox (if the term can be used for people who were themselves regarded as being far from orthodox) of the decadents were sharply critical of mystical anarchism which represented the radical wing of the new religious consciousness in the same way that the orthodox liberals were critical of the radical liberals such as Berdyaev and Bulgakov. The connection between mystical anarchism and Christian radicalism was a strong one and all four of the major figures – Chulkov, Vyacheslav Ivanov, Berdyaev and Bulgakov – collaborated on the journal *Voprosy zhizni* in the years 1904–5.

The point made by Filosofov, that any social immersion resulted in a lessening of individuality, revealed the core of the decadent outlook. For them the individual had no goal greater than his self-perfection. This was not a social task. It was in the first instance an aesthetic task and it was understood as such by the symbolist painters and poets, and for many, such as Filosofov, it was ultimately a religious task.[69]

Mystical anarchism itself showed that the connection between individualism and religion (however defined) was a strong one and resulted from the fact that subjective experience lay at the root of many religious outlooks. Intuition, working in areas not always open to rational verification, was the source of ideas of the existence of an absolute, of God, or of an after life. This was true of religious experience of many types, from tribal religion to Wordsworth's 'Intimations of Immortality'. From Merezhkovsky to Gorky and from Berdyaev to Lunacharsky, the whole question of the validity and importance of subjective religious experience was being discussed, even if it were only to be dismissed as nonsense by people as diverse as Struve, Bogdanov and Lenin, none of whom had any time for mysticism or irrationality.

One of the major works of the new religious consciousness was written in 1904 by N. M. Minsky (1855–1937). It presented a classical example of awareness of death, brought on by serious illness, leading to religious belief. Minsky's book *Religiya budushchego* (*The Religion of the Future*) was an autobiographical account of such a spiritual crisis. Like mystical anarchism, the religion arising from this situation was a kind of sentimental response to fear caused by witnessing death and feeling its presence and inevitability. For Minsky this fear awakened him to many intimations of the existence of 'the inexpressible' and 'the unknowable', usually transmitted to him at night in the darkened corridors of the eerily silent sanatorium in which he was staying.

Minsky brought out an additional element of the thought of the new religious consciousness, the theme of death. There does not seem to have been any period in Russian thought when death had such a strong hold on the imagination as it did in these years. Isolated thinkers had tried to come to terms with it, the most original being Fedorov who believed in the eventual ability of science not only to prolong life indefinitely but also to reconstitute from the original molecules the bodies of all dead people. Fedorov's views were not at this point directly influential on a wide circle because of his refusal to publish his eccentric ideas, but they were known to Solov'ev, Dostoevsky and Tolstoy and each of these acknowledged a great indebtedness to him. But in comparison to these disciples of his he was unknown.

After 1905 the question of death was raised in many ways. It was a major theme of Artsybashev's novel *Sanin*, although the more sensational aspects of this novel have attracted greater attention. It was particularly strong in the writings of the individualists, symbolists and decadents because for them death appeared to be the negation of individualism, whereas the collectivists could gain some consolation from the survival of the race. It was also for the decadents a useful method of causing a sensation and could be used *pour épater le bourgeois*. For a combination of these reasons of genuine horror and sensationalism, a symposium was published entitled quite simple *Death*.[70]

i

The mystery of death was also central to the thought of the radical Christians and the God-builders, but the positivists and Marxists regarded discussion of it as a complete waste of energy. But, according to the symbolists, it was through such mysteries that one came to the knowledge that the truth of the universe was beyond man's grasp. Although the universe might have surface manifestations which could perhaps be correlated and explained scientifically, its essence remained impenetrable. In Russian poetry this feeling went back at least as far as Tyutchev who wrote that 'a thought which has been put into words is a lie'.[71] The French symbolists had a great influence in Russia, especially Baudelaire, Verlaine and Rimbaud and the symbolist school began to dominate Russian poetry and painting under the leadership of Bal'mont and Bryusov. Although the origins and development of Russian symbolism up to the early twentieth century is too broad a topic to deal with in the present study, it is possible to discern some of its main features in the major artistic journals of the period and also in the contributions to the debate about the relevance and nature of symbolism in the years 1909–10.

The three main artistic journals of the period were *Vesy*, published from 1904–9, *Zolotoe runo*, published from 1906–9, and *Apollon*, published from 1909–17. Despite differences these three journals were all descended from the same source, *Mir iskusstva* which was first published in 1899 under the editorship of Diaghilev and later Benois, and continued until 1904. *Mir iskusstva* had been quite a new phenomenon in the history of Russian periodical publication. Its concern with the arts was broader than that of any predecessor, and art was treated as an autonomous part of life, not subject to social and political priorities as had been the case previously. The journals were written for people whose chief interest was in artistic and cultural life rather than in politics. They became foci of ideas about the visual arts as well as literature. Each became the platform of a separate coterie and the editors spent much of their time denouncing one another. Despite this the journals indicated unmistakably that there existed in Russia a group of people whose concerns were aesthetic as well as social. Periodicals of a more traditional type continued to flourish and each political party had its own journal. *Russkoe bogatstvo*, edited by A. V. Peshekhonov, spoke for the SR's, *Russkaya mysl'* under Struve became a platform for a wide variety of liberals, while *Sovremennyi mir* (called *Mir Bozhii* until July 1906) was the chief periodical of the Social Democrats. A

number of important but less substantial and shorter-lived period-
icals, such as *Novyi put'* (1903–4) and *Voprosy zhizni* (1904–5), put
forward the ideas of particular groups or schools within the
intelligentsia at various times. It was, of course, greatly to the credit
of the intellectual voraciousness of the intelligentsia that it was able
to sustain such a variety of eminently serious periodicals, which
were normally of considerable length and overflowing with articles
on Russian and world politics and culture in addition to a literary
section devoted to short stories, novels and literary criticism.

Despite the differences between these various kinds of journal, it
could not be said that the symbolists closed their minds to their
intellectual and political surroundings and locked themselves in an
ivory tower of 'art for art's sake' aestheticism. All three of their
journals showed a lively interest in the intellectual discussions of the
day, although in many ways their avant-gardism led them to reject
most of the trends which lagged behind their own. *Vesy* in particular
devoted considerable attention to the debates in the intelligentsia
from its second issue, which published a review of the Marxist reply
to *Problemy idealizma*, right up to one of its last issues which published
a review of *Vekhi* some months before it finally closed down. Far
from showing lack of interest in social and philosophical questions
on the part of the symbolists, the journals indicate that the full
meaning of their movement can only be comprehended when
considered in relation to the intellectual environment.

In 1904 in the opening address to its readers, *Vesy* claimed to be
the younger brother of *Mir iskusstva* and *Novyi put'* which indicated
the extent to which it hoped to combine interest in visual arts with
literature and ideas. Unlike *Mir iskusstva* the main concern of *Vesy*
was with Russian art as an independent school, whereas much of the
work of *Mir iskusstva* had involved spreading knowledge of western
European classical and modern painting. To some extent *Vesy*
wanted to encourage the reverse process and help to acquaint the
western public with the achievements of Russian art. The major
vehicle for this was Diaghilev's *Ballet Russe* and there were major
exhibitions of Russian art in Paris in 1901 and 1909. *Zolotoe runo* was
an even more energetic and ambitious propagator of Russian ideas
and its early issues were published in both Russian and French, but
this was abandoned after a few months. Even so, it is justifiable to
claim that this was an important turning point in Russian art as it
had achieved a distinctive style of its own and was being accepted as
such in the Paris salons.

The appearance in 1906, some eighteen months later than *Vesy*, of *Zolotoe runo* under the patronage of Ryabushinsky provoked hostility from the older journal. Even in this hostility it is possible to discern the sense that a higher plane of artistic life had been reached because the essence of *Vesy*'s criticism was that *Zolotoe runo*'s opening manifesto was not of a sufficiently high cultural level for what its editors claimed was a European publication.[72] It is interesting to note that *Zolotoe runo* felt the necessity at least to make a formal genuflection to the liberation movement in its manifesto and to feel the need to justify itself by claiming that it was playing a role complementary to that of the liberation movement.

We sympathise with all who work for the renewal of life, we do not deny any of the contemporary tasks, but we firmly believe that it is impossible to live without beauty. In addition to free institutions, it is necessary to acquire for our descendants the free, vivid, illuminated sun of creativity by indefatigable search, and to preserve for them Eternal values, moulded by successive generations.

Art was, it went on, one, eternal, free and symbolic 'bearing in itself symbols – the reflection of the Eternal in the temporal'.[73]

Only *Apollon*, of the three journals, specifically rejected non-artistic values. The goal of the journal was a 'purely aesthetic' one, 'independent of all ideological nuances (social, ethical, religious)'.[74] For *Apollon* art was an end in itself. Unlike the symbolists, *Apollon* sought to return to the path 'of the dogma of classicism' embodied in ancient Greek and Renaissance art. Thus it took its stand against all forms of modernism and was the only justification for accusing the creative intelligentsia of having only aesthetic ideals. The falseness of this accusation on the wide scale is revealed by the fact that *Apollon*'s pure aestheticism was a conscious reaction against the tainted ideals for which the symbolists stood.

Symbolism was not without its defenders and at this advanced stage of its existence it produced some of its most profound self-analysis, illustrating the similarities and differences running through it. Belyi in a lecture on 'Symbolism and Russian art', took up arms against the realists, represented by the *Znanie* and *Shipovnik* groups (a realism which was at this time influenced by God-building and other semi-idealist tendencies). Symbolism was not entirely opposed to realism, said Belyi, and realist art such as that practised by Tolstoy, Gogol and Verhaeren had a great deal to offer the symbolist even though the realists were very involved with social issues. In this lecture Belyi took pains to separate the spheres of art and society, pointing out the mistake of Vyacheslav Ivanov in trying to harness aesthetics to a political programme, or to the people. 'Symbolism,' said Belyi, 'makes a sharp division between the political opinions of an artist and his creative work', a sharp division which was not, in fact, apparent even in the works of Belyi himself. He did, however, approve of Vyacheslav Ivanov's views on art, including one which claimed that art 'strengthens a new populism' which was, in all senses of the word, a political outlook, except that it stood outside the confines of a specific party programme. He agreed in particular with Ivanov's view that art had a 'religious essence' deriving from myth.[75]

In 1910 Vyacheslav Ivanov himself drew up a balance sheet of 'the heritage of symbolism' in which he again claimed that symbolism and the new poetry were 'vague reminiscences of the sacred language of cult priests and Magi'.[76] Symbolism appeared to be an anticipation of that hypothetical specifically religious age of language when it would embrace two distinct kinds of speech – speech about empirical phenomena and relationships and speech about pre-suppositions and relationships of a different order revealed in inner experience, the sacred speech of prophecy. Symbolism was a reminder to poetry of its original primordial tasks and means.[77] In a reply, Blok reaffirmed and complemented much of what Vyacheslav Ivanov said, quoting Fet, that the business of the artist was 'to express the soul without words'. 'The first duty of the artist', said Blok 'is to point out, not to prove.'[78] V. Ya. Bryusov (1873–1924) was violently opposed to Vyacheslav Ivanov's 'servile speeches' in which he put art at the disposal of non-artistic ends. In opposition to this Bryusov redefined the doctrine of art for art's sake. The artist's work, he said, had no use-value. The artist for Brysov had no duty but to art. 'A hammer', he said, 'is used to hit nails, not to draw pictures. Weapons are better for shooting with than for drinking liquor from. A cookery book has to teach the preparation of various foods. But a book of poetry . . . what does a book of poetry give us?'[79] Symbolism was not, as Vyacheslav Ivanov suggested, whatever one liked it to mean but it was a 'definite historical phenomenon, connected with definite dates and names'. 'Symbolism *wanted to be* and *always was only art.*' Art had been made to serve science and society; now people sought to make it serve religion but, Bryusov cried, 'give it finally its freedom'.[80]

Bryusov's voice was, however, very much in a minority. The final analysis of symbolism and its religious and intellectual significance was given by the literary critic Ellis in his book *Russkie simvolisty* published in 1910. Ellis's basic view of the essence of symbolism was that it presented an ideal world, where thoughts, emotions and perceptions were refined to their highest state. For Ellis symbolism was the antithesis of the mediocrity of the everyday life which made up the essence of realism in literature and art. Symbolism transcended this level. It was, in his words, 'a mystical cult of beauty'.[81]

The fundamental impulse of symbolism was the creation of a new higher culture, the opening up of 'a great new cultural era, in its essence opposed in all aspects to our contemporary materialist and positive—utilitarian culture'.[82] The vanguard of this new culture was Nietzsche whose role in the movement was, according to Ellis, to capture the spirit of the oriental religions and transform them into definitive expressions of man's new religious sensitivity.[83] The other intellectual sources were what he called intellectual and emotional adventurers, such as Plato and Schopenhauer rather than lawgivers like Kant and Hegel. Platonic dualism and Schopenhauerian idealism were, he said, stimulants to symbolism and provided a background to it.[84] In poetry Baudelaire's *Correspondences* contained 'the programme of all contemporary symbolism'.[85] The Nietzschean influence was very strong in Ellis and he went further than many of his fellows in asserting it. Above all he borrowed from Nietzsche the idea of 'aristocratic individualism'. It was the search of the aristocratic individualist for freedom and even higher achievements that saved symbolism from falling into a pseudo-realistic vein which glorified banality and mediocrity.[86] The aristocratic character of symbolism was opposed to all dead and decaying forms and values, for example, historic Christianity, and struggled for a new religious sensitivity, a religion of the future, a third testament.

Thus the new religious consciousness was close to and yet distinct from philosophical liberalism. Both groups were idealist, individualist and, as a consequence of these, religious; but the way in which each of these was understood by the two groups was very different. On the one hand Schopenhauer, Nietzsche and the Greek myths inspired the new religious consciousness while on the other,

Kant, Solov'ev and Christianity inspired the philosophical liberals. At many points the divisions were obscured, particularly in the tangle of sources common to both – above all Solov'ev and Nietzsche, and also, perhaps Plato – but the interpretation of these common sources differed widely. Similarly the many internal disagreements, which meant in practice that each thinker stood for his own ideas and not those of anyone else, meant a great variety of intermediate positions.

Perhaps the most significant and puzzling feature was why symbolism should consider itself to be religious at all. It was, after all, derived from western Europe and America and few of the Western symbolists felt the same need to associate their views with any kind of religion. Many possible answers to this suggest themselves. First, the absence of a rationalist 'revolution', a renaissance or an enlightenment in Russian society, meant that religion in the traditional sense still had a much more prominent place in Russian thought as a whole. Arising from this but going beyond it was the figure of Vladimir Solov'ev. His genius was central to Russian symbolism as well as to Russian philosophy and Russian liberalism in general but he was a profoundly religious thinker in any sense of the term, almost a theologian, and this gave a religious coloration to the outlook of all his followers. Religion was so integral to his thought that hardly any part of it could be detached and made independent of its religious significance.

In addition to these, however, perhaps the main meaning of the term 'religious' as applied to *all* the people dealt with in this chapter was 'anti-positivist' or 'anti-materalist'. This was the thread which united Trubetskoi, Struve, Berdyaev, Vyacheslav Ivanov, Belyi, *Vesy*, *Zolotoe runo* and even *Apollon*. All were resolutely opposed to the dominant positivist, scientific and materialist world outlook of the intelligentsia and what their collective achievement showed beyond all doubt was that this positivist outlook was undergoing perhaps the most severe attack it had faced in Russia. The result of the activities of these people was the creation of a thorough-going, non-positivist body of thought, not confined to aristocratic or academic circles but stretching down into all sections of educated Russian society and including many of the country's major creative talents. This new phenomenon, limited and fragile though it was in many ways, presented a challenge to the revolutionary intelligentsia which made many attempts to refute it. This was particularly true of the discussions among the Social Democrats. These had been provoked by the tactical dispute between Mensheviks and Bolsheviks, but on a philosophical plane the divisions went even deeper and the years 1905–9 were crucial in the development of Bolshevik philosophy. In 1905 Bogdanov seemed to be on the way to becoming the official theortician of the Social Democrats on philosophical matters. But his views were subject to suspicion both by Plekhanov, whose work *Osnovnye voprosy marksizma* was published in 1907, and Lenin, who also published his major philosophical work, *Materialism and Empiriocriticism*, at this time. It is to these defenders of positivism that we now turn.

2 Philosophy and the revolutionaries

This chapter is an attempt to outline very briefly the fundamental positions of the 'revolutionary' element in our equation. A great deal more is written about such figures as Lenin, Plekhanov and the Social Democrats than about their opponents. For this reason the full range of their views will not be examined in the same detail as those of the less thoroughly studied groups. The purpose of this chapter is to sketch the context in which the debates among the revolutionaries occurred and to show the relationship of the better known works of this group, such as *Materialism and Empiriocriticism*, to the less well-known, such as *Empiriomonizm* and *Ocherki po filosofii marksizma*, and beyond it insofar as it interacts with idealism.

Up to this point the subjects of this chapter have been referred to under various names as socialists, as positivists or as revolutionaries. None of these titles is fully adequate and yet each one has a certain degree of accuracy. In terms of our classification of thinkers according to the content of their ideas, the people in this section have precisely the opposite world view from that of the liberals. Where the liberals were idealist, the revolutionaries were materialist; where the liberals were individualist, the revolutionaries (with certain exceptions, such as the anarchists, who will be considered elsewhere) were collectivists. It is because they represented the reverse of what the liberals stood for that they are considered at this point. The theoretical foundation of the two poles of social thought of the period will thus have been presented in outline, leaving an examination of the relationship between intermediate groups to later chapters.

For the history of idealist philosophy in general, the volume *Problemy idealizma* had little significance for it was not an original work. It was more significant as an attempt to re-establish fundamental idealist concepts in the mind of the Russian intelligentsia. However, its influence was decisive on the history of

Marxist philosophy (and not only in Russia). When *Problemy idealizma* appeared it was attacking Marxist positivism in areas which had been ignored because Russian Marxism was a mainly social and political movement and, like the intelligentsia movement as a whole, largely ignored philosophical issues. Consequently it was the attack launched by the idealists which caused the Social Democrats to formulate a philosophical position compatible with Marxism.

From 1903–8 various major attempts were made to refute the idealists. The first published reply was in a collection of articles entitled *Ocherki realisticheskogo mirovozzreniya* of 1904. At the same time the first Russian edition of Engels' *Anti-Duhring*, the major work on philosophy of the Marx-Engels corpus of writing, was published. In 1906 Aksel'rod-Ortodoks on Plekhanov's initiative, produced a collection of essays called *Filosofskie ocherki*. In the same year Bogdanov completed publication of his three volume *Empiriomonizm* (1904–6). In the next three years appeared several major monographs, for example, *Materializm i kriticheskii realizm* of Yushkevich (1908), Valentinov's *Filosofskie postroeniya marksizma* (1907), Lunacharsky's *Religiya i sotsializm* (1908), the collection of articles *Ocherki po filosofii marksizma* (1908), and Lenin's *Materialism and Empiriocriticism* (1909). In addition to these there were many articles in the intellectual periodicals. Thus at a glance it can be seen that this was a most important moment in the development of Social Democratic philosophy and, following from this, for the history of Soviet philosophy after the revolution.

The first attempt at definition of the materialist position was made in the collection of articles entitled *Ocherki realisticheskogo mirovozzreniya (Notes on the Realist World Outlook)* in 1904.[1] As it was the Socialists' first incursion into the philosophical field the tone of much of the volume was, as might be expected, tentative. The contributors contradicted each other at times and a facade of unity was provided only by the lowest common denominator of 'realism'. The essence of realism was not defined at this stage but its implicit meaning was that the world existed independently of human consciousness. In keeping with the book's function as an instigator of debate rather than as a lawgiving text, the editor emphasised to the reader that 'realism is not a complete cognitive *system*, but a particular path towards systematic knowledge of everything given to us in experience'.[2] The task of realism was, he continued, to provide man with the knowledge he needed to enable him to transform nature through his labour. Realism did not acknowledge the right of human reason to impose its laws on nature but rather the function of reason was to deduce laws from nature. Beyond this there was room for dispute: 'Like truth, realism is one, but at the same time, also like truth, it is many-sided . . . but the differences should not prevent the reader from seeing clearly among us a *basic unity* – the unity arising from a particular orientation of life.'[3]

A much more advanced attempt to fuse philosophy with materialism was being attempted at the same time by A. A. Bogdanov (1873–1928) who adapted the positivism of Avenarius and Mach. For Bogdanov these two represented the philosophy of science and of matter developed to its highest point. The central feature of Bogdanov's thought was the abolition of the distinction between matter and spirit. In his opinion all previous philosophers, including Plekhanov and Lenin, were guilty of dualism. In its place Bogdanov substituted monism, the identity of thought, spirit and consciousness with matter. Bogdanov's idea that thought was a function of matter was greeted by his disciples, for example Shulyatikov, as a revolution in philosophy.[4]

Most of Bogdanov's ideas at this period were developed in articles which over these years repeated the basic points of his outlook rather than developed them. His major work of the time, *Empiriomonizm*, was also rather fragmentary. It appeared in three small volumes and was largely devoted to discussion of separate questions rather than to a methodical exposition of his views. From all these works it can be seen that the question which interested him was the nature of matter itself. Bogdanov claimed to be the only true materialist and it was indicative of the atmosphere of the period that Bogdanov, Plekhanov and Lenin accused each other of being idealists, the worst possible slander in their eyes, and even today one of the objects of Soviet philosophy is to reduce ideological opponents to the status of idealists.

Bogdanov's concentration on the question of the nature and meaning of sensory perception and experience led him into the field of psychology, indicating the particular closeness of Russian thought to psychological questions. Bogdanov was, of course, a doctor of medicine and this perhaps made him more susceptible to a physiological materialist explanation of life. Be that as it may, Bogdanov's views were certainly extreme and extended the views of his mentor, Ernst Mach, to a far greater significance than their originator would himself have claimed. In the words of Izgoev, a wry observer of the dispute among the Social Democrats over Machism, the modest professor from the 1870s Mach, would have been astounded at the furore surrounding his name in Russia. Where he had thought simply that he was adding his own little stone to the building of Western thought, his talented Russian followers were acclaiming him as the demolisher of the old philosophy and the harbinger of a new era.[5]

It is not the task of the present work to evaluate or to expound in full the thought of Bogdanov. This has been done elsewhere.[6] However, certain observations can be made about it. Uncritical acceptance in Russia of it by many Social Democrats probably resulted from the fact that it seemed to fill the philosophical void in materialism revealed by the idealists without conceding any ground on either of the two major premises of the materialists; namely the primacy of science and scientific law to which all aspects of nature could be reduced, and secondly, the demand that a phenomenon should be judged by its value as either a help or a hindrance to the revolution.

The first characteristic can be seen in the article Bogdanov published in *Voprosy filosofii i psikhologii*. The first of these articles gave examples of some experiments carried out by German and French psychologists of the late nineteenth century on hypnosis, hysteria, personality change, 'double consciousness' and perception, which indicated that in the performance of certain activities, consciousness could be by-passed.[7] For instance, in one of the experiments a patient under anaesthetic wrote out with his right hand metal letters felt through the fingers of his left hand. Bogdanov's conclusion from these experiments, and from experience of patients who had changed their personality as a result of physiological trauma, was that the central nervous system was of overwhelming, probably decisive, significance in explaining the flow of human psychic existence. The whole of Bogdanov's thought was an attempt to develop a view of human psychic and social life based on this conception of the central nervous system. From this attempt arose Bogdanov's monism and his debt to Avenarius and Mach.

The central feature of monism was the denial of a duality between spirit and matter. Following from this was a denial of metaphysics in general and the assertion that nothing could reside in the central nervous system, and hence in the mind, in life, that had not been put there through experience, and nothing existed for men which had not been experienced through the senses. As an example of this Bogdanov constantly referred to perception to prove the importance of environmental conditioning. In common with modern psychologists, Bogdanov concluded that what a person saw in a given situation was dependent on the way the brain organised and interpreted the sensory data received, which in turn was dependent on the experience of that particular person. The result was that a complex event would not be seen in exactly the same way by two different people. From this arose, according to Bogdanov, a division between the 'physical' sphere of experience and the 'psychological', the former being 'objective' experience – that is, common to all people and socially organised – and the latter being 'subjective' experience – that is, individually organised and therefore subject to the quirks and idiosyncracies of individual perception. In Bogdanov's view, therefore, the group or the collective was the source of truth, of scientific accuracy in perception, while the individual was fallible, the source of error in perception.[8] Thus Bogdanov provided a theoretical basis for the collectivist outlook of the intelligentsia. Not only was the individual less reliable than the group, he was its greatest weakness.

To solve the dilemma of what constituted an objective majority and what was simply individual distortion reflected by a whole group, Bogdanov turned to conceptions common to many thinkers who based their views on progress, including Solov'ev. Only the human race *as a whole* could, he said, possess this objective truth. The task of scientific enquiry was to eliminate such distortions and to lay the foundations for the objective evaluation of experience common to humanity as a whole.[9] This was reflected in his three-stage view of the fate of human nature which Bogdanov shared with, among others, Engels and the Old Testament. In primitive communist society, said Bogdanov, the 'I' was less defined than at present because man had not learned to separate the self from the group – 'his experience was directly united with the experience of other people, the word "I" referred to his own body with its specific needs, but not to a complex of emotions and aspirations of other people, as happens in contemporary society'.[10] In the higher society of the future, with its 'collectively organised labour', the contradictions between individual psyches would be eliminated and 'harmoniously organised collective experience' would give people 'that grandiose fullness of life of which we, people of the epoch of contradictions, cannot even form a conception'.[11] Thus, the phases of human development – primitive communist society, the epoch of contradictions, and the grandiose fullness of life to come – appeared as an extreme secularisation and rationalisation of the Judaeo-Christian view of innocence, fallen man and the coming kingdom of God on earth.

The final objection to monism, the assertion that the distinction between spirit and matter was obvious to any individual simply from reflection on his own inner nature, was met by Bogdanov in his article 'Avtoritarnoe myshlenie' ('Authoritarian Thinking'). The hierarchic view of man's nature, reaching its peak in the Middle Ages – of soul, conscience, intellect, will, brain, body and limbs – arose, he said, from the hierarchic nature of authoritarian society which also had a dictator at the top passing instructions through a chain ending with the slaves.[12] In this way the metaphor of the body politic was turned upside down by Bogdanov. The fact that the dictator ruled society gave rise to the view that, in the individual, the psyche ruled the body, not the reverse.

The revolutionary task of philosophy, in Bogdanov's view, went hand in hand with the task of revolution in society. Theory should be united with practice. The elimination of social contradictions was to be carried out together with the elimination of the contradictions in the experience of the individual. The latter contradictions gave rise to what Bogdanov saw as a series of 'fetishes'. The chief contradiction in all previous philosophies was that between 'nature' and 'cognition'. It had never before been recognised that they were united.[13] Secondly, man had to be liberated from the fetishes of the 'cursed questions' of immortality, the origin of life, and so on, in order to realise his true nature and free himself from primitive fears, animism and religiosity which were at the root of all such questions. To resolve them, man should see himself as a completely material being.[14] Revolution united both the social and the individual process in Bogdanov's definition that revolution has one aim – 'the harmonisation of human existence'.[15]

The acclaim which Bogdanov received resulted not from the originality and merit of his ideas but from the extreme readiness of part of the intelligentsia to accept a philosophy which coincided with the fundamental propositions of its social outlook. Bogdanov's philosophy was scientific and evolutionary in its content; the intelligentsia's favourite reading included Darwin. His philosophy negated the individual and enthroned (or deified according to some of his disciples) the collective as the source of 'objective' truth. It appeared to take Marx's view that being determined consciousness to its extreme conclusion. It saw revolution as the path out of the epoch of contradictions in which modern man found himself. It established as its goal a future society from which all evil would be banished and complete harmony would reign. Thus Bogdanov's fundamental views seemed to carry the banner of intelligentsia hopes into the formerly ignored sphere of philosophy. Monism swept through the ranks of social democracy in Russia and seemed to fit its positivist world view like a glove. His conception of the liberated monistic man seemed to be a natural extension of the traditional revolutionary hero. Bogdanov had outlined the philosophy of a Rakhmetov.

The reception of Bogdanov's views among the Social Democrats within Russia was somewhat ambiguous. He was acclaimed and revised at one and the same time. While Bogdanov's natural scientific approach to philosophy was the starting point there were many differences of emphasis and opinion among his fellow Social Democratic thinkers within Russia. The fullest cross-section of this new outlook was provided by the collection of essays published under the title of *Ocherki po filosofii marksizma (Notes on Marxist Philosophy)*. This volume appeared in 1908, some time after Ortodoks and Plekhanov had begun their joint assault on Machism but before Lenin felt it necessary to define his own position. It was the volume which was for Lenin the last straw. He called it *Ocherki protiv filosofii marksizma (Notes against Marxist Philosophy)*.[16] To what extent Lenin's silence in these arguments and the eventual timing of his attack were the result of political calculation and the necessity of maintaining good relations with Bogdanov, who controlled considerable Bolshevik funds, is not known for certain, but Bogdanov was one of the major contributors to *Ocherki po filosofii marksizma*.[17]

The contributors started out by saying that the book was not linked to any complete philosophical system: 'The reader will see that the separate authors differ between themselves not only on points of interpretation of secondary problems but also in their conceptions of basic gnosiological problems.' But there were unifying principles. The first of these was socialism, by which term they meant the bringing to birth of a new form of social existence 'which must correspond with new types of thought'. They rejected ethical socialism, the editor continued, and substituted scientific socialism, the aim of which was not to lament the power of natural forces over man but to put them to work for him. In achieving this aim, positive (*polozhitel'nyi*) science was of great interest to the Marxist, and, in that it extended man's power over nature, it had to be assimilated by Marxists. The second characteristic shared by all the authors was that they were critical of two tendencies. On the one hand the dogmatists of scientific socialism were attacked for trying to pin man's knowledge of nature and society at the level already achieved and for refusing to permit further advance. On the other, they attacked those who rejected rational scientific methodology, proclaimed the bankruptcy of reason itself and preached non-rational or super-rational methods of exerting influence over nature and society. 'In this way, although the authors are not able to call themselves supporters of one or other philosophical system, none-theless they set out from a common starting point and aspire to a common goal.'[18]

It is clear that the writers considered themselves to be bringing socialist thought into line with contemporary ideas. They stood alone in opposition to Plekhanov's dogmatism and to the old enemy idealism. Their relatively receptive attitude to new discoveries in thought was more than just a pose and it strongly distinguished this group from Plekhanov and Lenin, neither of whom showed much inclination towards, or enthusiasm for, innovation. It was this characteristic which brought them closest to the other seekers of truth of the time. The question was posed, 'Are the God-builders and God-seekers friends or enemies?' and it is clear that they shared at least a similarity of temperament.

Of all the dissident Marxists within Russia P. S. Yushkevich (1873–1945) was the most eloquent and outspoken protestor against dogmatism. 'At worse', he said, 'Machism is a living error; materialism, at best, is dead truth. But there is more truth in a living error than in a dead truth.'[19] Showing both his relatively tolerant outlook and his depth of culture, both sharply distinguishing him from Lenin, he turned to parables to make his point. The two possible attitudes to knowledge were represented by Caliph Omar on the one hand and the pharisee Gamaliel on the other. The caliph had all the books in the library of Alexandria burned, his reason being that if what was in the books was also in the Koran then the books were unnecessary and if the knowledge were not in the Koran, then it was contrary to God's teaching. Yushkevich's sympathy lay with Gamaliel who, according to the Acts of the Apostles, requested the Sanhedrin to relax its persecution of the apostles because if they were acting with only human power they would destroy themselves anyway, but if they were from God, persecution would not be able to destroy them. 'Take care not to prove yourselves opponents of God', warned the pharisee.[20] In a similar fashion Yushkevich pleaded that Marxism should not shun or fear contact with other ideas and the Marxist should be confident of the victory of truth in a conflict of opinion. 'If Marxism is a "divine" teaching full of energy and strength, then it should not be fearful of any contact with bourgeois theories: it will assimilate them itself and not be assimilated by them.'[21] Yushkevich then went on to ask himself 'What ought Marxism to be?' Potentially Marxism was universal

> nothing human or cultural is alien to it. Religion, ethics, aesthetics, philosophy, literary problems, criticism, to all of these it should give its answers – positive or negative – but in any case defined, clear, and linked in one, structured, organic whole. Actual Marxism has barely touched on them even in the most timid way, normally keeping absolutely silent about them, at best satisfying itself with scorn, with casual remarks about the bourgeois or anti-democratic nature of existing ideological forms.[22]

Lunacharsky himself said that the writers of *Ocherki po filosofii marksizma* might be mistaken but were at least on the path to truth.[23] Lenin was most scornful of this suggestion. It was, he said, the task of his book to disprove their views.

> At the moment I would only remark that if our philosophers had spoken not in the name of Marxism but in the name of a few 'seeking' Marxists they would have shown more respect for themselves and for Marxism. As for myself, I too am a 'seeker' in philosophy. Namely, the task I have set myself in these comments is to seek out what it was that stood in the way of these people who under the guise of Marxism are offering something incredibly muddled, confused and reactionary.[24]

In this way Lenin set out to deal with the 'mutiny on its knees', as he characterised the movement.

The epistemological problem played a major role in the dispute between Lenin and Bogdanov. The following paragraph will serve as a representative sample of Lenin's rejection of Machism as a subjective idealism and therefore solipsistic.

> If only sensation exists in the world (Avenarius in 1876), if bodies are complexes of sensations (Mach in *Die Analyse der Empfindungen*), then we are obviously confronted with a philosophical subjectivism which inevitably leads to the denial of objective truth. And if sensations are called 'elements' which in one connection give rise to the physical and in another to the psychical, this, as we have seen, only confuses but does not reject the fundamental point of departure of empiriocriticism. Avenarius and Mach recognise sensations as the source of our knowledge. Consequently, they adopt the standpoint of empiricism (all knowledge derives from experience) or sensationalism (all knowledge derives from sensations). But this standpoint gives rise to the difference between the fundamental philosophical trends – idealism and materialism – and does not eliminate that difference, no matter in what new verbal garb ('elements') the standpoint is clothed. Both the solipsist, that is, the subjective idealist, and the materialist may regard sensations as the source of our knowledge. Both Berkeley and Diderot started from Locke. The first premise of the theory of knowledge undoubtedly is that the sole source of our knowledge is sensation. Having recognised the first premise, Mach confuses the second important premise, that is, regarding the objective reality that is given to man in his sensations, or that forms the source of man's sensations. Starting from sensations, one may follow the line of subjectivism, which leads to solipsism ('bodies are complexes or combinations of sensations'), or the line of objectivism, which leads to materialism (sensations are images of objects, of the external world).[25]

Thus, in the field of philosophy there existed for Lenin only black and white. On the one hand there was the subjective idealist who was equated with the solipsist and, on the other, the materialist. There was no intermediate position. All idealists were fundamentally in agreement with Berkeley. An idealism which recognised the existence of an external world was not possible according to Lenin, despite this being the fundamental characteristic of almost every religious philosophy and explicitly acknowledged by Berkeley himself. None of the Russian idealists were solipsists and none of them, including Solov'ev, considered it to be even a problem and they devoted little attention to it. Secondly, Lenin followed Engels' judgement in *Ludwig Feuerbach* that philosophers were divided into two great camps – materialists and idealists – the fundamental distinction between them being that while for the materialists nature was primary and spirit secondary, for the idealists the reverse was the case.[26] This question of the primacy of matter and spirit was the crucial issue of the debate. Lenin's constant confusion of this complex question with the more 'commonsense' issue of solipsism blurred his argument but sharpened it as a polemical and propagandist weapon because solipsism was, to almost everyone, an absurdity, and if an outlook could be called solipsist there was, among the naive, no need for further discussion. It was not surprising, therefore, that Lenin failed to provide further argument in favour of his views. He did not go beyond the statement from Engels that there were two camps and only two camps in the philosophical sphere. Any attempt to break down this simplification was treated by Lenin as a distortion and all attempts to stand between these two camps was dismissed by him as 'agnosticism', a term Lenin, again following Engels, used to characterise neo-Kantians. In discussion of the central issue of the debate, the nature of matter, Lenin had this to say:

> One expression of the genius of Marx and Engels was that they despised pedantic playing with the new words, erudite terms and subtle 'isms', and said simply and plainly: there is a materialist line and an idealist line in philosophy, and between them there are various shades of agnosticism. The vain attempts to find a 'new' point of view in philosophy betray the same poverty of mind that is revealed in similar efforts to create a 'new' theory of value, a 'new' theory of rent and so forth.[27]

This clear exposition of Lenin's anti-intellectualism and his ultra-conservative equation of poverty of mind with new ideas boded ill for the future of Bolshevik philosophy. His dogmatic view was based on the opinion that truth had all been revealed and only 'an inmate of a lunatic asylum'[28] or 'a charlatan or an utter blockhead'[29] could possibly disagree with Lenin's views. Avenarius wrote 'gibberish',[30] the Machists 'sheer nonsense',[31] Bogdanov was a 'jester'.[32] Nowhere in the book did Lenin argue the case for materialism except in terms of appealing to Engels to prove a point without discussing it or by saying that the truth, or in other words Lenin's views, was so obvious that only an idiot could disagree with it. The question of the primacy of matter or of spirit was regarded by Lenin as a closed issue, in that all the idealists rejected matter while the Marxists based their views on it. There was no intermediate position. Yushkevich's call for intellectual freedom could hardly have been more distant from the Leninist position. If Lenin had to resort to scorn and invective on this scale in order to ensure the defeat of such second rate opponents as Bogdanov and Mach and Avenarius – whose views are taken seriously today only by Leninists who still try to refute bourgeois ideologies as though they were aspects of Machism when in reality the influence of Mach and Avenarius is negligible[33] – how could one expect less vehement tactics against first rate and original thinkers? The book mentioned Vladimir Solov'ev only once.

Bogdanov himself was unshaken by Lenin's assault and paid him back in kind. Lenin's attack on absolute truth was itself, he said, intended as absolute eternal truth. As Lenin had accused Bogdanov of being a Berkelian so Bogdanov accused Lenin of being a Schellingian. 'Thus Lenin fights with the idealists.'[34] Lenin's philosophy was 'idealism, clericalism, *popovshchina* and such like'.[35] Lenin's tactics in argument were, said Bogdanov commenting on Lenin's dispute with Lunacharsky, 'to conceal from the reader the true meaning of the opinions of the opponent'.[36] For Bogdanov the fundamental contradiction in Lenin's book, which explained all the others, was between 'the sharp anti-religious tone . . . and the deeply religious thought with its cult of the "absolute"'.[37] At the heart of all Lenin's views Bogdanov found not certainty but belief.

Bogdanov was not alone in his protest against Lenin. Yushkevich, as we have already seen, was moved to respond powerfully to the dogmatism of Lenin, and V. A. Bazarov (1874–1939) was also unrepentant and in fact visualised the struggle as being 'on two fronts'. In his book of that name, published in 1910, Bazarov opened with a half-admiring account of Solov'ev's attempts to justify absolutes which contrasted rather sharply with his scorn for Lenin's naive philosophical views which he expressed in the same article. Lenin's book was of great psychological interest, he said, despite the misunderstandings and contradictions which it contained, for they were characteristics which were very typical of a person who had a realistic, commonsense (*zdravyi smysl'*) outlook which was not completely stifled but only somewhat confused by the metaphysics of one or other school.[38] For Bazarov Lenin was himself guilty of idealism. One can see from this that for the monists, only by accepting that man's mind was itself part of that so-called external world and ceasing to distinguish between inner and outer worlds, could this basic epistemological problem be solved. If Lenin persisted in a dualist outlook, differentiating between 'spirit' and 'matter', then he was just as much an idealist as Kant.

Until Lenin's open disagreement with him over philosophy, Plekhanov had been the major defender of orthodoxy in the dispute over materialism. According to his Soviet editors, Plekhanov 'with great polemical talent criticised and revealed the untenability and the reactionary essence of idealist theories' in this period, at the head of which were placed Machism and God-building.[39] According to Samuel Baron 'probably no other follower of Marx and Engels took philosophy as seriously as did Plekhanov'.[40] This view perhaps reflects our ignorance of the topic of Marxist philosophy rather than Plekhanov's pre-eminence. First it was other Marxists, such as Bogdanov, who forced Plekhanov deeper into philosophical controversy than he had formerly gone; secondly, he was criticised by Bazarov and others precisely for his unphilosophical formulations of problems; and thirdly, it was Plekhanov himself who greatly admired Franz Mehring 'whose knowledge of philosophy is the best and probably unique among German social democrats'.[41] In the Russian fashion of the time, Plekhanov asserted that Marxism was an 'integral world view'[42] and that 'each of its aspects is connected in the closest way with all the others',[43] but this was as far as he would go in agreement with his contemporaries. He set out to differentiate his views from those of the younger men and one of his major philosophical works of this time, *Materialismus militans* (1908), took the form of three lengthy epistles to Bogdanov, while other of his works were directed as Yushkevich, Bazarov, Shulyatikov and their German mentors. His motivation in opposing Bogdanov was founded partly on fear of the growth of idealism in Russia at this time and he thus showed clearly that the revival of idealism was taken seriously by the revolutionaries and was not, as Soviet histories suggest, regarded as an ineffective and insignificant phenomenon. In Plekhanov's words, the confusion brought about by Bogdanov was

> particularly harmful to us at this time when under the influence of reaction and under the pretext of a review of theoretical values idealism of all colours and shades celebrates in our literature a veritable orgy and when certain of the idealists – probably in the

interests of propagating their ideas – announce their views as Marxism of the very latest pattern.[44]

For both Plekhanov and Lenin the ultimate test of a philosophy was in its practice – was it capable of transforming reality? If so, then it was true; if not, false. Both of them took reality for granted and judged a philosophy only according to its effectiveness in interacting with that reality and, not surprisingly, they were materialists since materialism was the necessary presupposition of such a view. The nature of matter itself, which preoccupied several of the Machists, was not of such importance to them. To Plekhanov and Lenin, the important feature of materialism was that thought arose from matter – meaning that which was not thought – rather than the reverse. Having established that man and his culture were the product of matter, they were satisfied. Further elaboration of materialist theory would come but this crucial issue was for them definitely proved.

Historians have tended to minimise the significance of these philosophical differences from the point of view of the part played by them in the history of social democracy at this time. For Lenin philosophical issues were 'completely irrelevant to the question of social revolution'[45] and in fact philosophical discussion had been regarded since 1906 as neutral ground in the conflict within the Social Democratic Party. Further credence to this view of the neutrality of philosophy was given by the example of the German Social Democratic Party in which questions of religion were regarded as a private matter for each member of the party, thus permitting private interpretation of the human condition, providing it did not conflict with the fundamental political views of the party. Indeed, it is hard to see what justification there was in the writings of Marx for any other position. He had written that 'religious questions have no social significance. Nothing more can be said about religious interests as such.'[46] There was next to nothing about death or even about evil in the writings of Marx, Engels or Lenin. In that they treated evil, they saw it as a result of social conditions. Remove oppressive social conditions and one could remove the evil tendencies from within man. The implied abolition of evil in the future communist society was perhaps the most optimistic and utopian feature of the Marxist socialist outlook. In it there would be no offenders of the rights of others once oppression has been ended. Criminals and evil-doers were to be abolished alongside the conditions from which they originated. This optimistic outlook remained at this naive level because, for Marx too, the problem of evil was very much a side issue for the socialist movement and did not affect the immediate political situation.

Was this also Lenin's position? If so, then why did he devote a great deal of time and all his energy in late 1908 and early 1909 to philosophical questions? It is probable that up to 1906 or 1907 Lenin was quite prepared to overlook philosophical differences, particularly as, in the case of Bogdanov, crucial issues of party finance were at stake. But the stormy attacks on orthodox Marxism as he saw it in 1908 were the last straw and, in the interests of party discipline (*partiinost'*), Lenin felt that the party line in philosophy had to be drawn and no one could do it better than himself. Russian Marxism had, since the idealist religious onslaught, begun to develop from being a limited social and economic philosophy into an integral world view. The idealists had occupied intellectual territory left unguarded by the Marxists whose attempt to regain the lost ground had led them into areas of great danger for positivism of any sort. Russian religious idealism was rooted in the supernatural, a sphere the existence of which could only be denied by positivists, even though they were not able to give an adequate explanation since their *a priori* assumption was its non-existence, or at least its unknowability. Since Marxism and positivism had allowed themselves to be pushed by the idealists into a position requiring them to establish their opinions on supernatural problems, Lenin was no longer prepared to tolerate any further dalliance with metaphysics. For him, metaphysics in general was only an attempt to obfuscate the 'real' issues, that is, man's terrestrial, material, social life, which was the only legitimate concern of Marxists, positivists and revolutionaries.

Thus, although it may be true, from the point of view of party history, that in early 1908 the dispute between Lenin on the one hand and Bogdanov and Krasin on the other 'had little connection with the nature of sense perceptions',[47] this does not explain Lenin's energetic attempts later on in the same year to refute the philosophical systems which he regarded as unmarxist. In addition, the idiosyncracies of Lenin's personality have to be taken into account as does his personal response to these developments, so well illustrated by Valentinov in his memoirs of Lenin. According to Valentinov, Lenin wrote *Materialism and Empiriocriticism* in a sustained burst of passionate hatred directed at the intellectual deviants of the party.[48] For these reasons it would seem likely that Lenin did consider the actual issues involved to be important and this raised the more significant question of what importance Lenin actually gave to the issues. Lenin's mind was not of a philosophical or calmly reflective type and he was always much closer to political issues. Thus, one can surmise that for Lenin philosophy was important because it could delineate the various political affiliations of the time. For him *Materialism and Empiriocriticism* was a declaration of war on the political fractions. Around it could stand the true Bolsheviks, beyond it stood the enemies of Lenin, not only Bogdanov, who was expelled from the party at this time, but also Plekhanov who, as far as Lenin was concerned, had outstayed his welcome among the revolutionaries and was a generation behind the movement. Thus Lenin felt that in order to preserve his authority over a disintegrating party it was necessary to crush all sources of intellectual diversity within it. This helps to explain the predominance of personal vituperation over philosophical content in the book. Its publication meant, above all, the politicisation of philosophy in the sense that henceforth for Lenin, philosophy, as much as literature, was a political weapon to be used in the interests of revolution. Lenin rejected the fundamental premise of philosophy – the search for truth. For him this was a chimera used by the bourgeoisie to divert thinkers from the revolutionary path, and so it has remained in the opinion of Soviet ideologists. For the revolutionaries, as for Sherlock Holmes, it made absolutely no difference whether the earth went round the sun or the sun round the earth. Either way social problems and the given situation in which man found himself – 'reality' in the meaning given to it by Lenin – was not affected in the slightest. The purpose of philosophy was to show that man was a real being capable of transforming his environment through rational, collective, social action.

The politicisation of philosophy and its downgrading to ideology were noted at the time by Izgoev, who was one of the most perceptive social commentators. He had no doubt that one of the main issues at stake in the dispute was leadership of social democracy, and philosophy was only being used as a pretext. The squabble between the Machists and the orthodox reminded him of the story of a French explorer in Africa. In the course of his travels the Frenchman lost a clock. It fell into the hands of a tribe who proceeded to worship as a god this clock, the mechanism and function of which they did not understand. Not only that, but a 'rebel' group seized upon the new god to use against the established witch-doctor, whose regime only survived because the clock stopped at the crucial moment. 'Just such a clock is foreign philosophy among the Russians', concluded Izgoev.[49]

Ironically, Lenin's philosophical philistinism left a vacuum in the Soviet Union into which God-building and other quasi-religious cults were drawn. Both God-building and monism of a sort have taken a position in the modern Soviet Union that Lenin sought to deny them. In his memoirs Berdyaev recalled that Bogdanov was of the opinion that Berdyaev's own conversion to liberalism was a result of psychic illness and in Vologda often asked Berdyaev how he had slept in order to establish whether the disease of religion was advancing or receding.[50] Similar attitudes have been noted in the present day Soviet Union among, for instance, security police officers and others in authority who treat dissent from the party line as a suitable case for psychiatric treatment. Also, the cult of Lenin's own personality, in which he is portrayed as the all-wise, all-powerful and immortal protector of socialism, has also occupied the areas left vacant by his own attitudes.

3 Religious revolutionaries

The idealist, liberal, religious assault of the early 1900s had exposed the revolutionary socialist movement to attack from an unexpected direction. A number of the radicals felt that idealism had exposed a critical weakness in Marxism and that socialism, though it was more than adequate to explain social phenomena, was powerless to discuss the fundamental questions of life itself. In response to this, two closely related outlooks developed among those interested in such questions. On the one hand there were radical Christians, such as Bulgakov and Berdyaev, who attempted to unite certain aspects of the social movement with Christianity to produce, in Bulgakov's case, Christian socialism, and in Berdyaev's, Christian anarchism. While these people were attempting to show that Christianity had to be in a real sense revolutionary, liberating and socialist, another group reversed the emphasis and proposed that socialism should be raised from the status of a political movement to that of a religion.

These two groups, the radical Christians and the God-builders, were not movements having great influence among the intelligentsia at this time. For instance, Struve was suspicious of all socialists and anarchists, even those disguised as Christians, and among the revolutionaries the philistinism of Lenin was more representative than the openness of the God-builders. But even so the religious revolutionaries were among the most original thinkers in Russia at this time.

It was remarked in the previous chapter that certain of the revolutionaries used the word 'religious' in a pejorative sense, for example, Bogdanov in a reference to Lenin's *Materialism and Empiriocriticism* where he said that Lenin was a 'religious' thinker. In this case Bogdanov was using the word 'religion' as a synonym for clericalism, dogmatism, dualism and authoritarianism, and it had an extremely negative significance. This kind of usage of the term religious was not confined to Bogdanov. In *Vekhi*, Frank said that the intelligentsia could be regarded as 'religious' if one meant by that, dogmatic, intolerant and fanatical.[1] A pamphlet published in

1907 also attacked the intelligentsia for assuming the unpleasant characteristics of the Orthodox Church and the writer detected a kind of dogmatic Orthodox mentality among the Social Democrats. In this pamphlet, entitled *Ortodoksal'nyi marksizm i pravoslavie*, the writer compared the spirit of the teachings of Christ and Marx with those of their various disciples in the socialist political parties and the Christian churches.[2] In place of the dogmatic, scholastic approach the writer proposed a creative approach which he saw as being the true spirit of both Christ and Marx. If Christ were to return to earth at that time, the author wrote, He would once again reject the building of altars to Himself and drive out of the temple all those who justified their commerce by using His Father's name. If Marx were to come back from the dead he would deny that he was a Marxist and would refuse to acknowledge dogmatic socialists as his followers.[3]

But this sense of the word religious was not the one used by the thinkers dealt with in this chapter. For all of them, religion, however defined, was an integral part of human psychology. It was for most of them the most important and most noble element of the human character. There was a great deal in common between thinkers as diverse as Struve, Berdyaev, Bulgakov, Gorky and Lunacharsky on this question of religion. For them religion was the hope that there was more to human life than its sorry contemporary condition suggested. It was the striving of man for a better future, the bond of brotherhood uniting all men, the submerging of one's own individuality in the greater collective, and the denial of self in the interest of the other. This similarity, and also the undeniable difference, between these men, was symbolised by their adaptation of Solov'ev's term Godmanhood (*Bogochelovechestvo*). The Christians used it to mean that man was intended to work jointly with God in the business of creation, transformation and salvation of the world. Only by uniting his efforts with God as a co-worker in the great task of history, could man fulfil himself. On the other hand, the socialists changed the term into mangodhood (*chelovekobozhestvo*) in the Nietzschean sense that man was himself God and that he was himself the ruler of the universe. Both of these conceptions gave the same role to human activity, to human history, because for both of them man was the agent of creation in the world and it was to the task of transforming it into the ideal condition that man was called. Thus, in the practical affairs of the world, the gap between the two groups was not insurmountable. Similarly both used the old

Russian religious term *sobornost'* to exemplify the ideal relation between man and society. *Sobornost'* meant for them the *extension* of the individual through his *submersion* in the collective, in the Christian sense that a man could only live truly by denying his own life in its everyday sense, or in other words, that man was called to a higher task than that of securing his own personal comfort.

CHRISTIAN ANARCHISM AND CHRISTIAN SOCIALISM

The political views of Berdyaev and S. N. Bulgakov (1871–1944) distinguished these two men from each other more than their philosophical outlook. Both had strongly individual opinions and in fact were distrusted both by their liberal colleagues – such as Kizevetter and Struve who, as editors of *Russkaya mysl'* occasionally disclaimed responsibility for the views of these two men when an important article by either of them found its way into their journal – and also by the revolutionaries who saw the attempt to combine socialism with idealism as a dangerous move which might lead to a split in the liberation movement, separating it into bourgeois and proletarian fragments. They also differed considerably from each other. Bulgakov was far more socialist than Berdyaev in the sense that his views retained a great deal of the Social Democratic outlook, whereas Berdyaev, although he too retained an interest in the same problems as the socialists and often spoke the socialist language, was deeply hostile to the authoritarian implications of socialism. Those who had set out on the journey from Marxism to idealism, travelled at different speeds and came to rest at different points. While in 1901 the reconstruction of Marxism on an idealist base was still considered a valuable objective by Struve, he soon came to realise the difficulties of the task and his Marxism suffered as his idealism developed. If Struve travelled the furthest, it was Bulgakov who travelled the least. In this period, he made an attempt to set up an active Christian socialist party, or more precisely perhaps, pressure group, as it never showed any sign of becoming a mass party to rival the established ones.

The term Christian socialist was chosen by Bulgakov to describe himself and it indeed sits rather oddly on one who was a vehement attacker of socialism and who could in no respect be thought of as a revolutionary Marxist. Indeed it was in these years that he made a decisive break with the revolutionary movement and, as he related in his *Avtobiograficheskie zametki*, *(Autobiographical notes)*, became a tsarist. He explained that he was far from the support of the reactionary elements of tsarism but loved the tsarist idea because in it he saw not the reality but the potential.[4] Thus Bulgakov freed himself from the mystique of revolution only to fall immediately under the mystique of absolute monarchy, or more specifically, of theocracy. During the remainder of this period, Bulgakov devoted his attention to the elaboration of the theocratic idea based on a separation of the two powers, the sacred and the secular, which, he claimed, distinguished the tsarist idea, of which he approved, from the Caesaro-papism, of which he disapproved.[5]

The fundamental motif of his thought at this time was that the human race was faced by a religious dilemma – one had to choose for God or against Him. There was no other way. This was the fundamental question facing every man. Thus for Bulgakov, the world consisted only of fighters for God or fighters against Him.[6] This simple division was applied by Bulgakov to the sphere of thought.[7] At the centre of the ideas of Schopenhauer, Marx, Comte and Spencer, Bulgakov detected pantheism and cosmotheism, so that, for example, one of the primary motivations in Marx's thought was militant atheism derived from Feuerbach. This dilemma existed because, according to Bulgakov, man was a religious being and only religion could form the basis of society. 'Religions are various', he said, 'but religion is universal.'[8] In the same essay he wrote:

> Religion is the yeast of society, that 'basis' on which various 'superstructures' develop. In this sense religion is the universal unifying principle, and man is a social being (Aristotle's *zoon politikon*) only insofar as he is a religious being. Even though various causes or factors of a spontaneous, impersonal character are at work in history, in the final count they serve only as the passive material which is conquered and shaped by the human spirit, by the active principle of history.[9]

This conception of history was of great importance to him. Man's task was to change the world, to give order to it in accordance with his ideal. This, it will be immediately remarked, was the same impulse behind socialism, both utopian and Marxist, and Bulgakov was himself aware of the similarity, but for him it was not a similarity arising from the proximity of the two, as he had earlier thought, but from total negation.

The theme of socialism as a negative image of Christianity was developed by Bulgakov in a long essay, 'Apocalyptics and socialism', published in *Russkaya mysl'* in 1910.[10] The greater part of the work was devoted to a detailed theological study of Judaeo-Christian chiliasm, that is, the belief in the immediacy of the thousand-year reign of good on earth. But the heart of the essay lay in its application to the modern world. Bulgakov argued that the appeal of socialism arose from its role as the translator of the cosmology and theology of Judaic chiliasm into the language of rational political economy. 'Socialism is the apocalypse of the natural religion of mangodhood.'[11] Socialism, he continued, had in the proletariat its chosen people, the bearers of the messianic idea and the elect who were to realise the coming kingdom. The class of capitalists played the role of the devil, their metaphysical tendency to evil expressing itself in their tendency to accumulate capital. Finally, there was the '*deus ex machina*' which would, inevitably, effect the transformation. In socialist theory this role was played by the 'laws' of society, especially those of the growth of productive forces. This, said the socialists, was the locomotive that would pull the train of history from the realm of necessity into that of freedom.[12]

In view of this irreconcilable difference between Christianity and socialism, how could Bulgakov be imbued with a socialism which survived the revolution in his metaphysical outlook? For him the historical task set itself by socialism was the same as that facing the Christian – the transformation of the world into a condition in which social justice, equality and the good were dominant. The weakness of socialism, for Bulgakov, was that it was a blasphemous perversion of the kingdom of God, stolen in the name of the kingdom of man. Thus, what Bulgakov was attempting was to return the socialist impulses of Russia back to the Church from whence they sprang.

Bulgakov referred to Dostoevsky's statement that Orthodoxy was 'our Russian socialism'[13] and his own conception of the Church reflected this belief. He did not simply say that the Church should be socialist or that Christ was the first communist; in fact quite the reverse. Christianity was, in his view, ambiguous in its attitude to the social question and to the world. While the Church was hostile to existing social forms of slavery, feudalism and capitalism, the social question was not at the heart of religion.[14] In a religious outlook, the central aspects were morality and individualism and it was from these that the Christian set out. Wealth was a *moral* issue, as was property. It was, for instance, wrong to have a strong *sense* of ownership, of oneself having exclusive rights over particular material objects. At the same time the Christian had to be aware of the danger of immersion in the world.[15] This ambiguity extended to the Christian conception of history. In the Christian consciousness there was, he continued, an unavoidable struggle between two conceptions of history. On the one hand there was the optimistic, chiliastic view, that is, that the triumph of good on earth was possible, and on the other the pessimistic, eschatological, which emphasised the transience of the world and concentrated the mind on thoughts of death and judgement, heaven and hell. The Christian was torn between immanence and transcendence.[16] Bulgakov usually sided with the optimists.

In Bulgakov's view, the socialist task arose from the Church, and its divorce from the Church – its transition to atheism – made it impossible for it to succeed. 'Only the Church can propose and be capable of solving the task which socialism takes on, the task of uniting and organising humanity on the basis of beneficial gifts given by the Saviour, on the basis of love for Him, which is at the same time personal and general.'[17] It was, then, the duty of the Church to shoulder the task of modern culture and to carry it further than was possible for the secular man.[18] According to Bulgakov, the real Church had to be synonymous with society, with culture, with the whole of humanity. Indeed, he said, it was the division into spheres of influence which had robbed the Church of its vitality,[19] and it was only by reuniting them that Christianity and society could reach their full potential.

It was to these views that Bulgakov had come. The desire for social justice which brought him to the revolutionary movement had found a new and more lasting dwelling place. In standing for the Second Duma, he had called himself a non-party Christian socialist[20] because he was under the impression that around that time in Russia there was a movement afoot which was both religious and revolutionary, but this, he admitted, turned out to be a 'senseless dream'. In Moscow, he recalled the business did not go beyond sticking crosses on revolutionary proclamations, but he did try to set up a 'Union of Christian Struggle', the name and idea of which were both borrowed from Solov'ev.[21] What he had in mind was, he said, 'an early prototype of the living church'.[22] Bulgakov's initial attempt to set up a Christian political party devoted to social reform, came in 1905. In the last issue of *Voprosy zhizni* (September 1905), he set out a five-point basis for such a party. These points were: (1) the cultivation of Christian society in which political activity would be regarded as a fulfilment of religious duty; (2) the uniting of all Christians irrespective of creed, who understood the fundamental tasks of Christian politics; (3) the political and social liberation of the individual, based on the anarchistic communism of the early Christian communities, as the fundamental task of the party; (4) a declaration of irreconcilable war on all 'hatred of mankind' of the Black Hundred type and an alliance with non-religious parties of a similar democratic type as the Union, in order to achieve common goals, while at the same time struggling against their atheist ideas; (5) the creation of a Christian literature and newspaper press to propagate its ideas and the construction of organisations of people who agreed with its principles in town and country and among the intelligentsia, as the immediate task of the Union. Finally, the slogan of the society was to be *Bog i narod* – God and the people.[23]

As Bulgakov admitted, the wave of optimism which had led him to these proposals was insubstantial and the practical proposals came to nothing. Their importance for the present study is that they show the first form taken by Bulgakov's attempts to unite religion with a social policy. They contained elements of both liberalism and socialism. For him, the whole weakness of classical liberalism, which recognised the value of the individual, was that it found no way to realise this ideal in society. Thus Bulgakov distinguished himself from liberalism and socialism as such because for him liberalism was insufficiently democratic, in the sense that it did not actively promote its ideals in all areas of society and the economy, and social democracy in its Marxist and economist forms was insufficiently liberal. Genuine liberalism had to be liberal—democratic or liberal—socialist.[24]

At this point Bulgakov did not claim that the Church, as he understood it, was the only means of solving social problems, but he did feel that for the Christian, political action was a categorical imperative. The Christian could not be indifferent to politics because politics was the means of the external arrangement of mankind – to deny politics was to deny society and to deny society was to split mankind into separate individuals. To do this was to deny Godmanhood and ultimately to deny Christ and Christianity.[25] The absence of Christians from the political arena had had fatal consequences. The socialist movement which, he said, was not simply a political and social movement but first of all an atheist, quasi-religious, philosophical movement, gained strength from the weakness of its opponents in this sphere. This gave atheism a monopoly over the defenders of the working class so that materialism and socialism were almost synonymous in the same way that religion and reactionary obscurantism had become synonymous.[26] In a later attempt by him to promote his Christian Brotherhood of Struggle and his Christian Political Union, he pointed out that by having such an organisation to attack abuses in the Church and in the government, it would be possible 'to knock the weapons from the hands of the Black Hundred leaders' who claimed to represent religion but who in fact engaged in religious deception and hatred of mankind, which was very far from true religion. In the immediate context of 1906, when this article was written, Bulgakov claimed that his proposed organisation would bridge the gap between the Kadets and the people, a gap caused by the irreligiousness of the party, which prevented it from becoming a party of the whole people, as Struve and others hoped.[27]

Such was the basis of Bulgakov's political views at this time. He combined liberal individualism with religious collectivism and conservative cultural values with revolutionary ardour. The fate of his attempts to start an organisation based on these principles showed that he stood almost alone, but even so, many of the fundamentals of his outlook were comparable to those of Berdyaev, and even to Gorky, Lunacharsky and the God-builders whom he hated so much. Interestingly enough, Struve and Frank were very critical in 1906 of Bulgakov's views and appended to his article on 'Religion and politics' a sharply worded and very revealing refutation of these views. Bulgakov's mistake was, they said, that he had a dogmatic understanding of religion in an ecclesiastical sense, in the sense of an 'objectively ordered system' of belief which created a barrier between believers and non-believers.

> In distinction from Bulgakov we propose that for the Christian and the atheist, for the idealist and the positivist, there can be a common policy having a single religious root. . . . True socialism based on recognition of the individual as the highest value is completely independent of any dogma whether it be materialistic or theological.[28]

Clearly, Struve and Frank had not yet given up the hope of achieving a united liberation movement in which people could work together despite intellectual and metaphysical differences and which could still claim the name socialist, though in the British Fabian sense rather than the Marxist one.

Although he is often spoken of in the same breath as Bulgakov, Nikolai Berdyaev presented a very different variation on the theme of Christianity and revolution, even at this immature stage of development when they had both recently emerged from a similar change in their ideas which had led them from legal Marxism to Christian idealism. In their social views they stood far apart as Berdyaev's view of humanity was an extremely libertarian one whereas Bulgakov's theocratic outlook was unavoidably authoritarian. In Berdyaev's way of thinking no power, not even God's, had the right to compel or constrain the individual, whereas for Bulgakov individualism implied a free submission to a just authority. Another major distinction between the two was that Berdyaev attached far less importance to theology and apocalyptics. From similar principles of idealism and individualism tempered by a collectivist view of individuality – that is, the inseparability of individual and collective – Bulgakov and Berdyaev were travelling on diametrically opposed paths – Berdyaev towards freedom, Bulgakov towards authority – leading in Bulgakov's case to ordination.

If Bulgakov followed a path leading towards theology and the official Church, Berdyaev was at this time much more influenced by mysticism, not in its institutionalised Christian sense but by its pagan form as expressed in the new religious consciousness, particularly by Vyacheslav Ivanov. In the years 1904–5 Vyacheslav Ivanov and Chulkov were close collaborators with Bulgakov and Berdyaev on the journal *Voprosy zhizni*, and in his autobiography Berdyaev acknowledged the influence Vyacheslav Ivanov had on him at this time, although Berdyaev claimed that the influence was only a temporary one.[29] It did, however, have enduring results in that it opened Berdyaev's eyes to the mystical side of the human personality which was ignored or denied by the materialists. For Berdyaev, the reality of mystical experience became as unquestionable as the existence of an external world was for the materialists. This must have played a considerable part in preparing Berdyaev for one of the major events in his intellectual life, the encounter with Jacob Boehme, which he said happened in 1912.[30] If his meeting with Boehme was still in the future, his discovery of mysticism itself was occurring at this time and, like other members of the new religious consciousness, the immediate impulse to mystical individualism and the perfection of the self as an imperative had been provided by Nietzsche.[31]

Many of Berdyaev's works of this period expounded his views on various aspects of religion and mysticism. Whereas, for the materialist mysticism represented a turning away from reality, Berdyaev accused the materialists themselves of being the ones who were unrealistic. He talked of mystical *realism* at this time and claimed that the decadents and the positivists were anti-realist while the mystics truly expressed a higher reality.[32] In the foreword to *Novoe religioznoe soznanie i obshchestvennost' (The New Religious Consciousness and Society)* Berdyaev characterised himself as 'a realist and an objectivist'[33] and this extended to his mysticism which was, he said, '*objective* mysticism' in that it was 'linked with the *meaning* of universal history'[34] and from this arose his religion because religion was a necessary corollary of this view of the world. 'Religion is necessary to me so that the *meaning* of my existence and the meaning of history can be revealed and in order that my own meaning is united, linked for ever with the meaning of the world.'[35] Death, the separation of the individual and the world, as Berdyaev saw it, could only be given meaning by religion.[36] The first aim of the true Christian religion was, he said, to banish fear and to establish a courageous attitude to life.[37]

There was nothing specifically Christian in many of these statements. When Berdyaev wrote 'our religion must be greater than Christianity'[38] or 'in the light of the new consciousness is born another dilemma: *Christianity or Christ.* Christianity is the old world, the old way of life: Christ is the new world, opposed to all ways of life'[39] he seemed to be voicing the views of the God-builders, or even of Nietzsche. However, Berdyaev was a Christian and based his views on the personality of Christ, unlike the God-builders or decadents. Since Christ, he wrote, religion had been the path to actual union with God.[40]

While he showed less interest in the theological apocalypse than Bulgakov or Merezhkovsky, he was imbued with the secularised apocalyptic idea of revolution. His support for revolution arose from the fundamental element of his social outlook which was a very highly developed social conscience which had led him, as so many others, to the socialist, revolutionary and liberation movements in the first place. For him Radishchev was the founder of the Russian intelligentsia and Radishchev's confession that he could not be happy while his countrymen suffered,[41] applied *a fortiori* to Berdyaev who, like Radishchev, was full of the spirit of *noblesse oblige*, which had always been a significant motivating force of many members of the intelligentsia.[42]

One aspect of Berdyaev's sympathy for the oppressed and hatred of the oppressor was his extreme dislike of the middle class and particularly its philistinism (*meshchanstvo*) which he chastised whenever it appeared. Berdyaev's aristocratic disdain for the tradesman mentality even affected his view of thinkers whom he admired and respected, such as Chicherin and Leont'ev in Russia and Windelband in Germany. Windelband, whose lectures on Kant Berdyaev had attended in Heidelberg,[43] and German academic idealism in general, were criticised by him because they were too 'bourgeois' and the morality they preached was that of petty-bourgeois manners. He added, as did the Marxists, that such a philosophy 'from the social—political point of view serves the forces of conservatism which are hostile to liberty.'[44] Elsewhere, he criticised Chicherin and the old Russian liberalism for having 'bourgeois ideals' rather than 'universal' ones.[45] Like Windelband, Chicherin was too conservative and did not share Berdyaev's desire for innovation or revolution. 'For him [Chicherin] religion is not a liberating force but a conserving one. It preserves the old economic, family, state and suchlike foundations of life. About the birth of new forms of life he says nothing.'[46]

This philistinism was not confined to the middle class but was also at the heart of its intelligentsia offshoot, according to Berdyaev. In *Vekhi* he complained about the intelligentsia's lack of genuine culture but even before 1909 he was making similar remarks and many of the arguments of *Vekhi* were used at this time. In *Dukhovnyi krizis intelligentsii (The Spiritual Crisis of the Intelligentsia)* he outlined his view of the intelligentsia as a spent force which must be reactivated by a change of heart and of mind. A crisis had come about in the views of the intelligentsia.

The whole traditional outlook and traditional psychology of the Russian intelligentsia has become bankrupt not only in an external material sense but in an inner spiritual one. The initial idea, the position at the basis of our revolutionary movement, did not withstand the test of life when it was called into question. A new idea, a new faith, a new spiritual atmosphere are needed.

With the old means nothing further will be achieved. We must give birth to a new intelligentsia which should borrow from the old only its thirst for justice on earth but in the soil of a new consciousness, of a different content for our soul.[47]

The intelligentsia's conservatism expressed itself for him in, amongst other things, a complete lack of artistic sensibility which he berated in an article of May 1905 in *Voprosy zhizni*. 'In this area the ignorance, lack of culture, and vulgarity of taste of the advanced Russian intelligentsia surpass everything.'[48] None of them took the arts seriously with the result that, for example, *Mir iskusstva*, 'which would have been the pride of any other European country,' said Berdyaev, was not read by the greater part of the intelligentsia.[49] Russia possessed very talented poets such as Bryusov, Bal'mont, Gippius, Sologub and Vyacheslav Ivanov, but, he continued, the intelligentsia did not understand them.[50] For Berdyaev it was not the 'nihilistic—ascetic' intelligentsia which was revolutionary but rather those in sympathy with the new consciousness. As a journal *Novyi put'* had had its shortcomings, he said, 'but it also had a truly revolutionary thirst for religious creativity and for a new transfigured culture'. The intelligentsia 'Old Believers' were, he went on, 'bearers of philistinism and bearers of distributive arithmetical truths'.[51] However, he said, the hour had then struck 'when facts and actions compel us finally to turn the attention of our radical, or rather conservative, intelligentsia towards the new and eternal that is being created in the contemporary consciousness'.[52] No other path could realise the hopes of the intelligentsia, 'the bringing into existence of our hundred-year-old political dreams must be connected with the great cultural and religious renaissance of Russia'.[53]

Thus, for Berdyaev the nature of the crisis of the intelligentsia and of the revolutionary movement was clear. He attacked the 'revolutionary intelligentsia' not because they were revolutionary but because their interpretation of the revolution had become stale and static when it should have been fresh and creative. Berydaev diagnosed a spiritual crisis in the intelligentsia resulting from the collapse of Marxism, not through defeat by reactionaries but as a result of its own shortcomings. He called for the intelligentsia to recognise this situation and to face up courageously to the task of reassessing its views and its presuppositions. Marxist materialism, he said, could not halt this crisis of revaluation because it was itself one of the causes.[54]

In 1900, however, Berdyaev was still at least half Marxist and some might even say that he always remained so. It was noted in the first chapter that Struve welcomed Berdyaev's first book *Sub"ektivizm i individualizm* because it marked the first step in an attempt to reconstruct Marxism on an idealist foundation.[55] This remained the objective of Berdyaev's efforts in the early 1900s though it gradually gave way to the growing feeling that this was impossible and that parts worth saving in the materialist socialist outlook could not be amputated and made to live independently of the parent organ. In 1901 Berdyaev published in the social democratic journal *Mir Bozhii* his article on 'The struggle for idealism'. In it he argued for a bringing together of Marxist socialism, which provided the means of life, with religion and idealism, which provided the meaning and purpose.[56] Recent years had shown, he said, that Marxism was going through a crisis. No longer was the main division of the intelligentsia that between its populist and its Marxist wings, but between the orthodox and the critical tendencies within Marxism itself. 'The motivation for theoretical work now is not the criticism of the *narodnik* tendency, but self-criticism and the necessity for the further development of a world view.'[57] It was this development of a world view which exactly described the activity of Berdyaev in this period. He and the idealists were forcing the Russian Marxists to extend and define their views on a much broader front so that philosophical questions came gradually to assume a greater significance in their arguments than economic or practical political disputes. This, said Berdyaev, corresponded in a sense to the attempts of Bernstein in Germany to revise Marx, but the critical Marxism of Russia was not simply an imitation of Bernstein. It was wider in its origin and related to the 'spiritual ferment' of the nineteenth century in general, so that, Berdyaev continued,

> I dare assert categorically that the song of positivism, naturalism and hedonism is sung, and everywhere *the struggle for idealism* is announced, the struggle for a more joyful and brighter understanding of the world in which the highest, eternal needs of the human spirit are satisfied.[58]

Before proceeding to a justification of idealism, Berdyaev felt it necessary to remove one basic misunderstanding.

This historical misunderstanding says: theoretical idealism is connected with reactionary social desires, with practical materialism: practical idealism and progressive aspirations can be linked only with theoretical realism or materialism.[59]

Far from being conservative, Berdyaev argued, idealism was devoted to the constant improvement of society and was aware that the perfect society did not exist. In this way Berdyaev's views were relativist in relation to reality, absolute in relation to the objective of progress. This was to be expected and applied to many dialectical systems because reality was always able to be improved upon. No culture, said Berdyaev, could claim to possess absolute truth; the content of humanity's spiritual culture was relative.[60] But he was an absolutist in that he saw perfection as the goal of this relative process.

Mental development is the process of approximation to the *truth*, moral to the good, aesthetic to beauty. Filling the life of the human individual with the highest content, we inevitably depend on the ideas of truth, goodness and beauty, which are shown to be higher than happiness and pleasure so that they only make elevated, dignified men happy, but not swine . . . From all the preceding arguments naturally arises that exceptionally important conclusion that *progress and perfection are higher than happiness and pleasure.*[61]

One aspect was, however, absolute in both reality and in theory and that was the absolute value of the individual as an end in himself, which took precedence over everything else and could not be deduced empirically.[62] Finally, for Berdyaev, the transition from science to philosophy went one step further, into religion.

If science turns into philosophy, then philosophy turns into religion. Without religious faith in the moral order of the world, in the vital link of the individual with the general, the undying significance of every moral effort, life is not worth living, life becomes meaningless.[63]

The central idea of Marx, not original to him but apparent in his whole conception of society and of the world, was the idea of progress, and this was also one of the twin pillars of Berdyaev's idealism, the second being absolute individualism. He summed up his own view of idealism – which he said was only one among a number of factions and offshoots within the general movement – in 1904 in an article 'On the new Russian idealism'.

> There are two problems, the problem of the individual, of the individual fate of the human soul, of its rights, of its value, and the problem of progress, of the fate of humanity and of the world, of the goal and meaning of history: in them interact the most abstract and theoretical and the most concrete and vital of our interests. All the most recent Russian idealism arises from the attempt to raise and to resolve these questions.[64]

His impatience with the revolutionaries grew in these years and he began to denounce them, but even in his denunciations he did not primarily question the desirability of revolution, nor of many socialist doctrines, such as the redistribution of wealth. What he attacked was the vulgar philistinism which made these doctrines into ends rather than means, and the irresponsibility of the intelligentsia which stood between it and the successful fulfilment of its aims. In particular two articles of this period discussed the questions of the revolutionary mentality and the place of revolutionary ideas in the history of Russian intellectual development which he examined in greater depth after the revolution and during his exile. The first one, written in 1906, was on 'The history and psychology of Russian Marxism'; the second written two years later, was devoted to 'The psychology of revolution'.

Berdyaev found at the heart of Russian Marxism an unmarxist utopianism, a 'religious thirst and an eschatological hope'.[65] Scientific and political argument was, he asserted, useless against the chiliasm of the mystical devotees of the new religion of the thousand year earthly kingdom not of Christ but of some other god. 'We hoped for neutral social development not this social passion and religious dreaming.'[66] Berdyaev explained this mentality by means of the yoke of autocracy which dominated life in Russia.

> Revolution is not characterised by the radicalism of its aims, nor by the depth of the renewal of social life and of human nature, but by the ardour of reaction to the evils of the past, to oppression, to reaction . . . The revolutionary cannot exist without the reactionary, without oppression, without prisons, and police. His

life would not be enriched, but impoverished if these abominable spectres were to disappear. He would lose his pathos.[67]

The case of Marxist revolution was somewhat different from this classic pattern, according to Berdyaev, because it had definite theories of social development. The revolutionary element of Marxism was, said Berdyaev, 'an optical illusion' because *social* revolutions have never occurred and cannot in fact ever occur.[68] A revolution can change a government but not a whole social system.[69] Berdyaev argued for the evolutionary interpretation of Marxism. Each turning point in social development could only be the outcome of a previous one, so that the production of wealth must precede its redistribution, and social and economic development as a whole was dependent on the forces of production.[70] The process of socialisation of production was seen by Marx, Berdyaev continued, as a gradual, many-sided long-term process,[71] and it was only by developing the forces of production and raising the consciousness of the workers that the revolution could come about. But the tactics of Plehve and the Jacobinism (sic) of the bureaucracy had given rise to a Jacobin understanding of the revolution in the eyes of the intelligentsia.[72]

Berdyaev's complex attitude to the intelligentsia, the revolution and to Marx was never clearer than here. He adopted the intelligentsia's ideas of transforming the present into a new and more humane society and recognised that economic development and the raising of class consciousness could bring this about, but at the same time he fervently attacked the revolutionaries for trying to precipitate the process. As a result they had set it back rather than promoted it. Berdyaev was only content when he had proved himself more revolutionary than the revolutionaries. He exposed the intelligentsia's mystical belief that the new society would spontaneously rise from the ashes of the old as a contradiction of all they professed – it was unscientific and unmarxist.

Berdyaev reiterated some of these arguments and presented others that were to be used later in *Vekhi* in a second important article on the revolutionary mentality written in 1907, but suppressed by Kizevetter, the editor of *Russkaya mysl'*, for a year. It was finally published in the July 1908 issue of the paper and was accompanied by a refutation from Kizevetter. The problem was that in this article Berdyaev widened his criticism of the 'fetishising' of revolution to include the Kadets who made a similar fetish of the .

constitution. 'Russia must experience constitutionalism' he said, 'and God grant that she may survive it with a minimum of idol worship.'[73]

His article started off in the by now familiar tone. The Left, he said, believed blindly and boundlessly in revolution, giving it almost absolute existence and almost divine attributes. In practice they had created the chimera of 'revolution', in theory the chimera of 'progress', so that, he continued in a manner very reminiscent of *Vekhi*, 'the criteria of revolution (*revolyutsionnost'*) and of progress (*progressivnost'*) have replaced the old criteria of good and evil, truth and falsehood, beauty and ugliness, godliness and atheism'.[74] Constitutionalism had presented a new situation. History, said Berdyaev, especially that of England, taught that the balanced, constitutional state had to grow gradually and organically. It could not succeed rapidly. Russia was at present in an ambiguous phase of constitutional monarchy and strong reaction to revolutionary excess, but the constitutional structure was slowly gaining ground.[75] But even so it had its dangers and the Kadets were not the least of the evils which Russia had to face.[76] The damage was that for them 'constitutionalism' was a fetish corresponding to the 'revolutionism' of the Left and the 'statism' (*gosudarstvennost'*) of the Right. They were in danger of believing that liberation could be achieved only through experiments in political alchemy.[77]

What annoyed Berdyaev most about the Kadets was their bloodless, soulless, rationalism, their 'neutral humanism' as he called it.[78] They were too rational to be popular among the people, their atheism drove a wedge between them and the Russian people who could not live without God and were forever seeking his kingdom. For the Russian people

> only inner revolution, the giving of life by the new Spirit, by the eternal Spirit, does not lead to decomposition, is not accompanied by putrefaction. Only this type of revolution is radical. May this great revolution conquer reaction and decomposition . . . The old revolution is finished in Russia, the old reaction calls forth ghosts. Is it not time for the new revolution to begin?[79]

Such were Berdyaev's views on revolution as expressed by him up to the time of the *Vekhi* debate. For him it was the religious renaissance that represented the real revolution of the early 1900s and the attempts of the conservative intelligentsia to oppose it were, as he said of Gorky's article, mere 'hooliganism'.[80] Gorky's article, 'Notes on philistinism', had, said Berdyaev, defined philistinism as being identified by its characteristics of individualism, metaphysics, mysticism, lack of contact with the proletarian revolution and a tendency to ponder the weightiest problems without recognising a duty to the people.[81] If we were to accept Gorky's definition, Berdyaev retorted, we would have to include, for one reason or another, all great cultural achievements, including Tolstoy, Dostoevsky, the Russian intelligentsia, philosophy, science, humanism and so on. And what was Gorky's alternative? – 'the cult of force, worship of the working people, as a fact, as the victorious element, spite against individual creativity, the negation of cultural values, a view of the human individual as a means and as an implement'.[82] 'I can only call this article of Gorky's', said Berdyaev, 'hooliganism in the widest and deepest meaning of the word.'[83] Again Berdyaev explained nihilism as a reaction to and a mirror image of the autocracy. 'The most important of all to understand is the psychological truth that reaction is not the antidote to revolution, but, quite the reverse: revolution and reaction are of one nature – twins.'[84] Similarly in 1905,

> Nihilism in the Russian revolution is the child of the nihilism of our historic past, of the nihilism of the Russian autocracy. The lack of culture in radicalism is the expression of lack of culture in conservatism, the vandalism of the old, official Russia. In revolutionary Jacobinism the spirit of political autocracy and despotism is always to be found.[85]

Thus Berdyaev felt alienated from both conservatism and radicalism for the same reason, because they were one and the same thing. His answer to the vicious circle of reaction breeding revolution and revolution breeding reaction, was in creativity, closely connected with individualism and religion. His hopes for such an increase in culture and spiritual creativity rose, but he was never optimistic of success in the short term. The disputes of the period showed that Russian society lacked sufficient 'creative spiritual power' to prevent the catastrophe of revolution.[86] For Berdyaev, only a new start, the encouragement of a new mentality, the effort to develop 'creative spiritual power' could solve the impasse in which Russia found herself. This new way of thinking would have to harmonise better with the Russian tradition and with the Christianity of the people than the old intelligentsia traditions had done. Only a liberated Orthodoxy, such as that of Khomyakov, Dostoevsky, Solov'ev or Fedorov, would provide a basis for this, and it was because it derived its ideas from traditional Russian sources, from nineteenth-century relgious thought, that Berdyaev welcomed the twentieth-century spiritual ferment. This Orthodoxy would have to be the Orthodoxy of freedom, exemplified in Dostoevsky's legend of the Grand Inquisitor and it ought to be the religion of the free spirit as opposed to authoritarianism. Looking back in 1928, when he had come much closer to the Church, Berdyaev claimed, like Bulgakov, that the ideal form of Orthodox theocracy represented a kind of utopia, although he had to add that it was an anarchist utopia. 'It is beyond doubt,' he said, 'that in the Orthodox monarchism of the slavophiles and of Dostoevsky there was a strong element of anarchism. According to them the Orthodox monarchy was an ideal utopia, the perfected state and social structure, which put Christian truth into practice'.[87] This may have been the ultimate direction of his thinking but at the time of *Vekhi* he was particularly critical of the Orthodox Church as it then was, especially of its anti-humanist, ascetic practices, which, he said, attempted to gain victory over death by means of death and which showed a stronger belief in the power and reality of evil than in the power and reality of good.[88] Religion could not exist without humanism, he continued, and if a religion had inhuman forms and practices, like Orthodoxy it was the religion of Godless men.[89]

This combination of admiration and hatred was characteristic of Berdyaev. His dual attitude to the Church, to revolution, to Marxism, to the intelligentsia, to the new religious consciousness and to anarchism, makes it very difficult to categorise his thought. He idealised Orthodoxy and condemned its reality. He was an *intelligent*, but reviled the intelligentsia. He considered himself to be more revolutionary than the revolutionaries. He welcomed the new religious consciousness and mystical anarchism and worked with them, but considered their views 'mistaken' and 'false'.[90] He assimilated important elements from each of the tendencies he opposed, which made him more vehement in his denunciation of the elements which he rejected. The result of this eclecticism was that his writings seem valuable for their separate parts rather than for the ensemble of his ideas, and in fact it is very difficult to distinguish a consistent pattern of thought. Certainly there were *idées fixes* – freedom, individualism, mysticism, the conservatism and philistinism of the intelligentsia, the necessity for new ideas and for the conflict of ideas – but was there a unifying thread? The situation was complicated by the fact that his most substantial reminiscences of this period were written long after, and his memory of it was inevitably coloured by hindsight and by subsequent developments in his own outlook which led him to emphasise mainly those tendencies which were important in the light of what followed. As a reliable guide to his views at the time about which he was writing, they left a great deal to be desired. For example, in common with most of his commentators, he almost completely ignored the *Vekhi* dispute.

In view of this, the search for a common thread in his outlook is best pursued through the hints thrown out in his works of the period. Perhaps the deepest and most long-lasting of his ideas at this period was that of Godmanhood as the next step in human and divine progress which was at the heart of his view of the nature and meaning of human life. The history of religion was, he said, the history of man's gradual step by step discovery of the meaning of the world.[91] He elaborated his view of religion later on in the same essay.

> Our religion must be greater than Christianity. It must be the religion of Godmanhood, the religion of the perfected union of the Divinity with humanity, of the complete incarnation of the Spirit in the life of humanity, achieved by adding to and supplementing the truths of Christianity. The phenomenon of Christ was the overcoming of both Godless humanity and manless divinity but up to the present this overcoming was accomplished only in the person of the Godman. Now it has to be accomplished in humanity, in Godmanhood, in religious community.[92]

Up to that time, Berdyaev continued, God and man had remained separate. Human history was still dominated by the natural, tribal order, based on the superficially Christianised but actually pagan institutions of the family and the state, and on pagan morality and way of life. The Divinity had turned away from the earth, from history. Godmanhood was the coming together of these two separated entities, God and man. Human flesh would become divinised; the Divinity would become incarnate. That moment would mark the final liberation of humanity and the creation of true human community based on God rather than on tribalism.

In this conception of God and man uniting in freedom to transform the world, Berdyaev resolved the main contradictions of his outlook. It had room for the omnipotence of God and for the freedom of mankind, for collectivism and for extreme individualism, for his mysticism and for realism. It gave human action and human history an eternally significant role. It promised a salvation for man, attainable through his own efforts. In Berdyaev's view, religion and revolution became necessary complements to one another. Berdyaev's mystical nature and language were harmonised with his burning sense of injustice and his acutely developed social conscience. It was Godmanhood and *sobornost'* which brought him close, not only to Khomyakov, and, to a lesser extent, to Solov'ev, but also to Nietzsche and his mystical anarchist followers in Russia who turned these ideas into an atheistic assertion of the divinity of man himself. Thus Berydaev, like Bogdanov, presented one of the best examples of a religious revolutionary, whose religion and revolution were both integral to his outlook.

SOCIAL DEMOCRACY AS A RELIGION

The ideas of *sobornost'* and of Godmanhood were, as was pointed out in the first chapter, capable of a pagan, atheistic, irrational interpretation, such as that provided by mystical anarchism. A more carefully thought out attempt to harness these ideas to an atheist and humanist view was made by certain Social Democratic thinkers. These so-called God-builders (*Bogostroiteli*) did not form a coherent movement and each member emphasised different features of a common pool of sources, which included Christ, Marx and Nietzsche. It was built up partly as a response to idealist taunts that socialism ignored philosophical questions and partly because the general religious atmosphere of the time spilled over into this quarter. In any case, a movement which pretended to intellectual respectability and popularity in Russia had to come to terms with religious questions because they were so much part of the way of thinking of the Russian people. In addition, the peculiar position of religion in the state structure of the autocracy gave it a special significance, far greater than in any major western European country.[93]

The idea of socialism as a religion did not begin in Russia nor was it confined to that country. In England, for example, socialism had many intimate ties with organised religion and, like humanism, some of its varieties themselves took on the form of a church even to the extent of there being socialist rites and services.[94] In France Saint-Simon had long ago proclaimed socialism to be *Le Nouveau Christianisme*. This tradition, however had no influence on Russian socialism. One of the first people who did have an influence on Russia and pointed out that socialism was a religion, was the self-taught philosopher, Joseph Dietzgen.[95] His admirers considered him to be the supreme example of the common man who, naturally from his experience of and reflection on his work and on society, had undergone a development parallel to that of Marx and had arrived at a dialectical materialist conception of the world which had a great deal in common with that of Marx and Engels.[96] But perhaps more than any external influence, the main reason that Russian socialism had a religious interpretation lay in the Russian intellectual tradition and the place of religion in that tradition. For example, A. V. Lunacharsky (1875–1933), who wrote the most important and thorough treatise on the religious roots of socialism at this time, and Berdyaev, both recorded that in their early development religion played an important role as a phenomenon that had to be faced and explained.

The central work of the God-builders was, without doubt, Lunacharsky's two-volume work *Religiya i sotsializm (Religion and Socialism)* – the fruit, he wrote, of a long-standing interest in the phenomenon of religion.[97] The fundamental notions of the book, said Lunacharsky, had been fermenting in his mind for ten years.

> The basic ideas – the essence of religion in general, the meaning and direction of the development of religiousness, the connection between scientific socialism and the cherished expectations of mankind as expressed in religious myths and dogmas and the replacement of them by metaphysical systems, the central position of 'labour' in the new outlook – all [these ideas] arose at an early date in the author's mind and were not changed in essence, but were only clarified and consolidated in proportion to his deeper acquaintanceship with the history of religion and philosophy and with scientific socialism.[98]

The root of his interest in religion and in idealism may well have lain in his deeply humanistic openness to all aspects of human experience and to his respect for the artistic and cultural achievements of mankind. He was aware of the appeal of religious ideals to man, but for him Marxism was attractive because it was a richer tradition, and as a companion work to his book on religion, he hoped to write another which would disclose 'the great treasury of ideals concealed within Marxism, a treasury before which all the enthusiasms and highly scientific fabrications of the idealists pale'.[99] Thus for Lunacharsky religion had been a creative factor in human history and the argument of his book was that the creative and archetypal aspects of it were of value to the socialists and that socialism, particularly as it shared with the best of religion a thirst for justice and equality, had grown out of a religious—socialist tradition going back at least to Moses.

Lunacharsky's view of religion derived in its entirety from nineteenth-century German criticism of religion and theology. Lunacharsky was quite clear about the provenance of his ideas and in his chapter 'What is religion?' he showed how, step by step, transcendental religion had been replaced by humanist religion. The first and most important contribution was that of Feuerbach, whose work, according to Lunacharsky, resulted in the raising of anthropology to the status of theology. 'After Feuerbach, the philosophical religion of God is dead,' he proclaimed.[100] Thus Feuerbach substituted 'man' for 'God' and the religious problem was solved.

For Lunacharsky, as for Plekhanov and many other socialists, the root of the old religion lay in fear of natural forces arising from ignorance of their causes. Primitive man, aware of his own consciousness, attributed a similar consciousness to the natural forces which threatened him – hence the myths by which man explained the phenomena of the natural world. In his anthropological 'biological' definition of religion, Lunacharsky said that 'religion is that thinking about the world and that feeling for the world which psychologically resolves the contrast between the laws of life and the laws of nature'.[101] This rather obscure formulation was amplified elsewhere to show that by it Lunacharsky meant that primitive religion served to explain the mysteries of nature in a partial way and only with the fullness of scientific knowledge, which was not available before Marx, could the religious conception of the world, as opposed to the scientific one, be shown to be false. 'Scientific socialism' on the other hand 'resolves these contradictions puts forward the idea of the victory of life, of the subjugation of the elements to reason by means of knowledge and labour, science and technology'.[102]

But this was only the negative side of the socialist attitude to religion as it developed in nineteenth-century Germany. There was a feeling not simply that the religious era was over but that socialism, in some way, was destined to replace it in human life. In this period Joseph Dietzgen was one of the most influential of the writers who developed this theme and he devoted a major work to *Die Religion der Sozialdemokratie*. Lunacharsky quoted from this volume with enthusiasm:

> Dear fellow citizens – *in the idea of social democracy is contained a new religion* which, as distinct from all existing ones, aspires to be accepted not only by the heart but also by the mind. Social democracy differs from other ordinary objects of mental labour because it is a revelation of the human heart in the form of a special religion. *The aim of religion*, strictly speaking, *is to give relief from the sorrows of earthly life to the worn out human heart.* Up to the present, however, this had only been achieved in an idealist way, by resorting to dreams and allegories, invisible gods and promises of life after death. As for the Gospel, it genuinely promises to finally transform our vale of sorrow and grief by the most real, most actual and tangible methods.

'This,' said Lunacharsky, 'is a categorical and splendid expression to which we subscribe joyfully.'[103] Thus socialism attempted to construct on earth what was formerly thought could exist only in heaven. Like the apocalyptic thinkers such as Merezhkovsky and Vyacheslav Ivanov and even Berdyaev and Bulgakov, Lunacharsky asserted that the kingdom of God, the utopia, could be built on earth and that man and earthly society were perfectible.

The second element which Lunacharsky drew from Dietzgen was also analogous to a Russian religious concept, that of *sobornost'*, of the superiority of collectivism to individualism. The religion of socialism, said Dietzgen, rejected the possibility of the separated self attaining perfection. It could only reach perfection through social organisation, so the objective of social democracy was the perfection of social organisation, which would allow the individual to achieve his fulfilment. This, he continued, could be achieved only through love, about which religion only dreamt. In conclusion, for Dietzgen the social democrat believed not in God and spirit, but in the social democratic structure of society.[104] Dietzgen's argument was thus, said Lunacharsky, based on the thesis that 'man must have a system'.[105] A similar point was made by Liebknecht. Lunacharsky quoted one of Liebknecht's statements in the Reichstag to the effect that the devotion of social democratic people to each other and to their cause was like a religious love of one's neighbour. Liebknecht said, 'this is *a religion*, not the religion of the popes but *the religion of humanity*. It is a faith in the victory of good and of the idea.'[106]

With Nietzsche, Lunacharsky concluded that, 'Man: your business is not to seek meaning in the world but to give meaning to the world.'[107] 'The new religion,' said Lunacharsky, 'the religion of humanity, the religion of labour, gives no guarantees. But I maintain that even without God and without guarantees – the masks of that same God – it is still a religion.'[108]

Lunacharsky's own contribution to this debate was to elaborate a view of mankind evolving from primitive animism to socialism – the religion of labour. He saw five main stages in this process of development. The first one was cosmism which represented primitive man's fearful view of nature, followed by Hellenism, reaching its height in Platonism, which he put below Judaism, the third stage, because although Judaism was the religion of 'the slave-man' it was, even in this lowest form, the first 'purely humanist religion'.[109] The fourth stage was Christianity, which combined the previous two, its history being intertwined with the struggle of the fifth stage, the religion of labour, to emerge. In Lunacharsky's own words:

Ancient cosmism says: I bow down before the world and its laws.

Plato says: I do not accept the world, I build another better world in dreams, I worship them, I repudiate life for the sake of dreams, I proclaim them the sole reality.

Israel says: I do not accept the laws of the world. Over the world there must rule a mighty, living will similar to the human, leading it to enlightenment and to justice. We note at this point that *Christianity* combined the last two theses to the great detriment of both and then stopped to extricate itself from its unbearable contradictions.

The religion of labour says: I recognise the world as material requiring to be re-worked, we accept the ideal as a plan of the recreation. Freedom and justice or the rule of organised humanity, while it does not yet exist, is born only in suffering.[110]

It was the later stages of this process which occupied the greater part of Lunacharsky's attention. He was especially interested in Christianity because he saw it as the result of a fusion of Platonism and Judaism. Thus, for Lunacharsky, religious development and philosophical development were very closely allied. Each movement – cosmism, Platonism, Judaism, Christianity, pantheism, deism, idealism, materialism, socialism – grew organically from its predecessor, so that he traced a direct line from primitive religion through Plato, Christ, Augustine, Spinoza, Kant and Hegel to Marx and from Marx to the greatest Marxist philosopher, Bogdanov. From this vast canvas, the present study can only isolate and consider three aspects, which will be dealt with in turn: first, the relationship between Christianity and communism as it developed in history; second, the view that Marx's philosophy was religious; and third, the view that Bogdanov represented, as it were, the most advanced point of this process. In all these aspects the ideas of religion and revolution were closely interwoven.

The communist, socialist element in Christianity was, said Lunacharsky, present from the beginning and was indeed dominant at that period. Despite their errors, the early Christians were characterised by their 'beautiful tenderness and beautiful sense of brotherhood'.[111] Christianity in Rome and in Palestine was based on the idea of the brotherhood of man and was a proletarian movement containing communistic strains or 'the Christianity of earthly hope' in Lunacharsky's words.[112] This 'semi-revolutionary Christianity' was best expressed by Tertullian who 'preceded Rousseau in the radicalness of his revolutionary denial of all cultural values. He resolutely protested against the state and the fatherland and spread anti-militarist propaganda.'[113] This tradition, however, began to decay, so that, as a result of gnostic influences there were at least two struggling tendencies within Christianity. On the one hand the 'Christian communist proletariat' which was 'in significant measure penetrated by the collectivist spirit' and on the other, the teaching that 'each individual soul must seek its own salvation' which caused Christian communism to decay and endeavoured to replace it by individualism.[114] The final blow to the democratic structure and independence of Christian communism came from the developing hierarchy which began to turn the Church into an administrative and defensive organ and produced the hierarchy which (and here Lunacharsky quoted Kautsky) became a ruling class to oppress the masses.[115] The early Church structure, according to Harnack, came to reflect the imperial state structure – its popes were its emperors, Peter and Paul were its Romulus and Remus, the archbishops and bishops were its proconsuls, the monks and priests its legions. Finally, the praetorian guard of the new Church were the Jesuits (who, according to this account, were already performing mischief some ten centuries before the birth of their founder!)[116] In Augustine, the Church achieved its full self-consciousness. It turned, said Lunacharsky, to the Pauline doctrine of grace which minimised the merits of individual attempts to achieve salvation and maximised the role of the Church as owner and manager of indivisible saving grace. Christ had guaranteed the survival of the Church but outside the Church there could be no salvation.[117] In Augustine,

> the Church reached its peak. It changed from being a religious philosophy of the poor and created a new position saving its class ideology from pernicious aridity. The democratic Christian spirit and common sense demanded a struggle against the terrible, oppressive and stately building of Catholicism.[118]

Thus, in this period Christianity, according to Lunacharsky, performed the rather impressive feat, in Marxist terms, of being the ideology of no fewer than four conflicting social classes: first, the proletarians; second, the traders; third, the aristrocracy; and fourth, the new class of the hierarchy created by Christianity itself.[119] The emergence of the hierarchy did not end the struggle entirely and the socialist element kept reappearing at later dates, he continued, the most recent being the contemporary Russian Christian socialism of Merezhkovsky who tried to unite popular God-seeking and the religious philosophy of Gogol, Dostoevsky and Solov'ev with the political principles of Bakunin, Chernyshevsky and Herzen.[120]

Exactly what Lunacharsky's views have to offer to an historian of the Church is not our concern at this moment, nor is the question of what he owed to various sources such as Kautsky, whose book on the origin of Christianity appeared in 1908. What is significant in the present context is that Lunacharsky saw the existence of a natural communism expressed in Christianity which was suppressed by the ruling class. For Lunacharsky it was the function of Marx, among others, to show that the communist elements were the true and enduring ones while the ecclesiastical structure and doctrine had been used by the ruling class to suppress the legitimate hopes of the oppressed. Unlike others in the field, said Lunacharsky,

> I dare to say that this philosophy [of Marx] is a *religious philosophy*, that it has its source in the religious quest of the past, engendered by the economic growth of mankind, and that it gives the brightest, most real, most active solution to the 'cursed questions' of human self-consciousness, which were resolved in an illusory way by the old religious systems.[121]

The fundamental tenet of the new creed was the statement that thinking was determined by the social environment.[122]

According to Lunacharsky, it was Bogdanov who continued the tradition of Marx.

> In our opinion Bogdanov is the only Marxist philosopher continuing the pure philosophical tradition of Marx . . . In reality empiriomonism is for the most part a return to Marx, to genuine unvulgarised, unplekhanovised Marx. For the rest it marks a step forward, I would say, in a straight geometrical line in the direction projected by Marx.[123]

Lunacharsky's conception of socialism as the fifth religion, the religion of labour, found its philosophical equivalent in Bogdanov who was, as Lunacharsky went on to say, concerned with the questions of existence and consciousness, which were central elements in the new religion, and of the reconciliation of individual and collective through the medium of an ideology which expressed collective consciousness. In Lunacharsky's own words:

> The fundamental question faced by Bogdanov and all Marxist philosophers is the relationship between existence and consciousness. For Marxism this is not primarily a question of the relationship between physical and psychological . . . but of the relationship between *social existence*, that is of *co-operation* with society, and individual *consciousness* in the form of *ideology*.[124]

Bogdanov's views were important to Lunacharsky's conception because despite differences of terminology and sometimes of ideas themselves, we find in his [Bogdanov's] outlook – in his brilliant construction on the firm foundation of genuine Marxism – splendid soil for the growth of the socialist religious consciousness.[125]

A clear hint as to what Lunacharsky hoped to gain by considering socialism as a religion was given in the final stages of his work. 'I am of the opinion,' he said,

> that the singling out and understanding of these ideals, as realistic religious principles within proletarian socialism, must powerfully facilitate the development among the proletariat of the mighty rudiments of psychological collectivism.[126]

Although he did not emphasise it here, it was obvious that in a country such as Russia, where the Church and religion had perhaps a stronger appeal to the masses on whom the socialists were relying than among the relatively Godless townspeople and working men of France, Germany or England, an appeal in the form of religion might, as Lunacharsky suggested, help a great deal in the spread of the socialist ideal. Maksim Gorky, who had always expressed a deep love for the ordinary people of Russia, emphasises this aspect of the transformation of the natural religious characteristics of the Russian people into natural socialist ones in the novel *Ispoved'* (*The Confession*) which was one of the most straightforward expositions of the God-building ideal. In it the central character, Matvei, was searching for God and found his God in the people 'which is the only God that works miracles', and, continued Matvei, it was the people who created religious consciousness.

This novel was in many ways a remarkable diversion from Gorky's other works of the period and was, in fact, treated by Soviet critics and by Gorky himself later on, as an aberration brought about by the reactionary influences of this most difficult period for the revolutionary movement. In the early stages of the book, Matvei was under the influence of various conventional ecclesiastical conceptions of God presented to him by simple believers or by decadent aristocratic monks. None of these was satisfactory. He was driven from one to another by an irresistible inner drive.

The stars flicker restlessly to show their full beauty at the rising of the sun, love and sleep caress and intoxicate you and a bright ray of hope darts flame-like through your soul. There is, somewhere or another, a glorious God!

'Seek and ye shall find Him.' How beautiful are those words – words that must never be forgotten, for they are, in truth, worthy of human reason.[127]

While acting under this impulse, Matvei encountered the worker and political organiser Yonash who began to direct him to a more satisfying view of God. Yonash told him:

It is the people that creates gods – innumerable people of the world! Holy martyrs greater than those whom the Church honours. That is the God that works miracles. I believe in the spirit of the people – the immortal people whose might I acknowledge.[128]

Was it, asked Matvei, the peasantry who created God? Yonash replied:

I spoke of the working classes of the world, of their united strength, the one and eternal source of deification . . . Even now many are seeking the means of fusing all the forces on earth into one, and creating out of it a splendid and beautiful God who shall embrace the universe.[129]

The chief enemy standing between man and the fulfilment of this collective destiny was individualism. The present deplorable human condition originated on the day

when the first human individual tore himself adrift from the miraculous power of the people, from the parent mass, and from the dread of isolation and its own impotence, it transformed itself into a wicked skein of petty desires – a skein which was christened 'I'. This 'I' is man's worst enemy. For the sake of its self-defence and self-assertion on earth, it has fruitlessly killed all the intellectual forces and all the great faculties for creating spiritual wealth in mankind.[130]

Matvei's lingering doubts were resolved when, in one image, Gorky showed that the people could literally perform miracles when they, with the assistance of the icon of Our Lady of Kazan, restored an epileptic girl to health. Matvei underwent at that moment a mystical conversion which transfigured his perception of the world. 'I stood on the summit of experience,' he said

> and beheld the world as a fiery stream of living forces that strove to unite all in a single force, the goal of which was hidden from my sight. Nevertheless I joyfully recognised that ignorance of that goal was to me the source of infinite spiritual development and vast earthly beauty, and that in this infinity lay unbounded bliss for the living soul of man . . . . The earth stood before me in her luxuriant flowery garment of autumn, a field of emeralds for the great games of men, for the battle for the freedom of these games, a holy place of pilgrimage at the festival of Beauty and Truth.[131]

Matvei was moved to pray to the immortal people – 'You are my God, and the creator of all gods which you have formed from the beauties of your spirit in the labour and rebellion of your search. And the world shall have no other God that works miracles. This is my confession and my belief.'[132]

Such was the essence of Gorky's extraordinary and untypical novel, a far cry from realism and a great concession to the mysticism and idealism of the decadents who might have agreed with Gorky's view that life was 'games' played 'at the festival of Beauty and Truth'. This was an echo of the Gorky who in 1900 remarked in a letter to Chekhov, 'Solov'ev, I am reading him again. How clever and subtle.'[133] He was, however, and remained, an unrelenting opponent of the idealist group as represented by Struve, Berdyaev and Bulgakov and he worked hard to set up the socialist publishing venture *Znanie* as a direct counter to the idealists' *Voprosy zhizni* (*Novyi put'*).[134]

In *Ispoved'* Gorky saw in the religious phenomenon a powerful metaphor and analogue, although in distorted form, of the spirit of human brotherhood which inspired his socialism. But not only did Gorky use religious images to explain the essence of his humanist socialism in a very simple fashion which would be immediately familiar to his audience, he also suggested the conversion of the emotional energy generated by religious experience into that required to build socialism. This was one of the most attractive features of religion for the God-builders. It enabled them to fulfil the fundamental desires of the individual for truth and for immortality in a secular way and fulfilled the desire of each man for a satisfying faith which was deeper and more human than the philistine platitudes of the positivists. Only religion could provide a universal view to match Gorky's and Lunacharsky's love for all humanity and for all its achievements.

Be that as it may, another aspect of Gorky's novel was the fact that it was steeped in the spirit of God-seeking which was to be found in many quarters among the intelligentsia of this period. There is a tendency, perhaps stemming in part from the similarity of the terms in Russian, to mention God-building and God-seeking in the same breath. But whereas God-building might, as in Gorky's case, incorporate elements of God-seeking, none of the other God-seeking tendencies had much in common with God-building. God-building was strictly a Marxist heresy while many of the God-seekers were not in any sense Marxists. While both to some extent reflected and embodied the religious and socialist mood of the period, they moved in different spheres. For Berdyaev, Lunacharsky was a man 'from the other world', the world of political organisation, demonstrations, strikes, not that of the ivory tower of Vyacheslav Ivanov's Wednesday salons near the Tauride Palace.[135] For Lunacharsky, Berdyaev was a man who, from similar presuppositions to his own, had developed in a very different direction. In the introduction to *Religiya i sotsializm* Lunacharsky recalled a day in Kiev ten years previously when the idea of writing the book had been forming in his mind. On that day in 1898 he had read a paper on 'Idealism and Marxism' which contained the kernel of his ideas. On that occasion one of his opponents had been a social democrat who shared his preoccupation with and interest in such problems, N. Berdyaev. 'But,' said Lunacharsky, 'what a difference in the results!'[136] This initial contact was continued in exile in Vologda but neither Berdyaev nor Lunacharsky mentioned to what extent they exchanged ideas. Despite the coolness and the disagreement between them, Lunacharsky said that Berdyaev understood the tasks facing Marxism in the intellectual sphere better than the Marxists themselves because he was concerned not only with the sociological necessity of Marxism but also with truth. He also agreed with Berdyaev that a teaching which ignored the force of subjective ideals in the struggle with reality was a false one.[137]

The question of the relationship between God-building and God-seeking was one which interested members of both groups and discussion of it attracted attention in 1908–9. Socialists who rejected

God-building naturally rejected God-seeking too and tended to fail to distinguish between the two schools, but the God-builders themselves took up the issue. In particular Bazarov dealt thoroughly with the topic in a series of articles, which were all reprinted in *Na dva fronta (On Two Fronts)*,[138] and in a lecture at the St Petersburg Literary Society.

Bazarov's fundamental disagreement with the God-seekers lay in their false conception of individualism. 'God-seeking' is one of the symptoms of the very slow but very deep cultural crisis, the crisis of individualism,' he said in his lecture. He then went on to explain that

It is not positivism which turns science from being the revelation of truth into a means of comfort, but it is individualism which cuts humanity off from its capacity to understand the objective value of scientific and of artistic creativity. Individualism corrupts, devalues and reduces to the level of a comfortable pastime, to *je m'en fichisme*, that great culture which it itself created. This is an evident symptom that the cultural content of individualism is already exhausted, that its mission is already fulfilled, that it is time for the Moor to retire.[139]

Elsewhere he supplemented this by saying that the attraction of individualism was that it made it possible to believe that individual liberation could be achieved independently, but the revolutionary movement and the working class could not succumb to this delusion. Freedom could come only as a result of struggle by the progressive class as a whole.

Not the conscious communist, not even the most implacable enemy of the bourgeoisie can be fully liberated from the bourgeois psychology as long as bourgeois relations exist in reality. The new consciousness cannot be created by separate individuals or by groups of individuals, nor by religious sects, nor by political parties. It can only be the affair of all humanity once it has done away with the material bases of its bourgeois 'pre-historical' existence.[140]

Thus, even for this Marxist, salvation could only be universal, not individual. Indeed he was relying on a central theme of Marxism in this, which went back to the very roots of Marxism, because Marx's criticism of Proudhon and the utopian socialists rested to a large degree on Marx's belief that the reform of consciousness preached by these people was not sufficient to change society.

Bazarov was, as he said, fighting on two fronts, on the one hand against bourgeois individualists like Merezhkovsky and on the other against socialist dogmatists like Plekhanov and Lenin. Each side accused him of belonging to the other and his refusal to identify in any way with either resulted in powerful attacks by him on both. These attacks were returned, particularly by Plekhanov and Lenin and his associates. Though their views showed many differences at this time, they both agreed that the various attempts at a new start for the intelligentsia in this period, represented by the new religious consciousness, the God-builders and *Vekhi*, were part and parcel of one and the same retreat into religion and mysticism as a result of the setbacks to the revolutionary movement. Both treated the movement with complete contempt and worked energetically to re-establish 'orthodox' Marxism (though this meant different things to each of them) and 'orthodox' materialism.

The main thrust of Plekhanov's attack on 'the so-called religious-seeking in Russia' was aimed at Lunacharsky, Merezhkovsky and Gorky. His disagreement with Lunacharsky rested on the latter's assertion that religion was that conception of the world which resolved the contradiction between the laws of life and the laws of nature.[141] Plekhanov's own definition of religion was quite different.

> *Religion* can be defined as *a more or less structured system of notions, moods and actions*. The notions form the *mythological element* of religion, mood is related to the sphere of *religious feeling*, and actions to the spheres of *religious worship*, or, to put it another way, *of cult*.[142]

The remainder of the first article of this series of three was devoted to expanding this conception in anthropological terms with particular reference to the emergence of religion from nature and the environment, in accordance with Marx's conception that consciousness was determined by environment.

Turning from this hazy prehistory to the contemporary 'religious seekers' in Russia, Plekhanov showed that their conceptions were far from new. Marx himself devoted a great deal of attention to those socialists of his time and earlier who had seen socialism as a religion, for example, the utopian socialists, Saint-Simon, Fourier and Leroux, who all had religious elements in their outlook. Thus for Plekhanov the debate was ended by Marx himself and to continue proposing ideas specifically rejected by Marx proved the unmarxist nature of Lunacharsky's book. By invoking the highest authority and repeating his scorn, Plekhanov attempted to cut the God-builders off from the socialists. Gorky also fell under Plekhanov's anathema even though he was, according to Plekhanov, a wonderful artist, but

> even great geniuses are frequently helpless in the field of theory. One does not have to go very far to find examples: Gogol, Dostoevsky and Tolstoy are giants in the field of artistic creativity, but they displayed the feebleness of a child whenever they considered a fundamental question.[143]

Finally, he turned to the decadents, in particular Merezhkovsky and Minsky. They were suffering from the symptoms of a disease – individualism. Gippius complained in the introduction to her collected poems that 'up to the present we have not found the Universal God nor have we caught that which we are striving for. Until that time our prayers – our verses, alive for each one of us will be misunderstood by, and will be unnecessary for, some.'[144] Plekhanov offered an explanation of why the verses of the symbolists 'alive for each one of us' should be unnecessary and misunderstood.

> It is simply because they are the outcome of extreme individualism. When the human world surrounding him is not necessary to and not understood by the poet, the poet himself becomes unnecessary and is misunderstood by the surrounding human world.[145]

They also provided a distinction between the God-seekers and the God-builders and Plekhanov did not confuse them. Such fine distinctions, however, were far beyond Lenin, for whom, as was pointed out in the previous chapter, philosophy and propaganda went hand in hand. For him, Lunacharsky and other 'destroyers of dialectical materialism proceed fearlessly to downright fideism'.[146] Writing to Gorky in November 1913, Lenin said,

> God-seeking differs from god-building or god-creating or god-

making etc. no more than a yellow devil differs from a blue devil. To talk about god-seeking, not in order to declare against *all* devils and gods, against every ideological necrophily (all worship of a divinity is necrophily, be it the cleanest, most ideal, not sought-out but built-up divinity, it's all the same), but to prefer a blue devil to a yellow one, is a hundred times worse than not saying anything about it at all.[147]

Lenin was concerned only with the inroads God-building had made in the party and sought to attack its influence. For him God-building, God-seeking, 'otzovism' and 'ultimatism' were used interchangeably, but only to refer to Bogdanov and his followers. God-seeking as a phenomenon outside the party never provoked a response from him.

Lenin's views on religion at this time were formulated in his article on 'The attitude of the workers' party to religion', published in *Proletarii* in May 1909. Like Marx and Engels, Lenin's views existed on two levels, the theoretical and the practical, which were not always in step with each other so that while on the one hand he said that Marxism was 'a materialism which is absolutely atheistic and positively hostile to all religion'[148] and that 'we must combat religion – that is the ABC of *all* materialism',[149] on the other hand he added, 'we must not only admit into the Social Democratic Party workers who preserve their belief in God, but must deliberately set out to recruit them. We are absolutely opposed to giving the slightest offence to their religious convictions.'[150] For Lenin militant atheism could only play into the hands of the bourgeoisie. 'An anarchist who preached war against God at all costs would in effect be helping the priest and the bourgeoisie (as the anarchists always do help the bourgeoisie *in practice*).'[151] Lenin attempted to steer a course between this anti-religious mania and on the other hand the 'opportunism' of German social democracy which extended the principle of religion as the private affair of the individual, with which Lenin agreed, into religion as a private matter for the party, which he opposed. On the contrary, he said, the party must have a firm stand on the religious question.[152]

Lenin's own definition of religion differed from the others considered in this chapter in that it related only to the social form and functions of religion and not to its supernatural or philosophical claims. He said that Marx's dictum that religion was the opium of the people was 'the cornerstone of the whole Marxist outlook on religion'.[153] 'Marxism has always regarded all modern religious organisations,' he continued, 'as instruments of bourgeois reaction that serve to defend exploitation and to befuddle the working class.'[154] Far from taking into account Lunacharsky's view that religion contained great ideals which should not be lost sight of, Lenin saw nothing in religion beyond its social form and roots.

> In modern capitalist countries these roots are mainly *social*. The deepest root of religion today is the socially downtrodden condition of the working masses and their apparently complete helplessness in the face of the blind forces of capitalism which every day and every hour inflicts upon ordinary working people the most horrible suffering and the most savage torment, a thousand times more severe than that inflicted by extraordinary events, such as wars, earthquakes etc. 'Fear made the gods.' Fear of the blind force of capital, blind because it cannot be foreseen by the masses of the people, a force which at every step in the life of the proletarian and small proprietor threatens to inflict and does inflict 'sudden' 'unexpected', 'accidental' ruin, destruction, pauperism, prostitution and death from starvation. Such is the *root* of modern religion which the materialist must bear in mind if he does not want to remain an infant-school materialist.[155]

The social democrat consequently should fight religion as part of the general class struggle against capitalism. To eradicate the roots of religion was to eradicate capitalism itself.[156] Thus for Lenin religion was nothing more than an ideological arm of capitalism, an intellectual tool used for the mental suppression of the working class. The questions examined in the previous chapters of this study and in the earlier part of this chapter completely escaped his attention, even when he was confronted by them within his own party and his own faction in the form of Lunacharsky and Gorky. The philosophical issues for which the God-builders stood were completely integrated, in Lenin's mind, with the general question of the political struggle against Bogdanov.

The people dealt with in this chapter provide another variation on our basic themes. Bulgakov, Berdyaev, Lunacharsky and Gorky were all religious collectivists, the first two explicitly idealist, the latter two, at least according to their critics, were crypto-idealists. This distinguished them from religious individualists like Merezh-kovsky, Rozanov and the liberal philosophers. It also distinguished them from the materialist collectivists, such as Plekhanov and Lenin.

The central theme of these disputes was still idealism or materialism, individualism or collectivism, and it was on their attitudes towards these that the intellectual, and often political, position of the participants was based. The second part of this study will attempt to show how the theoretical positions defined above were related to the political divisions of the day and in particular the attitude of the intelligentsia to the central question of revolution.

Part II
The Intelligentsia and Revolution

4 Critics of the revolutionary intelligentsia

It is possible that crisis was a normal mode of existence for the Russian intelligentsia, but even if this were so, there can hardly have been another period in its history when the word sprang so readily to the lips of both its defenders and detractors than in the years 1907–10. From the Black Hundred right to the anarchist left there came claims that there was an intelligentsia crisis, a crisis of the revolution, a crisis in Marxism and a religious crisis. All these crises were inextricably linked with the thought of the intelligentsia and there was at this time criticism of the intelligentsia as a whole from outside its ranks, and a movement towards revaluation of its presuppositions and goals from within.

The debate over the intelligentsia had three main sources. The first was the traditional conservative opposition to the intelligentsia's reformist and revolutionary conscience. This group consisted of the supporters of Church and state who were Russian nationalists of either a Slavophile or chauvinistic anti-semitic outlook. Their main characteristic was a defence of orthodoxy in political and spiritual affairs in the face of the westernising and modernising tendencies of the intelligentsia. The members of this group without exception considered themselves to be quite separate from the intelligentsia. The other two sources were more closely connected with the intelligentsia itself. Of these the *Vekhi* group is the most important for our study and the debate surrounding it provides an extremely useful barometer of the intellectual mood of Russia in 1909–10. Finally there was the creative intelligentsia, in particular the symbolists and decadents who had a mixed attitude to the idea of revolution and an ambiguous relationship with the intelligentsia and politics. In this chapter each of these three groups are examined in turn, and in the following chapter the defenders of the traditional values of the intelligentsia will be examined.

In addition there was a fourth group, associated with Jan Vaclav

97

Machajski (1866–1926), who saw the intelligentsia as the exploiting class of the future socialist society in the same way that the entrepreneurial class had been in capitalist society. Machajski predicted that the monopoly of knowledge which the intelligentsia had would be sufficient to make them into a privileged order. His ideas, based on a literal version of Marxism, were elaborated by him while in exile in Switzerland and publicised in Russia by his closest (and almost only) associate, E. Lozinskii. Despite the originality of his ideas they attracted very little attention at this time and they will not be examined, therefore, in this study.[1]

So far, this study has outlined the ideas of, and the overlap between, the main protagonists in this debate in the field of theory. This chapter and the one following will deal with the disputes occasioned by these conflicting principles on the rather more practical issues of the role of the intelligentsia in society and of the correct political strategy for the post-revolutionary period which were the main themes of the debate of the period occasioned by the experiences of 1905, which massively accelerated the disillusionment of sections of the critically thinking people of Russia with crude revolutionary politics and vulgar materialist positivism. Never since its origin in the 1860s had the fortunes of the revolutionary intelligentsia been at such a low ebb. This state of affairs caused anxious reappraisal in the minds and hearts of the sensitive and open-minded sections of the intelligentsia. Only the conservatives, its traditional enemies, were delighted at the discomfiture of the intelligentsia.

THE CONSERVATIVES

The idea of renewal and the feeling that Russia was undergoing a renaissance had penetrated the Church in this period more thoroughly than the State. Rebel groups of priests were attempting to speed up this process within the Church.[2] The results were not inconsiderable and Nikita Struve, commenting on this period, came to the conclusion that the Church was better equipped than the State to face the revolution of 1917.[3] Be that as it may, the drive towards reform had opponents for whom the very idea of bringing the ancient faith up to date represented a blasphemy. They were hostile to the religious movement among the intelligentsia for the same reason. For them, all innovation in religion was impossible and could only diminish the great truths of Orthodoxy and represent a relapse into primitive pre-Christian forms and the rational, and therefore limited, humanism of ancient Greece.

I. G. Aivazov in a pamphlet entitled *Religioznoe obnovlenie nashikh dnei*,[4] spoke out against the Religious Philosophical Society intellectuals of the pre-revolutionary years and also against the *Vekhi* writers. There was nothing in the outlook of these people, he argued, that was not already in Gogol, Dostoevsky or Vladimir Solov'ev, but unlike these illustrious predecessors they rejected the Church and lacked the spiritual dimension of these great sons of the Orthodox Church.[5] The *novoputeitsy* had a mistaken idea of religion – they deprived it of its transcendental significance in their attempts to deprive God of his absoluteness. Religious truth could not, according to Aivazov, be derived from human knowledge, experience and reason. In attempting to arrive at truth through reason, the leaders of the religious movement in the intelligentsia were, he said, ignoring revelation and neglecting the contrast between the insignificant abilities of man and the might of the Divinity. Their so-called 'new way' was not a new way at all and it had nothing in common with the way chosen by Gogol, Dostoevsky and Solov'ev.

Other conservative writers were much more direct in their opposition and on the far right, among the Union of Russian People, agitators synthesised revolutionaries, the intelligentsia in general, the students and the Jews into the one common enemy of every right-thinking Russian. Pogroms against students as well as against the Jews were organised in this period. One of the instigators of such violence was D. Bulatovich from Kishinev who in 1909 wrote a series of articles on *Vekhi* in *Russkoe znamya*.[6] *Vekhi* was, he said, the work of 'seven *Russo-Jewish intelligenty*'[7] and he examined each contribution in turn and found them all guilty of being sympathetic to the Jews, if not actual Jews themselves. He dismissed Bulgakov's claim that the intelligentsia was innately religious. Bulgakov was correct in diagnosing with Dostoevsky that 'A legion of devils has entered the gigantic body of Russia and shakes it into convulsions, torments and mutilates it' but he had identified the wrong devils. For Bulatovich, 'the name of this legion is *Jew*'.[8] Bulatovich did not make any distinction between *Vekhi* and the intelligentsia in general, nor between them and the Jews. They were all part and parcel of the same thing. The Russian bourgeoisie as a whole, he said, was three-quarters Jewish and the constitutional movement had a Jewish nature.[9]

Another right-wing critic of the new mood of the intelligentsia was L. Volkov, writing in *Moskovskie vedomosti*.[10] He showed the development of a many-sided religiosity and a kind of neo-nationalism among the intelligentsia. He used the two collections of articles, *Vekhi* and *Kuda my idem?*, as his main examples. This transition on the part of a section of the intelligentsia from the 'cosmopolitanism' and 'international proletarianism' of 1905 to religious and nationalistic sentiments was, in his view, simply a new method to try to break the faith of the Russian people. One of the lessons which 1905 had taught the *intelligenty* was, he said, the powerlessness of atheism and materialism in the struggle with the Orthodox Church. The new religion and the sects were to be used to loosen the people's ties with Christianity and the intelligentsia's new-found neo-nationalism was intended to combat 'healthy Russian nationalism'. He warned his readers that the intelligentsia 'has new words for its propaganda, but its goals remain the same as before'.[11] It was, he concluded, all part of a Jewish plot.

Not all the conservative critics of the revolution maintained this simplistic and crude level of argument. A more substantial and more systematic opposition to the intelligentsia on grounds closer to the spirit of the nineteenth-century Slavophiles was to be found in a book published in 1904 by N. M. Sokolov, entitled *Ob ideyakh i idealakh russkoi intelligentsii (On the Ideas and Ideals of the Russian Intelligentsia)*. In Sokolov's view, the root of the problem lay in the intelligentsia's rationalism which was derived from western Europe. Their over-emphasis on reason, according to Sokolov, blinded them to the special qualities and achievements of the Russian people who were in many respects superior to the people of the West. Sokolov's criticism of the intelligentsia's outlook took three forms. First, he protested at the 'cultural imperialism' implicit in the intelligentsia's view that Russian society had to converge with the western European model. Second, Sokolov analysed the relationship of the Russian intelligentsia to religion, and third, he characterised the intelligentsia in terms of its isolation from Russian society in general.

Sokolov opened his work with a criticism of the intelligentsia for believing that there was 'no truth higher than that truth which only the Europeans know'.[12] The problem raised by Sokolov was one that to a greater or lesser degree confronted all underdeveloped countries. Was the European pattern of development the only one?

For Sokolov the answer was definitely no. The European model which was so admired by the intelligentsia was a very imperfect one and was based on hypocrisy. The Spanish conquistadores, after bloody wars, spoke to their victims about God and the modern imperialists of England (such as Robert Clive, Warren Hastings and Lord Kitchener) and Germany were equally hypocritical. For Sokolov, the culture of western Europe extended from Marx and Engels to Krupp and Mauser, who were all agreed that the western European capitalist model was the only path of development. Sokolov pointed out that this great culture depended upon the stock exchange 'in which is incarnated all the conscience of the European west', strategic railways, dreadnoughts, artillery and guns, not to mention South African concentration camps and class warfare.[13] The western European path was not relevant to the true aims of life and even its own anthropologists acknowledged that other less developed societies could be 'the happiest of people' as H. Fielding-Hall called the Burmese.[14] The life of this tribe was described by Fielding-Hall in almost utopian terms. What need had they, Sokolov asked, of Western civilisation, of Nietzsche?[15]

Sokolov found an example of the uncritical acceptance of this model in Milyukov whose liberal and rational exterior disguised what Sokolov saw as a despotic philosophy which would crush personal and national individualism and subject all people and countries to the same laws. The underlying assumption of Milyukov was that there should be universal convergence to one model of society. 'We have noted,' commented Sokolov, 'that the notion of the universality of European culture is the "ideological" veil for the very real aspiration of the European west to rule the world.'[16] Milyukov's own 'talmudic dogmatism' was itself a curtain which concealed similar imperialistic drives.[17] Milyukov had what Sokolov called a 'theory of automatic colonisation' that large nations 'naturally' expanded, and Sokolov also poured scorn on Milyukov's casual assumption in *Ocherki po istorii russkoi kul'tury (Notes on the History of Russian Culture)*, that 'unconscious' and 'spontaneous' elements had a special place in Russian culture.[18]

Sokolov's counter-suggestion to the universal convergence of the new westernisers was a Slavophilism which combined respect for the peculiarities of the Russian cultural tradition with measures to assist and protect the people. He did not fully define what he meant by Slavophilism beyond saying that it implied 'a great love of the Slavs and interest in their language, way of life and political movements' (characteristics absent from the intelligentsia in general) and 'greater attention to the law of diversity [of cultures] than the law of uniformity'.[19]

It is clear that for Sokolov religion and the Church played an important role in preserving the culture of the Slav people. Almost half of the volume dealt with the relationship between the Russian tradition, the Church, the sects and the intelligentsia. Again, using Milyukov as an example, Sokolov said that the indifference shown by Milyukov to the splendid religious tradition of Russia was astonishing. Milyukov accused the Church of obscurantism in the seventeenth and eighteenth centuries, but, for Sokolov, in these two difficult centuries the Church had accumulated a store of knowledge, spiritual experience and elevated thought. This store would have been greater had it been able to live under easier circumstances.[20]

The positive achievements of the Church among the Russian people had been overlooked by the admirers of the people who thought these achievements had occurred naturally.

> Our *narodolyubtsy* naively marvelled that the Russian peasant was neither a savage nor a beast, that he was kind-hearted and full of pity for the unfortunate. This seemed to them to be a miracle but this miracle is easy to explain: a great deal of continuous persistent work was put into his moral education. In village churches in the ecclesiastical festivals of the neighbouring parish, in hermitages and monasteries, from miracle working icons and from divine power, the *narod* received lessons in Christian morality and love for people. The *narod* now loves divine books. From where did it take this love? If it was not the Church that taught it, then who did teach it?[21]

Sokolov's interpretation of the current intellectual situation in Russia, of the alienation of the rational intelligentsia, was based on his belief that Protestantism was infiltrating Russian society, particularly through the sects.[22] Under the influence of Peter the Great this infiltration began at the upper levels of society and had been percolating downwards.[23] 'Without Luther,' he concluded, 'there could not have been a Russian intelligentsia, although, of course, Luther would refuse to have anything to do with it.'[24]

The result of the advance of Protestant-inspired rationalism was the alienation of the intelligentsia. In Sokolov's view the intelligentsia was defined by its outlook, which was characterised by five ruptures – the rupture with the state, the rupture with the Church, the rupture with the people, the rupture with science and the rupture with the past. On these were based what he constantly referred to as the intellectual convictions of the intelligentsia (*intelligentnaya ideinaya ubezhdenost'*).[25]

One of the effects of this isolation was the intelligentsia's lack of faith in the 'simple people'.

> The *muzhik* cannot be an *intelligent* while he is a *muzhik*, while he stays on the land, and holds property. Here originates the area of superstition, tradition and conservatism. The letters of Engels on the mood of the French peasantry in 1848 established the foundations of a very original literature. Among the Russian *intelligenty* lack of trust in the *muzhik* made its appearance comparatively recently. For a long time they looked rather flippantly on the notorious 'difference between the intelligentsia and the people': it appeared to be some kind of misunderstanding which would vanish during the first serious attempt to 'serve the people'.[26]

As a result of this lack of trust, Sokolov saw Russia divided into two hostile camps.

> Two forces stand face to face with one another. 'The city' declared war on the country, and 'the intelligentsia' is convinced that 'the city' will win – although of course, it will be, particularly in Russia, a Pyrrhic victory.[27]

'In this way,' Sokolov observed, 'a worker who is only partially literate can be an *intelligent* but a well-educated peasant can never be an *intelligent*.'[28]

Most of the five ruptures which Sokolov pointed out were unquestionable but to say that the intelligentsia was also out of touch with science was perhaps more surprising. It was an idea which Sokolov claimed to have put forward on other occasions. Its essence was that

> genuine science speaks rarely, little and very warily, but marketable science is garrulous, like a market trader, knows everything and is never in doubt. The possibility of an ambiguous

and sophistic misuse of the term 'science' is explained by the fact that technical and applied sciences actually made and at present make discoveries and adaptations, the validity of which cannot be doubted. Of course for victory and conquest in those fields the word 'science' is linked here with the notion of exactness and infallibility compulsory for every commonsense person. Social science is a completely different affair. There are no laws of that kind, no discoveries of that kind. But for all that, in order to impart an appearance of scientific compulsion to simple conjecture and supposition, the present-day doctrinaires and theoreticians either speak completely falsely in the name of 'science' or with more honesty and modesty in the name of 'scientific character' (*nauchnost'*) but this is still something very mobile and flexible.[29]

In addition to these five ruptures – the source of which was the rupture of ruptures, that between the intelligentsia and the past[30] – Sokolov accused the intelligentsia of two further shortcomings. First, there was its tendency to form factions. It was, he said, practically impossible to detect an underlying 'idea' or set opinion valid for the whole intelligentsia because each part was in conflict with every other one.

All of the 'best sections' of the intelligentsia find themselves in positions of intense mutual conflict. *Bellum omnium contra omnes*. Each 'section', for the other 'sections', *lupus est*. Temporary predominance is a matter of changing fashions. Today the *narodniks* celebrate their triumph, tomorrow the Marxists intrigue against the *narodniks*.[31]

He pointed out *Novyi put'* as the latest entrant onto this stage.

The second shortcoming of the intelligentsia was its impracticality and its bookishness. The phrase 'going to the people' was widespread, for example in the works of Gorky, said Sokolov, but it was as realistic as travelling to the moon was in the stories of Jules Verne. The countryside was actually full of ignorant peasants who got very drunk on holidays. To remedy this situation hundreds and thousands of young *intelligenty* were busy learning husbandry and agricultural economics to teach the peasants, and medical students were busy learning medicine with which to treat the peasants, and jurists were learning law for the benefit of the peasants.

But nothing of this kind occurred. The *intelligenty* are too accustomed to the town and to paper and to books. Before everything it is necessary to prepare the theory. Statistics pepper the calculations. It was calculated how much [the peasant] received to eat and drink, what house he lived in and how much space there was in it. They worked out the death rate and birth rate, the debts and credit ratings of peasants in various districts of south-eastern Prussia and their financial and economic position in the reign of Tsar Gorokh. Particular attention is paid to the budget of workers in Australia and New Zealand: there exists the workers' paradise. Astonishing statistical tables with inspiring columns of figures and diagrams with gaily leaping curves were thought up and brilliantly executed.[32]

Summing up the relative positions of the Church and the intelligentsia, Sokolov concluded that the intelligentsia – defined not as 'the whole of educated society but only people who have definite aversions and expectations' – was not part of the people whereas the Russian Church was the last stronghold and last refuge of the faith and conscience of the Russian people.[32] The intelligentsia, on the other hand, displayed fierce bitterness and the most primitive fanaticism. 'In comparison with them the Norman dukes in Sicily were downright lambs.'[34] The fault did not lie only with the intelligentsia. Society as a whole had to accept responsibility for the superficiality and morbid dreaming of the educated class. 'Undoubtedly, in a healthy society decadents, vagabonds and historical materialists would never be credited.'[35] His final conclusion came in the closing paragraphs of the book.

Intelligent has a majestic ring to it. Buoyant and extremely flippant pessimism, haughty and arrogant humility, merciless humanity and fanatical patience are the present-day chimeras which grow in that soil.

If we are correct, if these signs are at least to the obvious extent part of the conception of the 'intelligentsia', then it is high time to renounce this word. This will not be that difficult to accomplish. One could say 'spirit of the age' or more precisely 'spirit of idleness, despondency and curiosity.'[36]

Such was the substance of Sokolov's objections to the ideas and ideals of the intelligentsia. His book did not have an effect comparable to that of *Vekhi* or even of *Problemy idealizma* and in any case it was soon swamped by the more absorbing events of 1905. But even so, Sokolov's work was distinguished and in some respects even penetrating – for example, his prediction that the revolutionary intelligentsia would provoke a bloody conflict between town and country in Russia – despite some of its more obvious absurdities such as the assertion that without Luther there could not have been a Russian intelligentsia. Above all, his work was valuable because it revealed the underlying fear of the conservatives that if reason were to affect the people as a whole, chaos would result; and although it lacked originality, it did show that some of the underlying assumptions of the Slavophiles persisted into the twentieth century.

VEKHI (LANDMARKS)

Without doubt, the most important critique of the intelligentsia published at this time was a slim collection of essays, entitled *Vekhi (Landmarks)*, written by seven *intelligenty* several of whom had been Marxists, but all of whom, from different points of view, were now critical of the intelligentsia's traditional revolutionary solutions to Russia's pressing problems. The book was read by everyone and serves as a touchstone for the thinkers of the period. Most readers seem to have reacted sharply, almost always in a hostile fashion, treating it as though it were a conservative book. This was not the case. Conservative hostility to the intelligentsia was based on quite different grounds from that of *Vekhi*, although to the majority of the intelligentsia *Vekhi* represented simply another version of that conservatism. But whereas the conservatives were opposed to the intelligentsia because it was revolutionary, the *Vekhi* group accused it of conservatism. *Vekhi* as a whole did not stand in opposition to revolution as they themselves understood it, in the sense of the subjective revolution of moral conversion which each person could undergo himself, but they were opposed to the kind of defined and structured social revolution which other sections of the intelligentsia worshipped blindly. *Vekhi* attempted to persuade the intelligentsia to re-examine its uncritical faith in the efficacy of bringing about changes in social institutions and to turn instead to the inner life of each individual as a source of revolutionary transformation. Gershenzon in his preface to *Vekhi* pointed to this as the only unifying idea among the conflicting opinions of the various authors.

Their common platform is the recognition of the theoretical and practical primacy of the spiritual life over the external forms of community. They mean by this that the inner life of the personality is the sole creative force of human existence, and that this inner life, and not the self-sufficient principles of the political sphere, is the only solid basis on which a society can be built. From this point of view the contributors see the Russian intelligentsia's ideology, which rests entirely on the opposite principle – recognition of the unconditional primacy of social forms – as inherently erroneous in that it contradicts the nature of the human spirit, and in practice futile because it does not lead to the goal which the intelligentsia has set for itself – the liberation of the people.[37]

This major distinguishing feature appeared and reappeared throughout the work. Berdyaev said essentially the same thing in his article. 'We will free ourselves from external oppression only when we free ourselves from internal bondage, that is, when we accept responsibility and cease to blame everything on external forces.'[38] It had particular emphasis in the final article, that of S. L. Frank. The third section of his essay was an examination of the origin, development and consequences of the idea of materialist socialism. According to Frank, the result was a rational—mechanical theory of human existence from which point of view the problem of happiness was seen to be one of external social organisation, less the production of wealth, rather than one of distribution.[39] Berdyaev also emphasised the intelligentsia's concern with problems of equality and distribution rather than with essential questions of human existence. He formulated the thesis thus: 'In the consciousness and feelings of the Russian intelligentsia, the claims of distribution and equalisation always predominated over the claims of production and creation.'[40] This he claimed was equally true of material and spiritual spheres. 'The Russian intelligentsia regarded philosophical creation in just the same way as it regarded economic production.'[41] Contrary to this prevalent attitude, the emphasis throughout *Vekhi* was on creativeness, on finding new and individual ways of meeting personal and political situations in preference to accepting complete ready-made ideologies.

We are entering a period when no ready-made ideal will greet the young man at the threshold of life: each one will have to

determine the meaning and direction of his life for himself, and
each will feel responsible for all he does and all he fails to
do . . . . The tyranny of civic activism over young people will be
shattered for a long time to come until the personality, after
submerging into itself, brings forth a new form of social
idealism.[42]

From this personalist viewpoint, which recognised the absolute
value of the individual and the necessity for each to be as free as
possible to live his own life in his own way, there emerged the basic
difference from the revolutionary intelligentsia. For this group the
absolute value was the revolution. They thought everything should
be judged according to the criterion 'is the revolution advanced or
retarded by this idea or action?' There was no reconciliation
between these two outlooks. This utilitarianism of the intelligentsia
was the object of detailed and powerful criticism by the *Vekhi*
writers, whether it was expressed in the intelligentsia's attitude to
philosophy, law, education, work or political organisation. Sacrific-
ing all interests to the revolution was regarded as the best sign for a
revolutionary *intelligent*, and they were proud to acknowledge their
nihilistic morality. 'Ready to sacrifice himself for his ideas, he does
not hesitate to sacrifice others.'[43] This point of view was given classic
expression at the Second Congress of the Russian Social Democratic
Workers' Party in 1903 in a speech which has re-echoed as a point of
controversy up until the present. The speech was made by
Plekhanov and the focal point of it was his assertion that the good of
the revolution was the highest law – *'salus revolutiae* (sic) *suprema lex'*.
Kistyakovsky, in his article, reproduced a lengthy section from this
speech, the very section that was to cause so much dispute in 1918
when the dissolution of the Constituent Assembly was justified by
reference to Plekhanov's words, to the later annoyance of Plek-
hanov himself.[44] From this speech Kistyakovsky drew the moral
that the Russian intelligentsia was more concerned with the idea of
the rule of superior force and the seizure of power than in principles
of legality.[45] He deplored the lack among the intelligentsia of any
sense of the value of the great liberal freedoms, of the civil rights
which had been the object of so much dispute and discussion,
particularly in seventeenth-century England, eighteenth-century
France and nineteenth-century Germany. 'Where is our *Spirit of the
Laws*, our *Social Contract?*' he demanded.[46] He attributed this lack of
scruple to the absence of the rule of law from the everyday life of the

Russian people.[47] Izgoev extended the criticism further in his contribution on 'The intelligentsia youth'. In every sphere of personal and social life Izgoev detected a breakdown between the generations and a slack undisciplined outlook on life and work by the young people. He quoted from a sociological survey by Chlenov of Moscow students in 1908 to establish a picture of a lazy, unhealthy, cynical, bored and miserable student body. They did not work as hard as western European students; they took no part in the physical activities so widespread in English schools and universities; they ended up only half-educated and totally uninterested in their professions. Their chief characteristics were spiritual arrogance and ideological intolerance. The main tragedy of their position was the contrast between their admirable desire to help their fellows and their complete lack of spiritual and physical equipment with which to attain their chosen goal.[48] Izgoev's major conclusions were twofold. First, the majority of the intelligentsia did not like its work and did not know it well. Second, in a crisis the extreme elements come to the fore. Taken together this meant an extreme danger of the victory of the immature, unscrupulous and the incompetent in any future upheaval.[49] The detailed factual examination of the students was particularly important in the first place, because, as Izgoev said, the intelligentsia itself was almost coterminous with the university-educated elite, and secondly, because of the importance of the image of the revolutionary student in the intelligentsia's scale of values.

This latter point, intelligentsia heroism, was the theme of the contribution by Bulgakov. He detected an unnatural order of events whereby the old looked to the young for guidance and example, a state of affairs he termed 'spiritual pedocracy'.[50] To Bulgakov this was the greatest evil of society. The deification of ill-thought out and immature attitudes to life which this implied was contrasted with veneration of the traditional Russian hero, the ascetic Christian saint.[51] Bulgakov turned to the examination of this problem of revolutionary heroism made by Dostoevsky in *The Devils*, which portrayed the progression from maximalist goals to maximalist means so that 'inside each maximalist there is a little Napoleon of socialism or anarchism'.[52]

Nihilism, then, is a terrible scourge, a horrible spiritual ulcer eating away at our society. The heroic 'all is allowed' imperceptibly degenerates into mere lack of principle in everything that fills our everyday existence. It is one of the main reasons why, for all our abundance of heroes, we have so few people who are just orderly, disciplined and hard-working; and why these heroic youths, in whose wake the older generation follows, in later life so easily and imperceptibly turn into 'superfluous people' or into Chekhovian and Gogolian types ending up with wine or cards if not worse.[53]

Gershenzon made a similar point.

What has our intelligentsia's thought been doing for the last half-century? (I am referring of course to the rank and file intelligentsia.) A handful of revolutionaries has been going from house to house knocking on every door: 'Everyone into the street! It's shameful to stay at home!' And every consciousness, the halt, the blind and the armless poured into the square, wailing and quarrelling. At home there is dirt, destitution, disorder but the master does not care. He is out in public saving the people – and that is easier and more entertaining than drudgery at home.[54]

Thus several of the authors noted the connection between nihilism and disorderliness in the make-up of the intelligentsia. Desperate opposition was more suited to their temperament than attempts to convince their opponents by reason. In these circumstances negativism dominated the minds and hearts of the intelligentsia. Instead of acting, as Radishchev did, from love for their fellows, the pressure of autocratic opposition, which had prevented them from expressing their concern for others, had turned positive love into negative hatred. 'In their life hatred takes the place of a deep and passionate ethical impulse.'[55] Also Bulgakov pointed out that hatred and destruction were the natural consequences of their nihilist outlook.[56] The distinction between the prevailing mood of the intelligentsia and that suggested by Bulgakov was neatly and succinctly drawn by him.

Christian asceticism (*podviznichestvo*) is unremitting self-control, struggle with the lower, sinful aspects of oneself, spiritual *askesis*. If outbursts and a quest for great deeds are characteristic of heroism, the norm here, on the contrary, is an even course, 'measure' (*mernost'*), restraint, unflagging self-discipline, patience and endurance – precisely those qualities which the intelligentsia lacks.[57]

Finally, philosophical truth itself was not regarded by the intelligentsia as having any value, except in relation to the revolutionary struggle. In the very title of his article Berdyaev made a distinction between philosophical truth (*filosofskaya istina*) and the intelligentsia version of truth (*intelligentskaya pravda*). His basic thesis was that, in particular since the 1860s, the intelligentsia, knowing just what they required, felt free to pick and choose among philosophies, taking out the part which suited them and ignoring that which did not, or which needed philosophical training or an effort of comprehension before it could be understood.

> For most of the intelligentsia, interest in philosophy was limited to the need for philosophical sanction of its social sentiments and aspirations. These are neither shaken nor re-evaluated as a result of philosophical reflection; they remain fixed, as dogmas . . . . The intelligentsia is prepared to accept on faith any philosophy which sanctions its social ideals, while it will reject uncritically even the truest and most profound philosophy if it is suspected of being unfavourably disposed to these traditional sentiments and ideals, or even merely critical of them.[58]

This did not mean a complete absence of philosophical themes and problems in the outlook of the Russian intelligentsia. In fact, the reverse was the case because even the most prosaic problems were viewed 'philosophically' or 'theologically'.[59] But the overall generalisation to be drawn from the foregoing was that

> love for egalitarian justice, for social good, for the welfare of the people, paralysed love for truth and almost destroyed interest in truth . . . . The intelligentsia's basic moral premise is summed up in the formula: let truth perish, if, by its death, the people will live better and men will be happier – down with truth if it stands in the way of the sacred cry 'down with autocracy'.[60]

In short, the intelligentsia had succumbed to the temptation of the Grand Inquisitor.[61] This utilitarian approach to philosophy resulted in, on the one hand, a distortion of Western philosophies taken into Russia and on the other, neglect of the deep, penetrating philosophies of the native Russian thinkers. Berdyaev gave as an example Bogdanov's crude sectarian apologetics which would always be preferred to the original philosophy of Lopatin since Lopatin's philosophy demanded serious mental effort and did not produce partisan slogans, while one could comprehend Bogdanov emotionally and his whole system would fit into a five-kopeck pamphlet.[62] The deplorable shallowness of culture reflected by this state of affairs was, he said, a fundamental cause of the failures of the intelligentsia.

From all this emerged *Vekhi's* picture of the intelligentsia's absolute value, namely the success of the revolution and the destruction of the autocracy, to which end all else was subordinated. The very intensity with which this absolute value was adhered to was in many ways akin to religious faith and, speaking from the point of view of a traditional Christian outlook, the *vekhovtsy* were not slow to make the analogy. The question of the religiousness or religiosity of the Russian intelligentsia and the true religious attitude which the writers of *Vekhi* wished to substitute for it, was the next major thread running through the volume. Bulgakov in particular treated the intelligentsia with some sympathy in this respect. He had not lost his admiration for the novel ideals of the intelligentsia and their self-sacrificing devotion to them even though he was then aware of the danger they presented to Russia. He talked in terms of a lost attachment to the Church and an innate religiousness which was assimilated subconsciously by the *intelligent* through the influence of family, nurse, education and social environment in general. The basis of this idolatrous religion was, he continued, worship of the people, a desire to save them (from suffering, if not from sin) and belief in the natural perfectibility of man and in infinite progress. The evil so prevalent in the world was to be explained by the external structure of society, and this repeated the point about a utilitarian, rational—mechanical view of human happiness. Bulgakov described this religion as mangodhood.[63] Its characteristics were a utopian hope for a perfect future society and a puritanical, even ascetic, view of conduct.[64] But any values other than material ones were to be disregarded and atheism, the cement which joined the multitudinous strands of the revolutionary movement, was dogmatically regarded as being the unavoidable outcome of education which was synonymous with religious indifferentism.[65] The result was a paradoxical picture of an intelligentsia more atheist than any other, but one which had several features which related it to its church background. Some of the leading *intelligenty* came from backgrounds very close to church influence. Bulgakov mentioned especially Dobrolyubov and Chernyshevsky who were at theological college and had been raised in clerical families.[66] His conclusion was that Russian atheism was not a rational rejection arrived at after complex, agonising and prolonged effort of mind, heart and will, a result of personal experience, but

> Most often it is taken on faith and preserves the characteristics of a naive religious philosophy, only inside out. The fact that it takes militant, dogmatic pseudo-scientific forms makes no difference. This faith rests on a series of uncritical, unverified, and of course, in their dogmatic form, incorrect assertions that science is competent to provide final answers even to religious questions, and moreover, that these answers are negative. In addition, there is a suspicious attitude towards philosophy, especially metaphysics which is also rejected and condemned in advance.[67]

Bulgakov was far from being the only one to notice this similarity. In particular Frank and Berdyaev took a very similar view. Frank, also starting from a religious outlook, saw intelligentsia ideology as a kind of religion, dominated by dogmatism, fanaticism, and intolerance. He talked of the religion of socialism,[68] the nihilist religion of earthly well-being[69] and the religion of the absolute realisation of the people's happiness,[70] not simply to draw attention to superficial similarities but to make meaningful comparison of the commitment required by following these imperatives; a comparison in which the earthly religion, having the intelligentsia as its monks, was shown to fall short of the fullness of true religious humanism. Like other writers, he exposed the limitations of the utilitarian approach to society and posed an alternative of personalist ethics giving precedence to each individual rather than to the majority. The danger of the prevailing view was that the *intelligent* ceased to serve the people and instead began to serve his conception of what the people should be. He was ready to sacrifice himself for this idea and was equally ready to sacrifice others.[71] This was the main weakness of the intelligentsia in Frank's view. Its belief that structural reform of society would bring about the disappearance of evil from human life was viewed with extreme scepticism by all the *vekhovtsy*. The certainty with which the intelligentsia held the opinion that it had all the answers to human problems in its grasp, was contrasted with the humble and creative approach of the religious man. Berdyaev was also aware of the pseudo-religious aspects of the intelligentsia. This was noticeable in the detail of its thought and in its overall world view. Sociological doctrines were treated in an almost theological light, he said.[72] In fact, several of the authors made the same point, that external questions were given too much significance by the intelligentsia so that the development of railways and canals, telegraphs and the prospect of proportional representation were treated as matters of belief.[73] In the larger sense, the whole basis of the intelligentsia was the desire for the salvation (*spasenie*) of mankind and this in turn was to be achieved through the commonplace questions of agriculture and labour organisation. No matter how little philosophical method they had acquired, the intelligentsia, from Belinsky on, had wrestled with the universal questions but it had not learned to esteem highly the systematic thinkers who had best formulated these questions. Instead, the heroes of the intelligentsia were people like Chernyshevsky who did not have this philosophical education but claimed to provide the solutions to these eternal problems. The fact that these men were muddled in their approach to these problems (Berdyaev particularly criticised Belinsky, Chernyshevsky, Mikhailovsky, Lavrov, Plekhanov, Bogdanov and Lunacharsky in this respect)[74] did not detract from the religious nature of these questions nor from the devotion with which they gave themselves up to their consideration.

So there was a strong vein of criticism of the intelligentsia for retaining the bad elements of religion, dogmatism, fanaticism, intolerance, the sense that all the answers were known and that everyone must apply them in the same way without individual differentiation. In this sense the intelligentsia made a religion out of its irreligion and it was this irreligion that Struve regarded as the foremost characteristic error of the revolutionary intelligentsia. It was impossible to understand the intelligentsia without looking at its irreligion, said Struve, and all the other contributors would certainly have agreed with him on his point. For Struve, this irreligion of the intelligentsia was an expression of its fundamental characteristic, a complete break in relations between it and the state, resulting in unconditional opposition to the state. Like the other writers, he castigated the intelligentsia for not recognising the role of the individual. 'At the heart of it lies the notion that the progress of society is not the fruit of the perfection of individual men, but a wager to be won in the game of history by an appeal to the aroused masses.'[75]

These general criticisms of the intelligentsia made in *Vekhi* were not related to any one particular historical situation. But of course Russia was still reacting to the events of 1905 and 1906. The Government had not yet descended to the extreme depths of the Rasputin period, but many of its everyday operations were characterised by viciousness, inefficiency, blunder and cruelty. The period was one of violence. The right-wing reaction was expressed at its extreme in the proto-fascist Union of Russian People. On the left the socialist revolutionary policy of terrorism and assassination was reaching new levels to the extent of being eventually disowned by the party. Violence was widespread in the provinces. In 1906, 1600 persons, mostly local officials, were murdered. In 1907 the number was 2500.[76] Death sentences were handed out without the due process of law under the state of emergency. Stolypin admitted to 683 being carried out in the period September 1906 to April 1907, but the true figure was probably much higher.[77] In fact, a restricted war was being waged.

This pressure of violence and strikes could not be kept up indefinitely, particularly since it seemed to be achieving nothing and the mood turned from the exuberance of 1905 to despair and finally to apathy. There is some evidence that in this respect 1909 marked a watershed. Figures for political strikes in these years showed a decline by this time. From around 8000 in 1905 to 3500 in 1906, the figures were in 1907, 1600, in 1908, 464 and in 1909, 50.[78] The underground faced difficulties of recruiting; the figures for active Social Democratic Party membership fell from 100,000 in 1907 to 10,000 in 1910, though there can be no certainty about this.[79]

This picture indicates that the revolutionary energies were completely spent by the end of 1908. The polarisation of society which had occurred since Bloody Sunday, and the innate violence which had flared up in the ensuing years, made the situation unpropitious for any kind of moderation, yet *Vekhi* took the side neither of reaction nor of revolution. Nor was it at all sympathetic to the mass apathy which was so prevalent and which was mentioned with abhorrence in the work.

According to *Vekhi*, much of the blame for this depressing picture lay with the intelligentsia. They were behind the revolt of 1905, it was inspired by their ideas and prompted by their agitators. Bulgakov expressed it in these words:

> It was our intelligentsia with its world view, habits, tastes and social mores that provided the revolution's spiritual leadership. The *intelligenty* will not admit it of course – in this they are indeed *intelligenty* – and, each according to his own catechism, they name one or other social class as the motive force of the revolution. We do not dispute the fact that it took a whole a complex of historical circumstances (in which the unfortunate war, of course, occupies first place) and very serious vital interests to arouse the various social classes and groups and throw them into a state of ferment. Nevertheless, we insist that the intelligentsia gave the revolution all its ideological baggage and its whole spiritual arsenal, along with its front-line fighters, skirmishers, agitators and propagandists. It gave spiritual expression to the instinctive desires of the masses, fired them with its own enthusiasm – in short it was the nerves and brains of the gigantic body of the revolution. In this sense the revolution is the intelligentsia's spiritual offspring, and consequently, the history of the revolution is history's verdict on the intelligentsia.[80]

Frank also interpreted the 1905 defeat in a similar way. The liberation movement was totally dominated by the intelligentsia's aims and tactics, its beliefs, life experience, values, tastes and its intellectual and moral outlook. Its failure brought into question the value of its beliefs.[81] The most specific historical assessment of the intelligentsia in this context was in Struve's article 'The intelligentsia and revolution'. This essay was a penetrating political analysis of the role of the intelligentsia; it stretched back in time to show how, since 1598, revolutionary upheaval had been a constant element in Russian society, often associated with a particular class or group. It was formerly associated with the Cossacks, but since Pugachev the mantle had passed to the intelligentsia who were singled out from society by their total alienation from the state. Removal of the autocracy was their starting point and this had led them to misuse the opportunity for progress opened up by the October Manifesto which paved the way for a possible democratic, constitutional state. The ludicrous 'all or nothing' maximalism resulted in the failure to seize realistic opportunities whenever they arose.[82] He particularly condemned the stupid errors of 1905 which frittered away the possibilities of solid advance, above all the senseless and pitiful riots, the Moscow rising and the boycott of elections to the Duma.[83] These were typical examples of the pointless 'heroic deeds' which all the *vekhovtsy* saw as being part of the outlook of the revolutionary intelligentsia's Godless religion of service to the people. Again the intelligentsia was criticised for its utilitarianism which enthroned society at the expense of the individual. 'Bentham has overcome Saint-Simon and Marx.' The need now was for a creative struggle of ideas.[84]

Throughout *Vekhi* there ran a dual picture of the intelligentsia or rather two types of politically involved intellectual. On the one hand there was the *intelligent*, a negative, narrow, puritan fanatic, and on the other the positive, humanist, personalist Christian. The *vekhovtsy* distinguished these two types throughout the history of the nineteenth century, the latter looking back to Radishchev and Chaadaev, the former to Belinsky and Bakunin (without Bakunin, said Struve, there would have been no left-wing intelligentsia),[85] and it was this intelligentsia tradition of the left wing which was the subject of the debate. As the debate showed, this tendency had grown so strong that it had come to be thought of as the *only* intelligentsia, or at least as the typical intelligentsia, and this was probably what Berdyaev meant when he said he was using the word 'intelligentsia' in the traditional Russian sense.[86] This was borne out by the fact that almost every defender of the intelligentsia in the debate defended Chernyshevsky and Belinsky, but ignored Chaadaev and the rest. This bipartite division into materialists and idealists superseded the traditional division into Westerners and Slavophiles.

The mentality of the left-wing group as it was portrayed in *Vekhi*, accorded closely with the image that the revolutionaries had of themselves. Its main characteristics were embodied in Chernyshevsky's hero Rakhmetov and Turgenev's Bazarov and remained the ideal of the revolutionary *intelligent* for the next half-century.

The dedication to revolution led to an all-consuming pre-occupation with social questions and an abhorrence of all personal and individual questions. *Vekhi* commented on this in one place:

> Our public opinion is the most despotic in the world, and for three-quarters of a century now it has adhered stubbornly to the same overrriding principle: thinking about one's own personality

is egotistical and indecent, the only real man is the one who thinks about social concerns, is interested in society's problems, works for the common good. The number of *intelligenty* who put this programme into practice was, of course, negligible but everyone recognised the holiness of the banner. Even those who did nothing, platonically agreed that this is the *only* activity that brings salvation, thereby freeing themselves completely from the need to do anything else.[87]

In another place:

> The concepts of *personal* morality, personal self-improvement (*samousovershenstvovanie*) are extremely unpopular with the intelligentsia, (while the word social, in contrast, has a special sacramental quality). Although the intelligentsia's outlook constitutes an extreme self-deification, in its theories the intelligentsia relentlessly persecutes the personality, sometimes reducing it without trace to the influence of the environment and the spontaneous forces of history (in accordance with the general doctrine of the Enlightenment). The intelligentsia will not grant that the personality holds living, creative energy and it is deaf to everything that approaches the question; deaf not only to Christian doctrine, but even to Tolstoy (whose doctrine does contain a healthy kernel of personal introspection), and to all philosophical doctrines that force consideration of the problem. The absence of a correct doctrine of the personality, however, is the intelligentsia's chief weakness.[88]

Finally, Berdyaev summed up the tragedy and paradox of the stance assumed by the intelligentsia.

> Our intelligentsia cherished *freedom* and professed a philosophy in which there is no place for freedom; it cherished the *personality* and professed a philosophy in which there is no place for the personality; it cherished the *idea of progress* and professed a philosophy in which there is no place for the idea of progress; it cherished the *brotherhood of man* and professed a philosophy in which there is no place for the brotherhood of man; it cherished *justice* and all noble things and professed a philosophy in which there is no place for justice and for anything howsoever noble. This has been an almost continuous aberation of consciousness, a

product of our entire history. The best members of the intelligentsia were fanatically prepared for self-sacrifice, and just as fanatically professed materialism which denies all self-sacrifice. The atheistic philosophy which always captivated the revolutionary intelligentsia could not sanction anything holy, but the intelligentsia gave this very philosophy a sacred character and cherished its own materialism and atheism in a fanatical, almost Catholic manner. Creative philosophical thought must eliminate this aberration and lead consciousness out of its impasse.[89]

All the *vekhovtsy* would subscribe to the essence of these statements though on more specific points they might differ considerably. They did not claim to be adding anything original to the debate. They looked back to a long tradition of such criticism. The difference was that 1905, 1906 and the ensuing events comprised a test of the prevailing intelligentsia values and brought on a mood of self-examination unusual in the intelligentsia. In Gershenzon's words,

> Our warnings are not now: all of our most profound thinkers, from Chaadaev to Solov'ev and Tolstoy, tirelessly said the same things. They were not heeded, the intelligentsia passed them by. Perhaps now, awakened by a real shock, they will listen to weaker voices.[90]

Unfortunately Gershenzon's hope was not fulfilled and the intelligentsia remained deaf to *Vekhi's* call. It was, in any case, optimistic of him to expect *Vekhi* to receive wide support and agreement when its authors themselves differed in many respects. Far from being a united school, the *vekhovtsy* fell into three groups. In the first group were Berdyaev and Bulgakov who had worked together for several years and had come to *Vekhi* from the heady atmosphere of mystical anarchism and symbolism and were far more influenced by the new religious consciousness than any of the others. The second group was composed of the majority of the contributors – Struve, Frank, Izgoev and Kistyakovsky. They were more typical of the realistic and practical men associated with the Kadet party. Their main interest was in political and social problems related to a humanistic cultural concern rather than to a primarily religious outlook. Finally there was Gershenzon who stood apart from the rest. The impetus behind the book came from him and he was the most outspoken critic of the revolutionary intelligentsia out of all the contributors. He was motivated by a passionate hatred of the men of the underground. N. Valentinov, in his reminiscences, vividly described Gershenzon's hostility.[91] The depth of Gershenzon's feelings was obvious from his article in *Vekhi* which contained many provocative statements including the view that it was the bayonets and prisons of the regime which preserved the intelligentsia from the wrath of the people,[92] which was the most striking, and most quoted, sentence in *Vekhi*. It was obviously unpalatable to the great majority of the intelligentsia although it did prove to be more accurate than its critics believed.

These differences within the *Vekhi* group were made more obvious because Gershenzon, as editor, did nothing to bring the contributors together to discuss the theme of the book. They did not even see each other's contributions until after the book had been published.[93] Some of the resulting contradictions were quite glaring. For example, Berdyaev said that one of the weaknesses of the intelligentsia was that it did not prize truth, while for Frank one of its weaknesses was its tendency to sacrifice itself and others in the name of its abstract truth.

Despite these differences, Gershenzon and the other *vekhovtsy* were united in their desire for a revaluation in the Russian intelligentsia based on a concern for deeper spiritual and cultural values than those which the intelligentsia currently possessed. Looking back on the period, Frank said that all the contributors, with the possible exception of Gershenzon, shared a basic tendency which had two elements. The first was the need for a religious, metaphysical basis for a world view, as opposed to the prevailing positivist and materialist one. The second was a critique of the maximalist revolutionary aspirations of the radical intelligentsia.[94]

In any case, the writers of *Vekhi* did not desire intellectual conformity. They wished to start a debate. They did not claim to have ready-made solutions. They themselves only presented problems and asked questions. Clearly the intelligentsia as a whole did not want to concern itself with such problems and questions. Even so, many of the main points of *Vekhi* have been repeated and expanded later by the same authors and by others. The collection *Iz glubiny* written in 1918 showed how many of *Vekhi's* prophecies had proved to be true in the light of the revolutionary experiences of 1917.

THE CREATIVE INTELLIGENTSIA AND REVOLUTION: ARTISTIC CRITICS OF THE INTELLIGENTSIA TRADITION

To say that the non-socialist artists of the period had a political outlook is controversial. No one would dispute that there were many politically involved socialist novelists, poets and critics, such as Gorky, Bunin, Friche and Vorovsky. It is much less common, however, for the political views of non-socialist writers to receive as much attention as is devoted to their aesthetics. As a consequence, there is a mistaken belief that the symbolists were apart from, or above, politics and lived in a separate world devoted to art for art's sake. However much this may have been true of the 1890s, the excitement of 1905 penetrated deeply into the formerly aloof creative intelligentsia and they, to a greater or lesser degree, were affected by the politicisation and polarisation brought about by the events of 1905. Political positions were more closely defined and politics was given a greater value in their outlook than it had formerly enjoyed.

In what kind of politics did this part of the creative intelligentsia involve itself? First of all it must be made clear that most of them did not take part in the humdrum routine of party politics and were not active at political meetings, demonstrations and the like. They did not join political parties nor did their writing reflect any interest in the bread-and-butter politics of the Duma or in specific political questions like the redistribution of land or the wages of workers. Their concern was far more related to general principles and to ideas. While many of them declared themselves to be in favour of revolution of some kind, including even the mercurial Rozanov, very few of them expressed sympathy for the intelligentsia tradition and for its current upholders in the ranks of Social Democratic, Socialist Revolutionary and Kadet parties. Their political interest was confined to a growing sense of the social responsibility of the artist, the feeling that with great events surrounding him it was imperative for the artist to take a stand. Beketova's remark about the effect of 1905 on Blok could apply to many others. She wrote:

Aleksandr Aleksandrovich's indifference to the life around him changed into a lively interest in all that was going on. He followed the course of the revolution, the mood of the workers, but politics and parties as before were alien to him.[95]

The hostility to the old type of *intelligent*, the man imbued with 'the spirit of the sixties' as Gippius called it,[96] ran deep. Merezhkovsky, for example, welcomed the journal *Voprosy zhizni* because, among other reasons, it avoided the usual pitfall of Russian journals, namely, subjecting eternal values of art, philosophy, science and literature to vulgar everyday political ends. For *Voprosy zhizni*, he said, culture was and remained the end, not the means.[97]

The separation of art from politics did not mean that those artists had no political views. For several of them art itself had an important role to play in social transformation and it was often on the level of revolutionary messianism that the spheres of political opinion and artistic creativity met. Merezhkovsky was a revolutionary in a sense, as was Blok. Both of them felt that society could and should be transformed. For Merezhkovsky it was religion which would achieve this. Similarly, Belyi was not entirely free of the utopianism he warned against. He himself defended the idea of Russian religious universality, the unity of people and intelligentsia through religion.

> We might seem to ourselves not to be religious, but that is only in our conscious mind; in the unconscious, in our life force, we are religious if we are with the people (*narodnyi*) and with the people if religious. Religion is a universal bond. It is not in the outer appearance but in the spirit.

This arose from the fundamental difference between West and East. 'In the West each is against all. Among us all are against one, and for that reason Russian individualism always corrupts religion.'[98] This led, for instance, to Nietzsche misunderstanding Dostoevsky, Belyi continued. Nietzsche thought Dostoevsky was a great individualist and did not see that he was a universalist expressing the hopes of a whole people, not of an individual.[99]

Like many artists who dabbled in politics, the political views of these symbolists were often vague and very general in form, and naive, emotional and shallow in content, but their prestige as artists gave to their opinions a greater significance than they would otherwise have possessed. Sometimes these political conceptions were expressed directly in artistic forms ranging from political cartoons to poems. The remainder of this chapter is devoted to a brief survey of these views and expressions, with particular reference to religion, revolution and the revolutionary tradition.

As a noted conservative, V. V. Rozanov (1856–1919), might have been expected to see nothing but bad in the revolution of 1905, but his writings of this time showed a much more sympathetic, if whimsical, attitude towards it. Rozanov delighted in paradox even to the extent of proposing opposite views in the same article and he made contradictory statements about the revolution. However, a collection of some of his articles of the years 1905–6, published under the title *Kogda nachal'stvo ushlo (When Authority Went Away)*, showed a consistently sympathetic attitude.[100] The tone of the volume was one of school-boyish delight that the headmaster should be temporarily absent.

Rozanov was attracted by the revolution despite his firm belief in authority on which, he believed, the whole universe was constructed – even the sun held 'authority' over the planets[101] – and which he saw as being both natural and necessary. But its temporary absence was not without its brighter side. 'This moment "without authority" . . . was short and brilliant,' he wrote.[102] For him the great achievement of the revolution was to break up the 'universal boredom' of the turn of the century. There was boredom with 'progress', boredom with 'evolution'.[103] In contrast with all this, youthful revolutionary activism created a favourable impression on him. Revolutions, he said, were nearly always carried out by the young and could be defined in three words, 'youth has arrived'.[104]

Although a conservative by temperament, Rozanov was also hostile to tradition and he saw in the revolution the possibility of freeing Russia from the dead weight of its oppressive institutions which crushed the creativity and individualism which Rozanov cherished. The revolution was the fire, Russia the pheonix.

> Fatherland, religion, way of life, social bonds, ranks, philosophy and poetry have all burned up in the fire of the phoenix. Man is once again naked. . . . Let us then look on him not quite without hope . . . but let us be hopeful that when the universal fire comes to an end and the old phoenix is finally completely burned out, from its ashes will fly a new phoenix.[105]

His belief in the recuperative and creative powers of Russia, which was an aspect of his patriotism, set Rozanov apart from other conservatives such as Pobedonostsev who was, he said, a persuasive writer but like Hamlet was fearful lest he or anyone else should do anything or initiate anything.[106] What Russia needed, Rozanov suggested, was a release from traditional values in the spheres of aesthetic judgement, way of life, economic relations and so on. He used this opportunity to score off his old enemy the Church, as well as the state. There was no country in Europe, he pointed out, where 'general oppression and general tradition (for example of our Church) were so powerful, long-lived and acute as in Russia and with this we begin to arrive at the reason why nihilism, as "anti-traditionalness" and release, burst from the volcano within her'.[107]

Rozanov's attitude to the revolution was thus very distant from that of the revolutionary parties and was only loosely related to the actual social and political problems which had played a considerable role in the uprising. Like Rozanov, D. S. Merezhkovsky (1866–1941) was also attracted to the revolution and was moved to protest against the oppressiveness of the regime. With Filosofov and Gippius he contributed to a book published in Paris entitled *Le Tsar et la Révolution*, parts of which were also published in Russia though somewhat abridged by the censor.[108] Also like Rozanov, the ideas of Merezhkovsky and his co-writers about the nature of the revolution were vague and tended to be poetic, emotional and mystical.

In common with many others, such as Bulgakov and Vyacheslav Ivanov, Merezhkovsky and his fellow contributors had a sense of the impending apocalyptic transformation of the world. For Merezhkovsky this would result in the age of the Third Testament to follow on from the Old and New Testaments. This would be the result of a religious revolution leading to the construction of God's kingdom on earth. This religious revolutionism put them outside the ranks of official Christianity and of the revolutionary intelligentsia. Their religion alienated them from the revolutionaries, their revolutionism alienated them from the autocracy and the Church. They stood alone but were not aloof from the revolutionary issue. For Gippius, Filosofov and Merezhkovsky both the revolutionaries and the autocracy represented a kind of religion, but a false one. As the preface to *Le Tsar et la Révolution* explained, the autocracy was a greater blasphemy than the revolution because although the revolutionaries were atheist and hated God's name, they were less blasphemous than the Church which took advantage of the most solemn liturgical moment to proclaim the Tsar.

The great problem for a religious revolutionary was to dissociate religion from reaction as the two were so closely linked in Russia. Merezhkovsky had pointed out the existence of this problem in 'All against all',[109] but it was Gippius who set about solving it in a remarkable article entitled 'The true power of tsarism' in which she claimed that the revolutionaries had failed to turn the people against the tsar, to whom they were loyal even when they opposed the government and its institutions, because they had tried to use crude materialist arguments which were totally ineffective and did not influence the deeply religious soul of the people. To be effective, Gippius continued, it was necessary to expose the tsarist system as a blasphemy, to show that it was a perversion of those very religious conceptions from which it claimed its legitimacy. Although she agreed that socialism contained much that was true and valuable, when it came to the question of the just organisation of society, it failed to respond to deeper, more fundamental questions. In short, she concluded, the differences between the revolutionary socialist religion and the autocratic religion was that while socialism was a half-truth the autocracy was a lie, but a complete one, and derived its power solely from the perfection of its lie.[110]

The three contributors shared the opinion that only a complete, thorough-going, revolutionary transformation was both possible and desirable in Russia. Half measures would not suffice. Merezhkovsky said 'The Lord's anointed must be an autocrat or he is nothing. In Russia a constitution is less possible than a republic.'[111] Gippius also spoke of the irrelevance of the centre in the face of the polarised situation in Russia at that time. The Kadets, she said, had spoken out against revolution without thereby gaining any compensatory sympathy from the government. 'Their role has become quite insignificant. It is between the extremists that the real battle is taking place.'[112] Filosofov also opposed the October Manifesto but for quite different reasons. In his view it was to be rejected because, as the tsar himself had granted it, there was no fundamental change in the situation. 'Constitutional absolutism' was no gain.[113] Despite these differences, all three shared an implacable hostility to the *status quo* and a utopian vision of a transfigured Russian society which would be just and holy, which would actually practise the principles which the autocracy claimed to represent. 'The Russian revolution,' said Gippius, 'must take a new self-aware path having universal value. And so believe firmly that it will do so because we all have faith in Russia and in the holy truth of our revolution.'[114]

Merezhkovsky's contribution was entitled 'Religion and revolution'.[115] In it he attempted to show how in the Russian situation religion and revolution came to be closely interrelated. The autocracy, Merezhkovsky argued, in its attempts to unite spiritual and temporal power had turned religious and intellectual dissent into an act of political rebellion and treason. Inevitably in these circumstances, said Merezhkovsky, revolution in Russia must have a religious significance. He was in fact inclined to see all revolutions as having their roots in something deeper than the mere social and political situation in which they occurred. The French Revolution, for example, was for Merezhkovsky, the first act in a continuing tragedy. It was an external, political expression of the personal and inner processes of secularisation which had been under way since the Renaissance.[116] But this religious content was even more noticeable in Russia because the autocracy, like the Roman papacy, was an attempt to unite Church and state. Where the popes were a spiritual power which had usurped the temporal, the tsars were the reverse but the end result was the same.[117]

Most of the remainder of the article was devoted to showing, with examples, how religious revolution developed in Russia from the time of Catherine the Great. In the eyes of the Tsarina, both Novikov and Radishchev, from their contrasting standpoints of mysticism and atheism respectively, posed an equal threat to Orthodox autocracy. The Russian God and its Russian tsar were indivisible.[118] He used many other examples to support his view, in particular Pestel' who wrote a revolutionary catechism, Chaadaev whose works were edited by a Russian Jesuit Prince Gagarin, Gogol, Dostoevsky and Tolstoy.[119] The last two were particularly important for Merezhkovsky. Dostoevsky's career went full circle from political revolution to religious revolution. Tolstoy's concept of the kingdom of God foreshadowed true Christianity. Dosteovsky's theocracy and Tolstoy's anarchy were the thesis and antithesis of a triad whose synthesis, said Merezhkovsky, had yet to appear.[120] Solov'ev, despite having opinions which were practically all considered to be either 'false or inadequate' by Merezhkovsky[121] did contribute two particularly important concepts, the collective view of religion and salvation and the view that historic Christianity was only a path to the new religion.[122] The common thread linking all these religious revolutionaries, Merezhkovsky said, was their preaching of the perfected Church, which would unite God with freedom, as the kingdom of God on earth. The present moment marked a turning-point for Merezhkovsky, 'We are on the eve of uniting our God with our freedom, of uniting the goal of the revolutionary movement with the goal of the universal religious movement,' he said. The result would be the discovery of a new unifying idea in the two movements, the idea of the Church, of the kingdom of God on earth.[123] He had proclaimed this idea elsewhere when he wrote that Russia was in the process of transforming itself from a positivist approach to social problems to a religious approach.[124]

Decadence, he claimed, had a particularly important role to play in this process. 'Decadence which seems to be death, the terrible underground, an impasse formed of deaf walls, is in reality the beginning of a new life, a narrow exit towards the obscure, starry sky of the people's soul.'[125] It was, said Merezhkovsky, a mistake to underrate the decadents who had a crucial part to play in bringing about the revolution. 'If all Russia is now a dry forest, ready for a fire, then the Russian decadents are the dryest and tallest branches in the forest. When lightning strikes they will catch fire first and from them the whole forest will be set ablaze.'[126]

Far from ignoring politics, Merezhkovsky and his circle saw it as an extremely important aspect of life and saw their own role in it, as diagnosers of past evils and as suggesters of future post-revolutionary values, to be of great importance for the revolutionary movement. Many artists who did not participate in political activity in the normal partisan sense shared this view of the crucial role of the artist in society and believed that their art was itself a revolutionary transforming activity.

The poet N. M. Minsky (1855–1937) was, like Merezhkovsky, a leading figure in the St Petersburg Religious Philosophical Society. He was also an extreme individualist and he was a sympathiser with religion and revolution. Despite all these similarities, however, Minsky had a very violent dislike for Merezhkovsky's ideas. He considered them to be even more objectionable than the God-building of Gorky and Lunacharsky. The substance of Minsky's complaint was that whereas Gorky and Lunacharsky's 'sham' was simply a use of religion for party ends to make the party better understood and more popular, Merezhkovsky had a falsehood at the very centre of his thought because he was a reactionary pretending to be a revolutionary. According to Minsky, Merezhkovsky's claim to stand as a bridge between people and intelligentsia was an empty dream.[127] Merezhkovsky's views, he said elsewhere, represented the reappearance of the most vulgar, most superstitious religiosity. The 'neo-Byzantine'[128] views of Merezhkovsky, Bulgakov, Berdyaev and their followers were an example of 'absolute reaction'.[129] They were 'burned out ashes, barren sand, aimless atavism'.[130] Until Merezhkovsky recognised 'sacred reason and sacred individuality' his words as a religious and social thinker would 'remain dead and dying ciphers'.[131]

Apart from his greater hostility to Christianity, Minsky differed from Merezhkovsky in his conception of individualism. Minsky, influenced by mystical anarchism, saw the individual as the most important revolutionary force.[132] In Russia, Minsky said, history had crushed individuals into an amorphous mass. For Minsky, lack of natural frontiers was the curse of the Russian nation and the search for them was Russia's 'thousand year nightmare'. Without the stability these would have given, there was no opportunity for individual development. European history differed from Russian, according to Minsky, in its search for individuality from the time of Dante. In Russia, on the other hand, history progressed through the centralisation and strengthening of the state at the expense of individuals and at the expense of the individual groups and sections of society which had brought about the diversification of state power in the west. 'Of all the European countries,' he wrote, 'Russia is the only one in which the individual was not the creator of state development but its victim.'[133]

For Minsky, progress came about as a result of contradiction. But how, he asked, could the contradiction of revolution have arisen in a Russia which consisted of a very powerful state and atomised individuals? The answer to this lay in the crisis facing the state itself. As weapons became more and more sophisticated the armed might of a state began to require a high level of education and culture on the part of the people who would have to use the weapons.[134] The whole Petersburg period illustrated this continuing crisis in Russia, said Minsky. From the '*narod*-polyp' no creative improvements in defence, whether tactics, strategy or improved weapons, were to be expected, though it would defend and die dutifully. Creativity, however, was not within its powers. For this it had no organs.[135] There were only two choices possible for a government in the situation described by Minsky. Both were equally disastrous. If the regime chose to educate its citizens, he said, it would strengthen the revolutionary movement. If it refused to educate them it would be unable to withstand even the slightest pressure put upon it from within or without.

Such was Minsky's diagnosis of the ills of Russian society. His prescription for them was equally individual. He proposed 'social-humanism', a system which combined fundamental features common, he claimed, to all the Russian thinkers of the nineteenth century, plus the worthwhile elements in Western socialism. The basis of this mixture was individualism and love.[136] Its fundamental characteristic, love, was the common denominator in many otherwise different Russian writers. 'In this respect,' Minsky said,

> our writers, with all their differences of political and religious ideas, present a surprising unity. One cannot imagine a greater abyss than that which separates the religion of Dostoevsky from the atheism of Chekhov, or Tolstoy's doctrine of non-resistance from Gorky's doctrine of revolutionary revenge. But between them they are all inspired by the same passion and burn with the same light. In the works of each of them the dark side of life is illuminated and transformed – underground bitterness, aristocratic callousness, intelligentsia flabbiness or the vagrant's despair. Father Zosim and Prince Neklyudov, the three sisters' officers and Luka the tramp, are all children of one family and all travel the same road from egoism to love, from their own 'I' to humanity and that is why all their words and actions are not rhetorical, not aesthetic, not tied up in themselves, but truthful, penetrating, powerful, universal.[137]

The Achilles heel of Western socialism was, in Minsky's view, its failure to consider any questions other than the means of transforming the production process and the redistribution of wealth. The western European socialist movement, he claimed, did not provoke questions of the use of riches or of the inner attitude of the individual to wealth.[138] It was exactly this missing dimension of individual experience that the Russian revolutionary movement could supply.

> We social humanists will borrow from the western socialists only their practical programme, political and syndicalist, the plan for the struggle with the capitalists worked out by them with the objective of removing them from their ownership of the means of labour and converting the system into one of collective ownership, exercised not only by the proletariat but by all mankind.[139]

Minsky did not at this point add that he had also borrowed a messianic view of the proletariat from the socialists but he made this clear elsewhere in his article. In Minsky's scheme, the proletariat had a crucial role to play, not only in the defence of its own interests but for the sake of civilised mankind in general. Every other part of society, including the political opposition and revolutionary movements in Europe, had been ruined by the spread of the commercial mentality, by philistinism. The bourgeoisie had even infected the socialist movement which had developed the vulgar materialism of the bourgeoisie into the ultimate materialism, historical materialism, which ought to be rejected. Minsky, like so many of his fellow writers at this time, from Gorky to Berdyaev, then allowed himself an attack on bourgeois philistinism, but extended it to include the socialist movement in his comments.

> Identifying all history with the struggle of economic interest and relating to religion (*religioznost'*) with a sceptical smile, the theoreticians of European socialism repeat the arguments of the philistine, they are smiling with the smile of the philistine, they recognise their spiritual solidarity with philistinism. It is possible to understand why the bourgeois cannot be anything other than a materialist and sceptic. He builds his whole life on distrust of truth, on compartmentalisation of conscience, on piracy and on brigandage of the good things of life which the capitalist by deception and violence snatches from the workers and from his own brother in competition. He hurries to devour them in his own corner laughing to himself. He is above the truth, which he, for reasons of personal security, wishes to inculcate into everybody else.[140]

In short, Minsky continued,

> The bourgeois gives his blessing only to those of life's riches which can be stolen and gulped down: hence his economic materialism. But being aware that he is in the wrong, he is powerless to justify and to consecrate these riches: hence his scepticism. The bourgeois can remain religious only under the conditions of impenetrable hypocrisy. The mingling of this hypocrisy, this empty religiosity, with the most naked ignoble materialism constitutes our contemporary Americanism.[141]

If this creeping philistinism were to be halted, there was only one hope and that was the working class. Minsky's reason for choosing this saviour was that in its oppressed condition it was still innocent of these evils. 'In its soul there is no compartmentalisation, its hands are clean, its eyes fixed proudly and brightly on the world.' The crux of the matter was, for Minsky, that the working class represented 'humanity's last reserve, the final stock of unused fresh forces'.[142]

Minsky's views, then, were a peculiar combination of socialism and anti-socialism, of religion and opposition to religion, of individualism and opposition to egoism. Revolution and creativity, two concepts which were very similar to Minsky's way of thinking, were for him the main positive values. Creativity did not, as so many of the Socialists, he said, seemed to think, stop with Marxism but it would continue to develop. Who, he asked, on looking at the works of Lomonosov and Derzhavin, could have foreseen the eventual development of a Dostoevsky or a Tolstoy? Similarly, who knew what would develop from 'the Plekhanovs, Lenins and Bogdanovs' who were the 'Lomonosovs and Derzhavins of Russian social- ism'?[143] He was thus in conflict with the dogmatism of the Social Democrats which he believed to be as opposed to culture as the forces of state reaction. Minsky had an excellent opportunity to observe the cultural attitudes of the Social Democrats as he was persuaded by Lenin himself to be the nominal or 'sitting' editor of the Bolshevik's first legal daily newspaper, *Novaya zhizn'*, which appeared shortly after the October manifesto had been issued and in which were published Lenin's articles 'Party organisation and party literature' and 'Religion and socialism'. Minsky's stay with *Novaya zhizn'* was brief and stormy but not so brief that he was unable to form an opinion of the Bolshevik attitude to the culture and creativity which were so important for Minsky. In a short polemical article entitled 'The story of my editorship'[144] Minsky issued a warning similar to that given by some of the *Vekhi* contributors.

If French revolutionary syndicalism shows that there is a deep split between the labouring class and the power-loving parties, then in a few days and weeks of the Russian revolution we saw with our own eyes that the interests of social democracy are similarly incompatible with the interests of culture, that the dogmas of politicking Marxism are no less hostile to the ideal hopes of the intelligentsia than bureaucratic tyranny and re- actionary violence.[145]

Minsky thus presents a very interesting example of the politically concerned poet imbued with the mystique of revolution and with the mystique of religion, the two main intelligentsia tendencies of the period. They came together in his populist vision of the religious intelligentsia, as distinct from the atheist—socialist intelligentsia, having a special role to play in guiding the people along the path of equality and justice. He accepted with enthusiasm Struve's view in *Vekhi* that the Petersburg period was characterised by the split between intelligentsia and people which had arisen from the immanent atheism of the former and the transcendental religion of the latter, and by the split between the intelligentsia and the state.[146] His mystical anarchist principles and his deep belief in creativity set him apart from almost everyone else. He criticised Merezhkovsky and he criticised the Socialists, both of whom he resembled in fundamental ways. He also criticised the revolutionary intelligentsia, even though he was himself so deeply a part of it. What cannot be denied is that Minsky was deeply involved, perhaps even more than Merezhkovsky, in the political intellectual issues of the time. He was a throwback to an earlier kind of *intelligent* moved by moral fervour rather than by political ideology, by creative idealism rather than by dogmatic materialism. He fused poetic creativity, love of mankind, Godless religion, anarchist individualism and socialist politics into one great personal synthesis, which included elements from all the main political intellectual movements which he had lived through in the late nineteenth century, ranging from populism through socialism to religious idealism.

Other writers presented a less heady mixture than this. For example, Aleksandr Blok (1880–1921) was also much concerned with the questions of revolution, the intelligentsia, religion and mysticism and attempted to analyse the role which the artist ought to play in society in the light of the answers he gave to them. Several articles of the period 1906–10 dealt with these themes. The conclusion that Block came to was that art should be seen not as the enemy of utility, as something separate from life, but as an integral part of it. The critical dispute over art and utility became superfluous in Blok's opinion because the two were not as contradictory as they had seemed. The contemporary artist, said Blok, added the category of 'duty' to those of 'form' and 'content' to which he had been limited in the past. This enabled the artist to reach the heights where 'in a wonderful way the sworn enemies, beauty and utility, take each other's hand'. The most perfect union between beauty and utility was to be found, Blok continued, in folk art where the two were linked rhythmically and inseparably in productive work.[147] Up until the present, Blok said, words remained words, life life, the beautiful useless, the useful ugly. 'The artist, in order to be an artist suppressed the man within him; nobody wishes this to continue, it is not right that it should be thus.'[148] This new path of duty and social responsibility which had been pointed out by Ibsen

> opens up before the contemporary artist a joyful, free and proper path between the valleys of contradiction to the peaks of art. . . Perhaps on the heights of the future tragedy the soul will experience the unity of the beautiful and the proper, of beauty and utility, in the same way that in former time the soul experienced their unity in the breadth of ancient folk songs.[149]

This was not simply an aesthetic conclusion but one which was intended to break down the barriers between life and art which would correspond to the removal of the barriers between intelligentsia and people. Art would help to change society. 'I am an *intelligent*, a man of letters,' Blok said at a meeting of the Religious Philosophical Society in November 1908, 'and the word is my weapon'.[150]

For Blok these barriers were very real and he was very scornful of the intelligentsia's futile efforts to overcome them through the gigantic irrelevancy of 'religious seeking' which consumed so much of its energy.

> The educated and spiteful *intelligenty*, going grey in arguments about Christ and anti-Christ, ladies, wives, daughters, sisters-in-law in decorous blouses, thinkers of many thoughts, priests shining from self-satisfied grease – all this inconceivable and disgraceful jumble is an idiotic, scintillation of words. And here a slender little priest in a poor cassock calls on Jesus and all are uncomfortable. One honest social democrat with a knobbly forehead, spitefully hurls dozens of questions but the bald man, gleaming with unction, replies only that it is impossible to answer so many questions at once. All this remains in fashion; so fashionable that it is accessible to the wives of assistant professors and to philanthropic ladies. But meanwhile on the streets there is a wind, the prostitutes freeze, people are hungry, people hang, in the country there is reaction, and life in Russia is difficult, cold and vile.[151]

Blok's bitter words about the religious seekers reflected the development of his views on revolution. Blok became increasingly aware of the political world in 1905 and began to follow the course of events with interest.[152] In many respects his atttitude to the revolution at this time went through the same cycle of enthusiasm and despair as in the years from 1917–21, although its impact on his poetry in the earlier period was slight. From the very outset of the disturbances in January 1905, Blok was gripped by the unfolding situation but by 1909 he had become totally disillusioned. His change of attitude was partly the result of his personal problems. This was a very painful period in his relationship with his wife Lyubov' Dmitreevna and his close friend Andrei Belyi, but despite this his depression was not solely the result of personal anxieties.

Blok's family background was a very conservative one. His stepfather, Frants Feliksovich Kublitskii-Piottukh, was a guards officer. The political outlook of the family can perhaps be best judged from the fact that the newspaper to which they subscribed was the monarchist *Novoe vremya*. According to Blok's aunt, M. A. Beketova, the family implicitly believed the reports in that paper of an approaching victory in the war against Japan and like many other such families in Russia at the time, were thrown into confusion by the military reverse at Port Arthur. The events of Bloody Sunday coming shortly afterwards caused a deep change of heart in both Blok and his mother. According to her sister, Blok's mother 'sharply changed her attitude to the Tsar and the old regime after 9 January. She at once began to hate it.' The chief cause of this change of heart was her proximity to the events (the family lived in an industrial quarter of St Petersburg) and horror at the cruel repression which she witnessed.[153] As a result of these experiences, she came to consider herself a revolutionary, welcomed the October Manifesto and the opening of the State Duma. The subscription to *Novoe vremya* was dropped and one to the liberal *Rech'* was taken up in its place.[154]

Blok followed a similar path. From 9 January he took a very great interest in the events in the capital city which reached a peak in the autumn. He attended a few political meetings though, according to his aunt, more as an observer than as a participant. He took part in street demonstrations and on one occasion even carried a red flag at the head of a procession.[155] In November 1905, he wrote to an acquaintance about his political involvement and declared, using capital letters to heighten the effect, 'I AM A SOCIAL DEMOCRAT'.[156] This involvement did not, apparently, go very deep. It had little influence on his poetry. Apart from one poem, *The Meeting*, its effect was negligible.[157] He himself made a sober evaluation of his experiences of that year in a letter to his father written on 30 December 1905.

My attitude to the 'liberation movement' was, alas, expressed almost exclusively in liberal discussion and at one time even in my feeling that I was a social democrat. Now I am withdrawing more and more having absorbed all that I can (from 'society') and having thrown out that which my soul will not accept . . . I no longer remain a revolutionary or a 'constructor of life' not because I did not see, in one sense or another, but simply as a result of the nature, quality and themes of my spiritual experiences.[158]

His concern did, however, express itself in new themes and interests in the ensuing years. During 1905 he associated himself with Bulgakov and Berdyaev and *Voprosy zhizni* and with mystical anarchism. His play *Balaganchik* was published in the first volume of the mystical anarchist collection *Fakely* in 1906. Perhaps the most important product of these new interests was his lecture 'The people and the intelligentsia'. He read the lecture on two occasions in St Petersburg. The first was on 13 November 1908 at the Religious Philosophical Society, and the second on 12 December in the somewhat grander surroundings of the Literary Society and in the presence of the stalwarts of *Russkoe bogatstvo* such as Korolenko, Annensky and Vengerov. It is interesting to note that this meeting, held two months before the appearance of *Vekhi* and dealing with themes closely related to those of *Vekhi*, attracted much the same sort of attention as *Vekhi* itself. The hall was full and Vengerov told Blok afterwards that there had never been such an attentive audience at any meeting of the society. He was treated by the old guard, he said, as 'a favourite nephew'.[159] The substance of his argument was that the intelligentsia's affection for the people was not returned. They were two different realities. 'On the one hand a hundred and fifty million, on the other a few hundred thousand, unable to understand each other in the most fundamental things.' The intelligentsia was in 'a state of hasty ferment' while among the people 'sleep and silence seem to reign'.[160] Blok warned that an attempt by the intelligentsia to rouse the people might result in its own destruction. 'When we rush to the people, we are rushing to certain death.'[161]

The increasing disillusionment noticeable in this lecture came to a head a few months later. The end of what Blok's biographer, K. Mochul'sky, has called his 'political and social period' came when he and his wife departed for Italy in 1909. On the eve of their departure he wrote to his mother. Russia, he said, had become a land of spitefulness and dissension. Everyone lived behind a Chinese wall and was half-contemptuous of everybody else. At the same time the single common enemies, the state system, clericalism, the taverns, the prisons, and the bureaucracy, did not show their faces but directed people against one another. It was not possible, he said, to remain human, to avoid being turned into a machine for the preparation of spite and hatred. It was necessary either to leave Russia, 'to spit in its ugly, drunken mug' or to cut oneself off from the humiliation of politics and from society and partisanship.[162] His vision became even bleaker and in June he again wrote to his mother, this time from Florence, saying 'I love only art, children and death'.[163] In this progression from involvement without participation leading to personal and political disillusionment and despair, Blok was perhaps typical of many of his contemporaries.

From a quite different point of view, Blok's friend Andrei Belyi was also very critical of the intelligentsia and he was one of the few figures of note who welcomed *Vekhi*. He had absorbed many of its fundamental ideas directly from Gershenzon whose friendship with Belyi began in 1908. Belyi had been very close to the revolutionary intelligentsia in the person of Valentinov up until this time and in his memoirs of Belyi, Valentinov gave a very dramatic account of the final confrontation between himself, Belyi and Gershenzon in Belyi's flat. Valentinov had been acquainted with Belyi for some time and Belyi had been more than sympathetic to Valentinov's social democratic opinions. However, in December 1908, during one of his frequent visits to Belyi, Valentinov met Gershenzon – a symbolic meeting between a *vekhovets* and a revolutionary. Belyi introduced him to Gershenzon and explained that Valentinov, like many others, was 'legalising' his existence and emerging from the underground. This triggered off one of, what Valentinov called, the 'explosions' or 'earthquakes' for which Gershenzon was well-known. 'It is not only from your friend's face that the mask has fallen,' said Gershenzon, 'it has been ripped from hundreds of thousands of others.' Valentinov was stung by this remark but his attempt to defend himself only provoked a further outburst. Gershenzon encapsulated his view which became public a few weeks later when *Vekhi* was published. The revolution, he said, was a 'smashed pot' and he spoke contemptuously of those who wanted to 'deepen' the revolution. Recent events since 1905 were, he went on, an indictment of the political leadership of the intelligentsia which had committed a series of criminal blunders from the events of autumn 1905 through the December rising to its stupidity at the time of the first and second State Dumas, all of which were, he said, a disgrace to the Russian intelligentsia. This explained why the revolutionary opportunity was lost. There was no doubt, said Valentinov in reply, that many errors had been committed during 1905 but there were also achievements, in particular an unprecedented freedom of the press, of speech, of assembly and to form unions. Gershenzon's fury grew greater. The intelligentsia, and not only its revolutionary parts, said Gershenzon, was alien to culture, lacked a legal consciousness and was 'not composed of individuals but of sick cripples'. At various points in the argument Valentinov turned to Belyi for support but it was not forthcoming. Belyi, to Valentinov's amazement, said nothing. The atmosphere in the room, Valentinov recalled, became suffocating. Rather than take the risk of coming to blows, Valentinov made a strategic withdrawal, overwhelmed by the fact that Belyi, who not long before had even argued in defence of Nechaev, should tolerate such an assault not only on the Nechaevs but on the whole intelligentsia. Valentinov's friendship with and influence on Belyi declined from this point, never to recover.[164]

Belyi broke that silence which so astonished Valentinov in an article published in the May issue of *Vesy*.[165] It was true, he said, that the intelligentsia did not value law, as Kistyakovsky had pointed out. It was also true that, as Berdyaev had said, the apologists of the intelligentsia did not value truth. 'We must raise the level of Russian culture,' said Belyi,

> Culture and freedom are synonymous. The Russian intelligentsia, considering itself to be the bearer of the freedom-loving idea, had, and often still has, an attitude of intolerable barbarity towards cultural values . . . . Above all we do not know what our interest in questions of theoretical philosophy is, and we have no idea of what art is.[166]

But this was not the main point. The value of *Vekhi* for Belyi was that it had pricked the bubble of the intelligentsia's self-deception. He wrote:

> An element of self-hypnosis was always present in the Russian intelligentsia. It was always completely right about everything. The Russian revolution was successful, Russian Marxism was not undergoing a collapse, Lavrov and Eliseev were more sensible than Gogol, Tolstoy, and Dostoevsky. There was no Azef. We were right about it all. But if there was an Azef, if the Russian revolution did not succeed, if Gogol, Tolstoy and Dostoevsky were forgotten in the searching, then you are to blame, writers of *Vekhi*. This is the answer the Russian publicists give to the poignantly experienced words of *Vekhi*.[167]

One of the sources of the intelligentsia's illusion was that it was responsible for forming its own image and writing its own ideology in the press – the 'obsequious mirror of the Russian intelligentsia'. 'The *intelligent*,' Belyi wrote,

> reads the newspapers and is moved because in them he is pictured like an angel. He is the summit of history, the saviour of Russia, the measure of all aesthetic and mental values. He knows very well the conceptual needs of the countryside even though in his whole life he has not left the town: why study it when he knows everything, and these are the consequences of omniscience?[168]

It was because it had disturbed this cosy, narcissistic relationship that *Vekhi* had brought such a barbaric reprisal[169] on itself and it was this very fury which was 'a sign that the book has found its mark'.[170]

Belyi did not, however, think that the critical remarks in *Vekhi* represented a complete renunciation of all that the intelligentsia had achieved in the past. He appealed for *Vekhi's* criticisms to be received in the spirit in which they were made. It was necessary only 'to take into account the personalities of the *Vekhi* authors,' Belyi said, 'to understand that the bitter truth of the condemnatory articles is not a judgment but a call to deeper introspection'.[171] In any case, Belyi said,

> the intelligentsia as a mentally privileged estate does not need

justification. It has many merits before the Russian people – the ability to sacrifice itself, to suffer without renouncing its ideals – but there are no more elements of creation, of reality. By the unjust judgement on *Vekhi*, the Russian press showed that it is intolerably biased. The authors of *Vekhi* did not think at all of passing judgement on the intelligentsia; they pointed only to that which prevented the Russian intelligentsia from changing from being a slave to abstract dreams of freedom, to becoming its creator. But it appears that the authors of *Vekhi* had no right to do this despite the fact that Bulgakov, Berdyaev and Struve are among the first who actually passed through that ideology which subsequently became the ideology of practically all of the Russian intelligentsia.[172]

In Belyi the *Vekhi* group found its most important, almost its only, convert.

Clearly there was wide support for revolution and hatred for the *status quo* among writers who were supposedly not political or not revolutionary. That this did not mean that they were all sympathetic to the 'spirit of the sixties' is equally obvious. What was less clear was that in many cases they were opposed to this old-style intelligentsia and its political parties because they were too closely linked with the autocratic system which they opposed. It was the similarity of a mirror image to the original object. In opposing it they had taken on some of its worst features. The parties were part of the 'bourgeoisie', the writers claimed. For Belyi the intelligentsia was the 'spiritual bourgeoisie'.[173] All the writers from Rozanov to Blok were united in opposition to bourgeois philistinism which was as obvious among revolutionaries as among the shopkeepers. Berdyaev's accusation that the Socialists were only interested in vulgar questions of money when they should have been concerned with a more fundamental spiritual task was echoed by many. The spirit of creativity common to them all would not allow itself to be confined within the outworn positivist creed of the political intelligentsia. The weakness of socialism in the cultural and spiritual sphere was a source of embarrassment to Marxists such as Lunacharsky, Bazarov and others. They too joined in the process of 'search' which characterised nearly all the new intellectual schools in Russia at this time.

The various people dealt with in the second and fourth sections of this chapter in no way added up to a movement but they did indicate that there was indeed a new spirit abroad in the intelligentsia. What each of these intelligentsia groups shared was a fundamental dissatisfaction with the 'traditional' utilitarian, materialist, positivist values of the remainder of the intelligentsia. They all felt that a new start was necessary, that a new mood was stirring in the country, that critical thought was replacing half thought out dogmatism. In the fight against scientific materialism, a form of religious idealism, loosely derived in most cases from one or other aspect of Solov'ev's work, was the handiest weapon. The intellectual seeds of this movement from a 'positivist' to a 'religious' social outlook, in Merezhkovsky's words,[174] had been sown before 1905, but it was the despair resulting from that year, the feeling that *the* Russian revolution, which had appeared so inevitable throughout the late nineteenth century, had failed and that the chance might never return, which hastened the process of disillusionment and popularised the new ideas. V. N. Il' in recalling those days, wrote that the lectures given by Bulgakov at the Kiev *Gimnaziya* in 1905 and 1906 were very popular and that the students, although not perhaps in agreement with it, were impressed by *Vekhi*, while Lenin's writings of the time 'evoked Homeric laughter by their backwardness, lack of culture and stupidity'.[175] Even though this may be a somewhat exaggerated memory, it is likely that something of that spirit was felt by a number of young people. It would be difficult to say how many. The serried ranks of the revolutionary intelligentsia establishment were unmoved by most of these new tendencies and met them with abuse. It is these defenders of the traditional intelligentsia who are the subject of the next chapter.

5 Defenders of the revolutionary tradition

The inheritors of the revolutionary and materialist tradition of the Russian intelligentsia had to defend their views against the various new movements of this period which threatened their fundamental principles. For the Social Democrats and certain other socialists, the various phenomena making up these new groups constituted a process which they interpreted as the impending *embourgeoisement* of the intelligentsia as a social class and the imminent danger of its permanently deserting the revolution, a process which they believed the tsarist government was encouraging by its policy of concessions, the chief of which was the October Manifesto. Other revolutionary intelligentsia groups were rather less abstract in their analysis and concentrated on attempting to refute various aspects of the new movement without seeing these separate phenomena as an interrelated, organic social-intellectual process.

Two features of the debate are indisputable. It provoked the interest of all sections of the intelligentsia and it revealed the absence of any kind of universal agreement or consensus among the intelligentsia on many of the issues raised. An unprecedented number of newspaper and journal articles were written about *Vekhi* and the book itself sold more quickly than any other of its type published at that time. It went through five editions within twelve months. Perhaps the best evidence of the extent of the debate and of its tone was given in the reports of discussion meetings of various learned societies which were devoted to *Vekhi*. All of them tell the same story of packed halls with people seated on window-ledges and crowded in the doorways and lively audience response to speeches with which they either agreed or disagreed violently. It was not only the great metropolitan centres of Moscow, St Petersburg, Kiev, Odessa and Baku which witnessed such scenes. Interest penetrated areas which were, in normal circumstances, intellectual wastelands. Even in late 1909 and early 1910, one year after the publication of

Vekhi, the discussion continued. By the end of 1910, however, this torrent of words had subsided. There could hardly be anything to say about *Vekhi* that had not been said.

The impression left by this clash of opinions was not one of clear thought organised in logical stages but quite the reverse. It resembled nothing so much as a Tower of Babel. On every issue the intelligentsia was divided. The debate showed that it could not agree on its own nature, its social role, its current tactics or its long-term strategy. It was not even completely united in opposing *Vekhi* which attracted some sympathisers, even though they tended to be few and isolated.

These divisions were apparent in the dispute over the nature of the intelligentsia tradition. In the Kadet reply to *Vekhi*, *Intelligentsiya v Rossii (The Intelligentsia in Russia)*, Petrunkevich expressed the common opinion that Belinsky was the father of the intelligentsia and Herzen, Chernyshevsky and Mikhailovsky were his heirs.[1] This definition was considerably narrower than that of other contributors to the same volume, two of whom even enrolled tsars in the intelligentsia ranks. Tugan-Baranovsky wrote that Peter the Great was one of the first *intelligenty*[2] while Gredeskul said that 'in his moral outlook Alexander I was a typical *intelligent*'.[3] Several commentators on the debate agreed that Radishchev and Novikov were the founders of the intelligentsia. Among them was Ivanov-Razumnik, who believed that the Russian soul originated with writers of the time of Catherine the Great, adding the names of Derzhavin and Fonvizin to those of Novikov and Radishchev whom he said marked the beginning of Russia's social self-awareness.[4] While he admitted that Belinsky was the 'banner of the intelligentsia',[5] he also included Pushkin and Dostoevsky among its membership because of their 'spiritual creativeness' which was for him the distinguishing feature of any intelligentsia.[6] Friche, speaking as a Bolshevik, enshrined Chernyshevsky as the embodiment of the best characteristics of the intelligentsia.[7] Steklov, also a Bolshevik, lamented the decline in influence of the revolutionary writers such as Lavrov, Eliseev and Shchedrin and the corresponding popularity of Solov'ev, Tolstoy and Dostoevsky, implying that there were two traditions within the intelligentsia.[8]

These differences of opinion were a reflection of deeper divisions of opinion within the intelligentsia about its nature and about the role it should be playing in the political and social events of the time. The earlier phases of the intelligentsia's development appeared to the men of 1909 to have been far more homogeneous than the current one. The liberal N. Gredeskul spoke for many when he divided the intelligentsia's past into five periods. The first was that of the repentant nobles of the 1840s, then the *raznochintsy* of the 1860s, the populists of the 1870s and 1880s, the Marxists of the 1890s and the current period which could only be termed heterogeneous (*raznorodnyi*).[9] This heterogeneity was not a superficial phenomenon but embraced fundamental differences of intellectual, political and social outlook and principles.

One of the main issues was the fundamental one of finding an agreed definition of the intelligentsia. While few people agreed as to what the intelligentsia was, most knew what it was not. It was not a sociologically definable group. Most of the participants in the debates of this period, therefore, did not have a definition of the intelligentsia based on sociological criteria such as its class background or its level of education. The idea that the intelligentsia was coterminous with the educated class in society was criticised for its anomalies. In a small pamphlet entitled *Intelligentsiya i narod*, A. A. Nikolaev argued that the spirit of true *intelligentnost'* could burn in the breast of even an unlettered peasant if he were aware of the injustice of his own and his neighbour's condition and sought to right it.[10] The intelligentsia, as Nikolaev saw it, was drawn from many sections of society and was to be found in many different social groups and occupations.[11] Where Nikolaev permitted the inclusion of illiterate people in the intelligentsia, Grigorii Petrov pointed out that certain highly educated men, and even eminent scholars, could never be considered as *intelligenty*. As examples he gave right wing politicians such as Purishkevich, a gold medallist at University, Bobrinsky, who received a degree from an English university, and Dubrovin, who was a doctor.[12] Milyukov described the intelligentsia not as the educated class but as a concentric circle within the educated class. For Milyukov the relationship between the intelligentsia and the educated class was based on a division of functions. The intelligentsia took the initiative in creative work while the educated class was the means of action, the transmission belt enabling the work of the intelligentsia to be effective.[13]

As an alternative to the difficulties of finding a strict 'scientific', sociological definition, many members of the intelligentsia still relied on moral and ethical criteria derived from Lavrov's definition of an *intelligent* as a 'critically thinking individual'. According to such a definition, the intelligentsia could be recognised according to its social aspirations and its desire to ameliorate the condition of the oppressed classes in Russia. Gredeskul said that the intelligentsia was the 'mind and light of the people'. For Gredeskul the distinguishing mark of the intelligentsia was its 'populism' in the general rather than specific sense, meaning its sense of oneness with the aspirations of the people.[14] For others it was not populism but socialism which marked out the intelligentsia. Tugan-Baranovsky, for example, made such a claim. He echoed many other writers when he defined the *intelligent* as an 'apostate and revolutionary, the enemy of routine and stagnation and a seeker of new truth'.[15] For Ivanov-Razumnik, too, 'spiritual creativeness was a major characteristic of the *intelligent*'.[16] The moral and ethical definition of the intelligentsia was the most widespread at this period as it had been previously but it was not unchallenged.

The existence of the intelligentsia had always posed something of a problem for the Russian Marxists. The question was particularly acute for them since it seemed that it was the intelligentsia, contrary to all their dogma, which was the most consistently revolutionary class in Russia. The very restricted aims and political objectives of the peasants and, later on, the proletariat, drove to despair their supposed leaders from the intelligentsia. The workers wanted wage increases; the intelligentsia socialists wanted to transform the world. The task of developing the class consciousness of the workers, to which Plekhanov had consigned the socialist intelligentsia, looked like being long and arduous. The problem was further complicated for them by the fact that the revolutionary intelligentsia did not spring from the people but from the sections of Russian society which approximated more closely the Western bourgeoisie than the proletariat.[17] By 1909, however, these old arguments had been further refined among the Marxists so that most of them had a dual view of an intelligentsia which was part bourgeois and part democratic (meaning socialist or proletarian).

There was considerable discussion of the nature of the intelligentsia in the years immediately before 1905. In 1902, for example, Gorky wrote in a letter to Pyatnitsky that there were two intelligentsias, one seeking self-perfection, the other struggling with its growing awareness of the importance of democratic development in Russia.[18] In 1904 Izgoev's article 'The intelligentsia as a social group' claimed that the intelligentsia was a new social group composed of mental labourers which was neither bourgeois nor proletarian.[19] At the same moment Tugan-Baranovsky also came to a similar conclusion. According to him the activities of the mental labourers lay outside the process of appropriation of surplus value and, as a consequence, the intelligentsia was a social group without a definite class character. It was quite possible, he said, that part of it could happily side with the people while the other part might support the exploiting class.[20] Vorovsky replied to these criticisms on behalf of the Bolsheviks. The intelligentsia, he said, was not a separate group having common interests but was actually a composite. The intelligentsia was made up of ideologists from each social class and their interests as a whole only coincided to the degree that the interests of the classes which they represented also coincided at a given moment.[21]

After the October Manifesto, the question became more acute. In the Social Democratic view the manifesto was an attempt to drive a wedge between the bourgeois and democratic wings of the revolutionary movement. They reacted with hostility to any move which seemed to further the polarisation desired by the government. In this scheme of things it was the defection of the liberal intelligentsia from the revolutionary camp that was to be feared and it was against the liberals most prone to come to terms with the government that the socialist fire was concentrated. In 1906 Trotsky wrote (under a pseudonym) a pamphlet attacking Struve's view that the time had come for the revolutionary movement to end its totally negative policy towards the autocracy and instead to try to bring about a democratic constitutional system in Russia. According to Trotsky the events of 1905 showed that the intelligentsia could not act independently. 'The intelligentsia on its own,' he wrote, 'does not represent a political force. Its significance is defined by its relationship to the revolutionary masses. Last year this was shown clearly in the "Union of Unions" which dreamed of uniting the revolution around itself but was swept away by it and did not play any role.'[22] The Constitutional Democratic Party, he continued, would fare no better. It represented a coalition of left *zemstvo* liberals and commercial bourgeois and the right wing of the intelligentsia, the liberation movement. 'This party' said Trotsky 'is less likely to draw off the bourgeoisie from the openly conservative Octobrist party than to bind the intelligentsia to the conservative bourgeoisie.'[23]

Trotsky was not alone in this opinion. Indeed the impending desertion of the revolution by the intelligentsia (meaning the class of mental labourers) could be verified from the highest western

European sources. Writings of leading socialists from Germany, France, Belgium and Holland on the intelligentsia question were translated into Russian at this time. Among them were articles by Kautsky, Bebel, Lafargue, Lagardelle, Mauerenbrecher, Paul Louis and Henri Beranger. All but the last were published in Russia in 1906.[24] The general opinion of the socialists of western Europe was that while the number of members of the intelligentsia in the socialist movement was growing and its influence was increasing and that this was a development to be welcomed, this process could not embrace any more than a few individuals from the intelligentsia. The whole class would never join the workers but would stay with the bourgeoisie. Thus, while many western socialist and syndicalist leaders were pointing out the bourgeois essence of the intelligentsia and considered its role in the socialist movement to be a peripheral one, in Russia Machajski was denouncing socialism as a smokescreen for the material interests of the intelligentsia. Perhaps the Russian publishers of these pamphlets intended them to be an antidote to Makhaevism. This was not, however, the main reason for them to circulate at that moment. They were mainly intended as a warning to show that a developing intelligentsia meant a developing bourgeoisie.

According to Aksel'rod, the failure of *Narodnaya Volya* and the ensuing decline in the belief that the peasant masses were revolutionary, coupled with the growth of a proletariat in St Petersburg and the proof of its militant qualities in the strikes of 1896–7, resulted in the appearance of separate bourgeois and democratic tendencies within a revolutionary movement which had formerly been united.[25] 'Both the proletariat and the revolutionary intelligentsia,' he wrote,

the two chief forces to which Russia is indebted for its entrance into the epoch of the universal movement for freedom, found themselves to be in the political sense servants of the oppositional bourgeoisie. The one because it had not *yet* succeeded in developing into a powerfully united independent revolutionary force, the other because it had already descended into the historical arena as a revolutionary element independent from society and from the popular mass. But in the given circumstances the workers played the part of the rank and file while the revolutionary representatives of the intelligentsia were the students who were leaders, organisers and skirmishers. Historically this role qualified as bourgeois democratic because in its objective social sense, it was of one nature with that played by the revolutionaries from among the bourgeoisie in the west in the period of the movement for liberation from absolutism. These revolutionaries also were far from caring for the well-being and rule of the bourgeoisie like our revolutionaries. No less than the latter they were inspired by the aspiration to general happiness, equality and freedom. But nevertheless history for very good reasons attached to them the name of bourgeois democrats, though by no means wishing to cast a shadow on the subjective sincerity of their love for the people, on their ideal aspirations and revolutionary slogans.[26]

Aksel'rod's conclusion was that the working class could not depend on these bourgeois democrats but must achieve its emancipation through its own efforts. The liberals and their associates, who also wished to clear Russia of its feudal remnants in order to establish capitalism, had to be opposed by socialists. Among these associates he specified *kulaks*, the commercial classes, industrialists and speculators. The socialist movement, he concluded, must be aware of this antagonism between the section of the liberation movement which wished to establish capitalism and that which desired to go beyond this to a socialist society.

Some years later Martov put forward a similar view in an article on intellectual tendencies in Russia 1870–1905 written in 1910 for inclusion in Ovsyaniko-Kulikovsky's *History of Nineteenth Century Russian Literature*. Martov's view was that the potential divisions in the movement were becoming actual as a result of 1905 and the divide and rule policy of the government. He pointed to the idealist movement of 1900–5 as the main indication of the development of a bourgeois liberal ideology. Martov was replying to views, such as those which Struve held up to 1906 as expressed in his writings in *Osvobozhdenie* and *Polyarnaya zvezda*, that the liberal movement should have no enemies on the left. Struve's dream of a united front of all opponents of autocracy evoked alarm rather than sympathy among the Social Democrats. Martov pointed out that the fundamental principles of Struve's policy fell short of those of the socialists and that socialists should not be fooled into winning the liberals' victory for them.[27] At the heart of Struve's outlook, Martov discerned patriotism, the monarchy, national sovereignty and the continuation of the links between Church and State. Consequently, liberalism, he concluded, was anti-democratic in its political views and counter-revolutionary in its strict economic individualism, its legal outlook and its national-soil attitude to the State and the Church.[28]

Among the Social Democrats there was an atmosphere of fear and watchfulness about the waverings of the intelligentsia. It was into this that *Vekhi* burst like a spark into a box of fireworks. The resulting display was colourful and spectacular, but chaotic. Nowhere was this clearer than in Lenin's writings on *Vekhi*. Lenin was no less aware of the danger of the intelligentsia choosing the bourgeois camp than were Aksel'rod, Martov, Trotsky and the western European socialists. Only in this light can one make any sense of Lenin's outburst against *Vekhi*. It was, he said, 'an encyclopaedia of liberal renegacy'. *Vekhi*, he continued:

> embraces three main subjects: (1) the struggle against the ideological principle of the whole world outlook of Russian (and international) democracy; (2) repudiation and vilification of the revolutionary movement of recent years; (3) an open proc-lamation of its 'flunkey' sentiments (and a corresponding 'flunkey' policy) in relation to the Octobrist bourgeoisie, the old regime and the entire old Russia in general.[29]

Lenin refused to see any distinction between the ideas put forward by the *vekhovtsy* and those of the Kadet party, despite the bitter arguments which had broken out between the two. *Really* (Lenin's favourite word in this article) they were one and the same. Gershenzon's statement about the bayonets and prisons of the regime protecting the intelligentsia from the anger of the people was, for Lenin, the central message not only of· *Vekhi* but of all Russian liberalism. He wrote of it,

> This tirade is good because it is frank: it is useful because it reveals the truth about the real essence of the policy of the whole Constitutional Democratic Party throughout the period 1905–9. This tirade is good because it reveals concisely and vividly the whole spirit of *Vekhi*. And *Vekhi* is good because it discloses the whole spirit of the *real* policy of the Russian liberals and of the Russian Kadets included among them. That is why the Kadet polemic with *Vekhi* and the Kadet renunciation of *Vekhi* are nothing but hypocrisy, sheer idle talk, for in reality the Kadets

collectively, as a party, as a social force, have pursued and are pursuing the policy of *Vekhi* and *no other*.[30]

Lenin's idiosyncratic view of *Vekhi* did not mellow with the passage of time. *Vekhi* remained in his mind as a symbol of everything he hated about liberalism. It was not the actual content of the book but the implications he saw behind it which he opposed so bitterly. *Vekhi* meant the end of revolutionary politics as they had existed in Russia up until that time. Indeed Gershenzon at least was suggesting a complete withdrawal from the tyranny of politics in general in the hope that the intelligentsia might put its personal life into some kind of order before it set about the infinitely more complicated and demanding task of changing society. This change of priorities would, as Lenin clearly perceived, lead in the short term to a decline in political activism. From this premise he concluded that all liberalism would lead to political inactivity which would of course serve the interests of the *status quo*. Hence, Lenin branded the *vekhovtsy* and the liberals as *de facto* members of the conservative camp. Lenin was not content with simply pointing this out. He had to prove that such a situation was an inevitable outcome of the class interests of the bourgeoisie. *Vekhi*, he repeated three years later, had not come about by chance.

> *Vekhi* is merely making a show of fighting against the 'intelligentsia' and is in fact *fighting against democracy* which it completely renounces . . . . The 'arguments' with the *vekhovtsy*, the 'polemics' of the Gredeskuls, Milyukovs and other such gentlemen against them, are no more than eyewash, nothing but a hypocritical disguise for the deep fundamental solidarity between the entire Kadet party and *Vekhi* . . . . The issue is obscured by those who present it *à la Vekhi* in terms of contrasting 'individualism' with 'altruism' and so on. The political meaning of these phrases could not be clearer – they are a *volte face against democracy*, a *volte face* in favour of *counter-revolutionary* liberalism. We must realise that this *volte face* is no accident, but a result of the class position of the bourgeoisie. And we must draw from this the necessary political conclusions as regards the clear demarcation of democracy from liberalism.[31]

Lenin's use of *Vekhi* in this way for his own propagandist purposes was quite in character with his other incursions into the field of thought at this time. Bogdanov, Bazarov, Yushkevich and Lunach-arsky had been turned into symbols of one kind of opposition to Lenin's own political views and political ambitions and through *Materialism and Empiriocriticism* they were made to stand as repre-sentatives for a whole spectrum of ideas to which they were themselves hostile. In the same way *Vekhi* was blackened by Lenin who recast its image into a form more suitable to his own immediate purpose. This method of falsification became common among the revolutionaries and was an illustration of the very feature of the intelligentsia denounced by Berdyaev, the subordination of truth to immediate practical ends. It had all the consequences foreseen by Berdyaev in that it opened the way to the unscrupulous and it was these elements, with Stalin at the head, which eventually triumphed over the more honest, if naive and unrealistic, of the revolutionaries. All this, however, lay in the future.

Martov's view of *Vekhi*, though it shared a fundamental similarity with Lenin's in general terms, was expressed very differently. Martov's analysis agreed with Lenin's in their belief that liberalism could not but become an ally of conservatism, despite Struve's belief before 1905 that liberalism should be with social democracy, not against it. In Martov's view, liberalism was reassessing its political position.

In *Polyarnaya zvezda*, published by Struve after the Moscow rising, in *Russkaya mysl'* and *Moskovskii ezhenedel'nik* and then *Vekhi*, liberalism has been attempting to revise its past, to snap the threads traditionally joining it with revolutionary and socialist ideologies, and to construct a system of views appropriate for a *ruling* class, or more precisely a class which tomorrow must become the ruling one and must prove its maturity in the quality of such views. Liberalism is attempting to become on principle monarchist, nationalist and anti-democratic in its political conceptions, counter-revolutionary in its legal views, strictly individualistic in the sphere of economics and national-soil in its attitude to the State and the Church.[32]

For both Lenin and Martov, then, *Vekhi* represented the same thing. They both saw in it a definite break between liberalism and the revolutionary movement and for both of them *Vekhi* was the very significant lurch to the right which they had expected and feared from the liberal intelligentsia. In other respects, however, their interpretations differed and Martov did not, for example, consider *Vekhi* to be representative of the Kadet party or of liberalism as a whole. The opposite was, in fact, the case. Liberalism, he said, did not possess a unified systematic body of ideas as did the Social Democrats and Socialist Revolutionaries. On the contrary it was a conglomerate of different intellectual shades and the only attempt, undertaken by Struve and the *vekhovtsy*, to create a systematic body of thought, was confined to a small section of liberalism. Since it was such a thorough break with the radical and revolutionary roots of liberalism, its influence, he concluded, was not likely to grow.

In this judgement Martov was undoubtedly correct and anyone familiar with the content of the debate *Vekhi* aroused among the intelligentsia could only agree that the most obvious feature of this great mass of material was *Vekhi's* isolation. Despite a few individuals who believed that it contained the bitter truth, *Vekhi* was greeted with universal opposition and, perhaps more significant, almost complete incomprehension. Only a handful of commentators seemed to understand the issues *Vekhi* raised. Its hopes that a creative self-assessment might be started were cruelly dashed beneath the waves of self-congratulation and complacency which it revealed in the intelligentsia. Though there was considerable disagreement as to what the intelligentsia tradition meant and what values the intelligentsia in fact stood for, the participants did not hesitate to defend the fundamental revolutionary orientation of the intelligentsia and to scorn the idea that Christianity or a religious sensibility was in any way necessary.

The almost universal misunderstanding of *Vekhi* is at first sight much more difficult to understand when it is recalled that in the years immediately preceding its publication discussion of all the issues had been widespread in the intelligentsia. Before 1905 an advance warning of the dispute was to be found in the exchanges between *Problemy idealizma*, and *Ocherki realisticheskogo mirovozzreniya*. After 1905 the pace was appreciably speeded up and a torrent of books, newspapers and journal articles devoted to the intelligentsia, plus two long critical studies of the development of its thought, appeared. The journals *Russkaya mysl'*, *Sovremennyi mir* and *Russkoe bogatstvo* provided space for combatants of various persuasions. The main thrust of the debate, however, was provided by collections of articles published in book form, such as *Ocherki filosofii kollektivizma*, *Iz istorii noveishei russkoi literatury*, *Literaturnyi raspad*, *Na rubezhe* and *Vershiny*, which were published in defence of social democratic positions. In response to *Vekhi* there appeared *Intelligentsiya v Rossii* from the Kadets and *V zashchitu intelligentsii* and *Vekhi kak znamenie vremeni* from the socialist revolutionaries. Other important contributions to the debate preceding *Vekhi* were the two histories of the intelligentsia, one being Ovsyaniko-Kulikovsky's enormous history of the Russian intelligentsia which began to appear at this time, the other, Ivanov-Razumnik's *Istoriya russkoi obshchestvennoi mysli*. Ivanov-Razumnik also published a volume entitled *Ob intelligentsii* devoted to a criticism of *Vekhi* and of Makhaevism. In addition to these major publications, there appeared a multitude of pamphlets, newspaper articles and so on. Thus *Vekhi* was as much a symptom of this wide-ranging clash of opinions as its cause. The debate had been under way before *Vekhi* burst on the scene in such dramatic fashion.[33]

As the revolutionary activities of 1905 and 1906 began to die away and the government's measures of physical repression began to restore order in town and country, the intelligentsia began to turn from direct practical involvement to the drawing-room tasks of analysis and assimilation of its experiences of the years of disorder. This passive role went against the grain for the most energetic members of the revolutionary intelligentsia whose spirit had been expressed by Gorky in a letter of 1902 to Pyatnitsky. 'At the present moment,' he wrote, 'the perfect man is not needed. What is needed is a warrior, an avenger of the workers. We can perfect ourselves after we have settled accounts.'[34] This comment Gorky made about the idealist school of that time, illuminated the whole revolutionary approach to idealism and expressed precisely the sentiment behind the opposition to *Problemy idealizma*, *Vekhi*, Solov'ev and to much of the non-revolutionary intelligentsia. The bourgeois intelligentsia, as he called it then, 'was afraid for culture which the democrat supposedly would not spare in the event of his victory'.[35] Perhaps Gorky's actions in 1917, when he spent his time and energy creating a Commission for the Preservation of Historic Monuments,[36] spoke louder than his words at this time, but those words expressed the feeling shared by many of the opponents of idealism and in-dividualism just as his later disillusion expressed the second thoughts so many of the creative intelligentsia had about the revolution after it had taken place.

The Social Democrats were also occupied with the question of individualism but they approached it from a quite different direction. V. Vorovsky was one of Lenin's closest associates in developing the spirit of *partiinost'* in literature which Lenin had called for in 1905. It was the decadent writers of the period who most aroused Vorovsky's wrath. The figure of Sanin, created by the novelist Mikhail Artsybashev, compared unfavourably with Turgenev's hero Bazarov, according to Vorovsky, although both were individualists. Bazarov's individualism was, however, subject to social utility while Sanin's was 'of a purely egoistic type'.[37] This analysis of Artsybashev's work was part of Vorovsky's general characterisation of the intellectual life of the period as unbridled literary reaction based on the idealist and liberal values of the petty bourgeoisie. Vorovsky was one of the most assiduous believers in the theory of the *embourgeoisement* of the intelligentsia and set to work to reveal the petty-bourgeois cancer at the centre of all the non-revolutionary literature and intellectual activity of the day. In 'The bourgeois essence of the modernists', written in 1908, he described the contemporary literary life of Russia as 'a bacchanalia of banality rising up completely unimpeded'.[38] This literature, he claimed, originated in the isolation of the petty bourgeoisie which, particularly since 1905, had felt itself to be caught between the bourgeoisie which it hated and the proletariat in which it could not believe. Its 'instinctive sense of self-preservation' prevented it from merging into the bourgeoisie towards which it adopted an attitude of bohemian disdain. It was the 'inner and outer life of this petty-bourgeois intelligentsia which found its expression in contemporary literature'.[39]

Vorovsky's views were important not so much on account of any intrinsic value they may have possessed, but because since 1917 they have been elevated to the level of orthodoxy and infallibility and form the basis for Soviet literary and aesthetic attitudes towards 'bourgeois decadence' in the outside world. They were also important because they were echoed in various degrees by other Social Democratic writers of the time whose orthodoxy has been more questionable. The main Social Democratic response to the art of the period came in the two volumes of articles entitled *Literaturny raspad (Literary collapse)* published in 1908 and 1909, most of the contributors to which have since been considered highly unorthodox.[40]

The tone of the book was certainly one of extreme hostility to the so-called bourgeois tendencies abounding in the literary and cultural life of Russia at the time and all the contributors echoed Vorovsky's hostility to Artsybashev. Vorovsky's own article 'Bazarov and Sanin' appeared in the second volume. The contributors also shared Vorovsky's view that these 'reactionary' elements originated from the class position of the lower middle class. However, in other respects they deviated from Vorovsky's Leninist line and, as the standard Soviet literary history of the period puts it, the work showed 'the influence of Machist, of God-building and Menshevik opinions'.[41]

The dominance of individualism in Russia at that moment was crucial to all of them. They also associated idealism and religion very closely with the emergence of individualism and generally considered the quite diverse strands of these movements as an amorphous whole embracing, for example, Vyacheslav Ivanov, Merezhkovsky, Sologub and even Leonid Andreev whose decisive move away from realism to mysticism at this time was a particularly bitter pill for them to swallow. Also included in this group were people such as Struve and Berdyaev who were not creative artists. Gorky summed up the attitude of all of them towards individualism when he said that socialists should strive to replace the word 'I' with 'we' and 'you' if the individual was really to be liberated.[42] Gorky's views on the miraculous strength of the collective as opposed to the helplessness of the individual[43] were shared by other contributors, especially Lunacharsky, Yushkevich, Bazarov, Mikhail Morozov, Voitolovsky and Shulyatikov, but in other respects their analyses of the social causes for the predominance of individualism, particularly in the form of mysticism, religiosity, fear of death, meaninglessness, a feeling of insignificance and all the other characteristics of alienation and *angst*, varied widely. As the preface explained the contributors all shared 'the proletarian outlook in its only scientific form – Marxism' but 'this of course does not predetermine a uniformity in the evaluation of the various phenomena of contemporary literature'. The only common feature of the contributors, the preface claimed, was that they recognised that 'there is a division on principle between the creativity of the contemporary period of decadence and the creativity of the future'.[44] All of them agreed that the roots of the individualistic decadence which they were attacking were to be found in the trying social conditions in which the petty bourgeoisie, the class they associated most closely with decadence, found itself at that particular historical moment.

For each of the writers, the petty bourgeoisie and their spokesmen, the decadents, were caught between hammer and anvil, but which hammer and which anvil? In the opening article, Steklov saw the petty bourgeoisie threatened by the trade unions on one hand and the great capitalist monopolies on the other. This social situation resulted in a sick mentality dominated by fear of dark mysterious forces which it saw conspiring against its interests.[45] For Morozov, they were caught between the state on one side and the revolution on the other.[46] But despite such minor inconsistencies as this, most of the contributors saw the growth of a technological, urban, capitalist society as the cause of the phenomenon. The crisis in Russian art was, said Voitolovsky, no more than a reflection of the general crisis in Russian society[47] as one might expect since 'art expresses life',[48] and no boundary existed between the two spheres.

The various essays in the two volumes attempted to interpret decadence in the light of the Marxist principle that the cultural superstructure of society was a reflection of its economic base. The first article in the collection, written by Yu. Steklov, was devoted entirely to 'The social-political conditions of literary collapse'. The increasingly rapid tempo of change in production relations in capitalist society, argued Steklov (in a way that is perhaps more familiar today than it was in 1909), had led to the spread of personal insecurity through rapid change in the social and economic environment. Increased mobility had torn the individual from his roots and the information explosion had led to a loss of personal identity in bourgeois society. More and more people were crying out for protection against being crushed 'under the wheels of the capitalist Juggernaut'.[49] The result of all this technical progress was, said Steklov, the natural development of fear and subconscious horror at the feebleness of the human grains of sand in the face of the enormous apparatus conditioning reality.[50] This sickness was expressed, said Steklov, in reactionary politics, in Roman Catholicism and in boredom and was exacerbated by the philistinism, selfishness and dishonesty characteristic of bourgeois life at the best of times.[51] A healthy, active society, he concluded, always had a materialist philosophy; a sick one always turned to idealism and mysticism.[52]

The articles by Yushkevich in the two volumes of *Literaturnyi raspad* echoed Steklov but with an altered emphasis. Urban life itself, said Yushkevich, aroused boredom because it cut man off from nature to which he must be reunited. For Yushkevich this necessary process of reunification was inevitably religious in the original sense of the word, remembering that the word itself was derived from the Latin *religare*, to tie together. The intelligentsia, he said, was particularly subject to this separation of man from nature because it was largely urban. 'Our life, that is, the life of the town-dweller and in particular of the urban intelligentsia is mechanical, artificial and stifling.[53] 'Urban life,' he said, 'is an uninterrupted kaleidoscope of people, things, ideas, feelings, and eternal jolts change one pattern for another.' In this situation the city-dweller longed for a reduced tempo, for a more measured and comfortable, natural rhythm. The city itself, he concluded, was ultimately a veil 'which conceals from our eyes the true reality – the universe, the cosmos, nature – one, unchanging, eternal'.[54]

The continual pressure which this way of life imposed on the individual could, in Yushkevich's view, only be relieved by resorting to religion, to reunification of man with man and man with nature, and in this sense of communication 'unites not only the single individual with the world, with the universe, but above all with the collective . . . . Religious feeling is, above all else, the most collective feeling.'[55] It was of course emotional. Yushkevich quoted Chateaubriand's words, 'The poetry of bells is a more convincing argument than the syllogism.'[56] It was in emotion rather than reason that man had to rediscover his true being and his true collective nature. In this way Yushkevich turned toward religious sentiment as the final validator of socialist collectivism even though he intended religion itself to be based on 'objective values' rather than 'subjective' ones and it was this attempt as much as anything else which caused Lenin in *Materialism and Empiriocriticism* to heap venom on Yushkevich and Lunacharsky for their 'kneeling rebellion'. Yushkevich tried to exonerate himself from the most obvious attacks of this kind by defining his own religious assumptions as 'subjective objectivism' rather than the 'objective objectivism' characteristic of science,[57] but this ridiculous verbal contortion did not stave off the hostility of those socialists like Lenin whose views were fundamentally and inextricably rooted in the 'spirit of the sixties', in Chernyshevsky, in fanatical, narrow, philistine materialism rather than in the more idealist school of impressionism which was the fashion to which Yushkevich was adhering, a mixture of Nietzsche and Bergson whose *Évolution créatrice* had been published in 1907.

At the same time another collection of articles entitled *Ocherki filosofii kollektivizma (Notes on the Philosophy of Collectivism)* attempted a more philosophic defence of collectivism. However, like so many previous attempts at philosophy in Russia, it was literary criticism which dominated the end product, even though more directly philosophical articles were contributed by Bogdanov and Bazarov. As in *Literaturnyi raspad* the emphasis was again on the 'healthiness' of materialism and collectivism and the 'sickness' of bourgeois individualism and idealism. The fundamental principle of *Ocherki filosofii kollektivizma* was that the world view of the proletarian class was based on collectivism, 'a complete, resolute collectivism of practice and of knowledge'. By developing this class point of view 'the proletarian frees himself from the innumerable individualistic illusions begotten in contemporary mankind through the economic anarchy of society and becomes a fully social and consciously social being.[58] In this way the working class would arrive at its own collective philosophy, 'a philosophy of labour and of union, a theory of social activity and active society'.[59]

The Social Democrats were not the only socialists interested in these issues, which received thoughtful treatment at the hands of the independent populist, R. V. Ivanov-Razumnik (1878–1946) who, in 1907, published his *Istoriya russkoi obshchestvennoi mysli (History of Russian Social Thought)*. The intelligentsia question was at the heart of Ivanov-Razumnik's book. As he wrote at the beginning of it, a history of Russian social thought was a history of the intelligentsia.[60] The remainder of his book illustrated the truth of this proposition. Ivanov-Razumnik traced the origins of Russian social thought back to the sixteenth century. Even though there was not an intelligentsia at that time there were, he claimed, individuals such as Kurbsky and Ivan Groznyi who could be considered as *intelligenty*,[61] presumably because of their concern with the fate of Russia and its people. The bulk of his book, however, was devoted to a study of the period 1825–1905. For him, the main characteristic of all sections of the intelligentsia was its anti-philistinism. Despite differences in other respects, this trait, according to Ivanov-Razumnik, was common to all sections of it. The word philistinism was of great importance to Ivanov-Razumnik and he used it frequently throughout the work to distinguish what he considered to be genuine intelligentsia thought from other types of thought in Russia.

After surveying the main ideas of the revolutionary movement, Ivanov-Razumnik turned to the contemporary period. In the 1890s the great schism in the intelligentsia had led, according to Ivanov-Razumnik, to the destruction of orthodox Marxism and orthodox populism. 'Populism' he said 'fell under the blows of the Marxists, and Marxism was destroyed by its internal contradictions'.[62]

Ivanov-Razumnik was thinking, no doubt, of the weaknesses in Marxism which had been pointed out by revisionists in Russia, Germany, Italy and elsewhere.

The result of this was, he said, that Russian social thought, after a long and illustrious history, had reached a point beyond which no further progress was possible. The main stream of its thought had dried up. At this critical point a new movement, idealism, had saved the intelligentsia from intellectual atrophy. As a result, although idealism did not become the leading tendency,[63] it did open a new period in the history of the intelligentsia. The old systems of thought received a new impetus from an unexpected quarter. The new critical tendency, he continued, quickly overcame its poorly equipped foes and forced them into a further stage of their own inner evolution.[64] The Epigoni of orthodox populism and Marxism had no philosophical reply to the idealists who were able to parry their weak blows without difficulty. The old guard, being unable to defeat the new critical tendency, attempted instead to discredit it by saying that metaphysical idealism was logically linked with reactionary social tendencies, even though, Ivanov-Razumnik said, the idealists had shown that democratic political principles could be linked to idealist, and even religious, philosophical principles.[65] The significance of the idealist movement, which had started with Berdyaev and Struve in *Sub"ektivizm i individualizm* and with *Problemy idealizma*, lay in the fact that it had destroyed the older intellectual fashions of the late nineteenth century. 'This significance,' he concluded,

> cannot be overestimated. Neo-idealism led Russian thought out of the positivist cul-de-sac in which it had helplessly lain for more than half a century. It showed it wider horizons opening on to the heights of critical philosophy; it demonstrated that this philosophy could provide a firm foundation for a world view; it overturned the 'putting of Hegel on his feet' and delivered a cruel blow to the philosophical conceptions of dialectical materialism. Finally, and perhaps most important, idealistic individualism consolidated on a new foundation and proclaimed with renewed strength the principles of ethical individualism, forgotten since Dostoevsky.[66]

Rather poignantly Ivanov-Razumnik concluded his book on the optimistic note that this new phase in the intelligentsia's history would be one of its greatest and that it would evolve and extend its struggle for the freedom of the individual and man on the basis of 'anti-philistinism, individualism and socialism'.[67] Ivanov-Razumnik thus had high expectations for the future development of the intelligentsia on the basis of a synthesis of all its better qualities, a synthesis which had been started by idealist criticism of ossified and previously unquestioned fundamental principles of the thought of the intelligentsia.

As a populist, Ivanov-Razumnik was especially aware of the peasantry and of rural Russia and turned to the work of the intelligentsia in the countryside as a vindication of the intelligentsia's role. The defence of the rural intelligentsia was undertaken by several writers. One of them, Olenin, wrote an article on 'The peasants and the intelligentsia' which was published in *Russkoe bogatstvo* in 1907.[68] Olenin argued that the rural intelligentsia had played a considerable role in guiding and organising the peasantry in 1905 and 1906 even though the rural intelligentsia itself was divided into liberal and socialist wings. The peasant unions in particular included intelligentsia leaders and even the revolutionaries, if they were known and trusted in the locality, would frequently play a part in organising them. According to Ivanov-Razumnik, on the evidence available the word which could best describe the 1905 revolution was 'populist'. 'All groups,' said Ivanov-Razumnik, 'all parties, even those like the Social Democrats who were hostile to populist doctrine, all had an enthusiastic faith in the necessity for a speedy realization of the old ideals of populism.'[69] He said 1905 had been a vindication of the ideal of the unity of intelligentsia and *narod*. This article, which was originally written in 1906, was expanded by Ivanov-Razumnik before it was reprinted in 1910, in order to serve as a refutation of Gershenzon's assertion that the *narod* would, given the opportunity, destroy the intelligentsia along with its autocratic protectors. For Ivanov-Razumnik nothing could have been further from the truth. According to him the question was not even arguable in theory because the facts of 1905 had proved that, far from using prisons and bayonets to defend the intelligentsia from the people's wrath, the regime had actually used its bayonets and prisons against the intelligentsia itself in the form of Black Hundred pogroms against intellectuals instigated by the regime and supported only by a handful of 'the people'. The armchair prophets were thus, said Ivanov-Razumnik, proved wrong as there had not been any sign of popular anger directed at the intelligentsia. Quite the reverse: 1905 proved the old populist dream to be quite practicable, concluded Ivanov-Razumnik. The distinction between intelligentsia and people was 'purely superficial' and 'lacked inner meaning'. The intelligentsia was of the people and the people were close to the intelligentsia, he said.[70]

It was clear from these and other writings that some of the oldest populist principles still survived. Ivanov-Razumnik's extremely optimistic view of the peasant and of his friendly attitude to the intelligentsia as a serious element in Russian social thought was usually associated with the 1870s, but in 1905 the old impulse of 'going to the people' was still in existence. Indeed the peasant rebellions of the period seemed to promise that at last the peasantry had reached the point where it could and would trust its intelligentsia protectors. Those who had maintained all along that this would some day be the case, felt encouraged and exhilarated by the thought that perhaps, at long last, their great day was about to dawn.

At the opposite extreme from Ivanov-Razumnik, who considered that the peasantry and the working class were on the point of seeing that the intelligentsia were their most trustworthy friends and allies, was Machajski who was warning the working class that the intelligentsia had nothing to offer it but fraud and deception. The debate about Machajski's views reached a peak in 1907 at the same time that Ivanov-Razumnik's *Istoriya russkoi obshchestvennoi mysli* was being published. Ivanov-Razumnik himself wrote a long and thoughtful article on Machajski's views.

In this article Ivanov-Razumnik felt that above all else Machajski showed the futility of having a sociological, class definition of the intelligentsia rather than an ethical one. 'Makhaevism', he argued, 'is the *reductio ad absurdum* of the social—economic definition of the intelligentsia' and was the best argument in favour of its opposite, the social—ethical definition.[71] The intelligentsia was of course partly a social group, Ivanov-Razumnik added, but Machajski was wrong to think that it was nothing other than that.[72] Makhaevism was not alone in this and other writers had, he admitted, tried to define it in a similar way and in fact the division between those who had a social—economic definition and those who had a social—ethical one, had been going on for half a century. By drawing the former to its logical conclusion, Machajski had at least demonstrated its absurdity, concluded Ivanov-Razumnik.

Machajski also confirmed Ivanov-Razumnik in views diametrically opposed to those of Machajski himself in another respect. The corner-stone of Makhaevism, said Ivanov-Razumnik, was class struggle, the theory of which the Makhaevists drew to preposterous but logical conclusions.[73] In this respect, too, Machajski showed the impossibility of holding such an opinion. On Machajski's practical complaint, that the intelligentsia dominated the revolutionary socialist movement, Ivanov-Razumnik had less to say.

Thus, in the areas of individualism and liberalism and on the intelligentsia question, various sections of the intelligentsia were taking part in a great defensive action in an attempt to preserve the pure revolutionary principles of the old intelligentsia in the face of changing social conditions which were breaking down the intelligentsia's traditional alienation from regime and society. Instead of intransigent confrontation, a small part of the intelligentsia was in favour of collaboration if not with the autocracy at least with the economic life of the country in the form of commerce and industry. It was in an attempt to restrict this influence, to keep *embourgeoisement* to a minimum, that this defensive action was being undertaken. *Vekhi* appeared to many commentators to be a further step in the process of replacing the revolutionary spirit of the intelligentsia by a more liberal one. If it illustrated nothing else, the passionate response to *Vekhi* showed that the fear that the intelligentsia might desert the revolution was, in the field of theory at least, exaggerated. Practically all the intelligentsia commentators rejected *Vekhi* and the debate revealed that, as with the autocracy after 1905, nothing in their outlook had really changed.

6 A continuing debate

Although the terms in which the debate was conducted are far different from those in use in modern Western thought, the rebirth in the last fifteen years of a fragile intellectual life in Russia independent of official Soviet channels has led to a new interest in some of the traditions abruptly ended by World War I and the October revolution. Some of the fundamental ideas of the period were preserved by being brought to the West through the enforced emigration of many *intelligenty* in the 1920s, some of whom, like Bulgakov and Shestov, remained relatively uninfluential while others, especially Berdyaev, transmitted some of the ideas to the rest of the world where they had a considerable, though as yet uncharted, influence on the mainstream of intellectual life. More recently Soviet ideologists have been assiduous in their criticisms of many of these influences and by devoting so much attention to the period and seeing it as a seminal one for twentieth-century art, literature and ideas helped to keep its influence alive. A brief examination of these three elements, namely the influence of emigres, dissent and Soviet ideology, show that the debate continues for Russia and for Europe.

In *Vekhi* Berdyaev predicted that a new way of thinking would emerge from Russia's and Europe's searching. Russian thought, which had, from the time of Khomyakov, been critical of Hegel's pure rationality, would restore the missing religious or mystical element in Western philosophy to produce what he termed 'concrete idealism' or 'ontological realism'. This would put back the living essence into European philosophy. 'It is impossible not to see in this,' he said, 'the creative dispositions of a new path for philosophy.'[1] It would not be going too far to argue that what Berdyaev meant was existentialism and that his injection of Russian ideas, notably from Dostoevsky, influenced the French existentialists and Camus in particular. Reviewing Berdyaev's book on Leont'ev in 1939, Camus wrote that Berdyaev's work had helped him to understand the underlying mystical element of Russian communism.[2] It is likely that Berdyaev's influence stretched more widely, particularly in Camus's works which dealt with the morality of the Russian revolutionaries, such as *L'Homme Révolté* and *Les Justes*, where there are clear reflections of Berdyaev's views. One source might well have been Berdyaev's work on Dostoevsky which was published in French in the 1930s and did a great deal to shape European views on Dostoevsky.

Within Russia itself, however, the debate has had a more direct influence. Aleksandr Solzhenitsyn, the central figure in the modern dissent movement, has been profoundly influenced by *Vekhi*. This aspect of his thought is to be seen more clearly in his non-fiction works. One of them, *From Under the Rubble*, consciously uses the format of *Vekhi* in that it is a collection of articles by people who have different views but shared principles, and, in its Russian title, *Iz-pod-glyb*, reflects the title of *Vekhi's* successor work *Iz glubiny (Out of the Depths)*. At a press conference to launch the book Solzhenitsyn was asked if his new collection was an attempt to bring *Vekhi* up to date. He denied that intention, but only because it would be 'immodest' of him to attempt to compare his work with *Vekhi*. *Vekhi* still pointed out the correct path, he said.[3] There are indeed elements of *From Under the Rubble* which might have come directly from *Vekhi*. In their overall approach the authors share a religious, specifically Orthodox, view of the world. Like *Vekhi* they criticise socialism for being unable to fulfil its promises because of its purely humanistic foundation. Also, like *Vekhi*, they see individual conscience and individual resistance to evil at whatever cost to be the only route to salvation for the individual and for his society. There is also a similarity in that the authors do not believe that an immediate transition to liberal democracy would be desirable or possible and some compromise with strong central authority has to be made. Looking more closely at the text, especially of Solzhenitsyn's three articles, one can find sentiments that might be equally at home in *Vekhi* itself. Before turning to this question it can be seen that the divisions within the dissent movement itself reflect the divisions in the pre-revolution intelligentsia. The main division, into Orthodox, liberal and liberal socialist, with fringe groups or individuals ranging from extreme nationalism to highly authoritarian socialism, all have their equivalents. The absence of enthusiasm for a capitalist system is also an enduring characteristic.

The programme of the recent *émigré* dissenters of a religious inclination can be found in their journal *Kontinent*.[4] Their first principle, according to the editors, is 'absolute religious idealism'; the fourth and final one is 'absolute non-partisanship'. Both of these could have come from *Vekhi* (as could the insistence that all four principles should be 'absolute').[5] It is clear that *Kontinent* is attempting to reintroduce elements of intelligentsia thought which were submerged after the October revolution.

Other elements in the debate also have their modern equivalent. Though very different in the shape of his ideas Andrei Sakharov represents an up-to-date version of pre-revolutionary Western-oriented liberalism, even to the extent that, like many Kadets, Sakharov is a leading scientist, having a tendency, in his earlier political works at least, to see a technocracy as the logical extension of any industrial society, whether its traditional political institutions are authoritarian or democratic. Another dissenter who might be classified as a liberal is Valentyn Moroz whose definition of the individual personality and its relation to society reflects, perhaps unconsciously, the views of Solov'ev. In Moroz's words,

> The very nature of creativity is rooted in the unprecedented and the *unrepeatable*, and the carrier of the latter is the individual. Each individual consciousness embraces one facet of the all-embracing boundless existence . . . with the disappearance of each individual point of view . . . one facet of the million-faceted mosaic of the human spirit stops sparkling.[6]

Similar sentiments could have been found in the articles by the Trubetskois in *Problemy idealizma*.

Interesting parallels can also be found between those trying to ensure that socialism should remember that it is, at least, more truly democratic and more truly libertarian than any other political philosophy. This question has become particularly confused because many modern analysts have found it possible to distinguish the legacy of Lenin from that of Stalin in this respect to the extent that one of the most distinguished, Roy Medvedev, in his biography of Stalin, has attempted to exonerate Lenin from responsibility for the worst of the perversions of socialism which Medvedev sees around him in the Soviet Union. For Medvedev it was Stalin who was the architect of monolithic, authoritarian socialism. However, for Lenin's socialist contemporaries, even before the revolution itself, it was clear that Lenin had peculiar views about the relationship of socialism to authoritarianism and dictatorship. Even in his dealings within the party Lenin showed only contempt for the spirit of free inquiry, debate, discussion and decision-making, which most socialists considered to be an essential part of socialism. Even socialists like Medvedev have more in common with the opponents of Lenin, like Yushkevich and Bazarov, than they do with Lenin himself when it comes to issues of democracy and intellectual freedom. It is of course argued on substantial grounds that Lenin in his last years came to see in certain respects the error of his ways and that a massive new effort would be needed to complete the revolution. As his critics had suggested long before, Lenin found that seizing power did not guarantee that the real intentions of the revolution could be fulfilled. Needless to say those critics were being imprisoned, exiled and executed for having had the impertinence to have been right.

Many Marxists who have opposed the authoritarian interprettation have been repeating some of these criticisms and have shared the values of Lenin's opponents. Like the latter, many modern dissenters have claimed that only fear and an abiding sense of insecurity can explain the Soviet government's opposition to democratisation and intellectual freedom. Leonid Plyushch the mathematician, complained in a protest about the trial of Galanskov and Ginzburg in 1968 that 'the times are gone when the Bolsheviks proudly proclaimed "We don't fear the truth for the truth works for us!"'[7] The 1909 debates at least suggest that this sentiment was not characteristic of Lenin but of Lunacharsky, Bogdanov and others. For Lenin it was peripheral to the revolution. For Medvedev, Sakharov and Valery Turchin the suppression of truthful information and suspicion of new ideas shows 'an obvious lack of confidence in creatively thinking, critical and energetic individuals'.[8] A Ukrainian dissenter, Vyacheslav Chornovil has even hinted that on the free circulation of ideas the capitalist states' attitude is more in line with that of Marx than is the Soviet government's attitude because the former allow any idea to circulate knowing that it cannot come to fruition unless the social soil is right for it.[9] Perhaps, however, the Soviet government realises the time is right for ideas which would be detrimental to their power and privilege. Again these resemble arguments used against Lenin in 1909. Left-wing critics in western Europe have challenged dogmatic Marxists in similar terms.

Other criticisms reflect other arguments we have come across in the pre-revolutionary period. E. Trubetskoi's comment that socialists had an unsubtle and mechanical view of the complexities of bourgeois legal thought is echoed by Medvedev in *On Socialist Democracy*. 'The fundamental principle of bourgeois democracy is the formal equality of all citizens before the law,' he says. It is important to stress, he continues, that 'all of these institutions and mechanisms [of bourgeois democracy] are the products of decades, sometimes centuries, of stubborn struggle by the people for their rights'.[10] For Medvedev there is a 'definite continuity' between bourgeois and socialist democracy, a view put forward by non-Leninists rather than Leninists, who were utterly contemptuous of bourgeois democracy.

It should not be forgotten that some of the least attractive strands of thought, extreme chauvinism and extreme authoritarianism, also survive in the contemporary USSR. The journal *Veche*, named after the general assemblies of medieval Russian city-states, has, under the editorship of G. Osipov, produced much that would have appealed to the editors of *Novoe vremya*, to Menshikov and to Archbishop Antony of Volynhia. One contributor wrote: 'Cosmopolitanism is spiritual slavery . . . on cosmopolitan soil grows the Antichrist, who promises freedom to all and brings them slavery.'[11] According to the unofficial *Chronicle of Current Events* another group presented

> the historical development of mankind as having taken the form of a struggle between order and chaos, chaos having been embodied in the Jewish people, who created disorder in Europe for two thousand years, until the German and Slav principles – the totalitarian regimes of Hitler and Stalin – put a stop to this chaos. [They] consider these regimes to have been historically inevitable and positive phenomena.[12]

An example of extreme nationalism can be found in a work of the early 1970s called *Slovo natsii (The Word of a People)* in which the writer claims that Satan carries on 'his corruption actively . . . preaching egalitarianism and cosmopolitanism – an ideology of the Jewish diaspora – thereby aggravating the process of universal blood-mixing and degradation'. Democracy is described as a 'state of ageing and decay'.[13]

A convenient focus for comparison with the *Vekhi* debate is provided by the contemporary debate surrounding the writings of Aleksandr Solzhenitsyn. Solzhenitsyn came to prominence as a writer of fiction but from the beginning it was clear that, in the Russian tradition, it was factual reality that interested him. His early novels are primarily about the retention of individuality and moral integrity in the midst of the apparently totally degrading circumstances of Stalin's Russia and of his prison camps. Solzhenitsyn's intentions always seemed to be closer to those of the historian, who attempts to describe and explain particular events, than to those of the novelist and he may have chosen the fictional form because there was more chance of publication, since no serious historical work on the period since 1930 has been permitted outside limited fields like military history. If so, then Solzhenitsyn was right in that a little of his work has been published in the Soviet Union and it is likely that his novel *Cancer Ward* came very close to being published. More recently, when it was clear that nothing further would be published, Solzhenitsyn has turned more and more to direct political and historical analogies, though not entirely forsaking fiction in that the project which he considers to be central to his life's work, the trilogy on Russia during World War I and the revolution, is a blend of historical imagination and a fictional form. These later works – in particular *The Gulag Archipelago*, the *Lenten Letter*, the *Nobel Prize Speech*, *Letter to the Soviet Leaders* and *From Under the Rubble* – have provoked sharp polemics within and beyond Russia.

It is much easier to parody or ridicule the ideas of Solzhenitsyn put forward in these works than it is to understand them. Perhaps the chief reason for this is that Solzhenitsyn owes a great deal to traditional Russian thought, which differed considerably from that of western Europe even before World War I. Because of this Solzhenitsyn can appear to be a relic of a previous age. His justification for looking backward in this sense arises from his conviction that a more healthy spiritual and intellectual climate can develop in Russia only by returning to the point at which the country's development was artificially interrupted by an alien political force, Bolshevism, and then embarking on an attempt to rebuild an indigenous mental environment more in keeping with what he sees as the traditional outlook of the Russian people. For this reason, among others, Solzhenitsyn believes that certain pre-revolutionary values, and those of *Vekhi* in particular, are as relevant today as they were before 1917.

Before briefly examining Solzhenitsyn's view of *Vekhi* it is possible to discern a certain similarity between his outlook and that of the *vekhovtsy*. This is most significant at the level of underlying values. For Solzhenitsyn, authentic values openly arrived at and defended without prevarication are the hallmark of the fully developed person. The formation and defence of these values is, as he says on more than one occasion, a more important duty than providing for the material well-being of self and family. He abhors the excuse used by many who cooperate with injustice that moral compromise is necessary for the sake of the children. 'That the moral health of their children is more precious than their careers does not even enter the parents' heads, so impoverished have they themselves become.'[14] This theme of moral integrity runs like a red thread through all Solzhenitsyn's writings from the early prison camp novels, through the impressive figure of Matryona in *Matryona's House* – 'that one righteous person without whom, as the saying goes, no city can stand. Nor the world' – to the later didactic writings. It explains some of the apparently odd judgements expressed in these latter writings; for example, the most controversial point in *Letter to the Soviet Leaders* is that the most damaging aspect of the contemporary Soviet system is its ideology. He tells the Soviet government that it is the 'antiquated legacy of the Progressive Doctrine that endowed you with all the millstones that are dragging you down'.[15] Its removal will not have disastrous consequences because, he continues, '*nothing constructive rests upon it*, it is a sham, cardboard theatrical prop – take it away and nothing will collapse, nothing will even wobble' because 'material calculation' has replaced 'ideological enthusiasm'. 'This ideology,' he concludes, 'does nothing now but sap our strength and bind us . . . Every thing is steeped in lies and *everybody knows it* – and says so openly in private conversation.'[16]

The same ardour is to be found in the Nobel Prize Lecture which he concludes by quoting the Russian proverb: 'One word of truth shall outweigh the whole world,' which is, he says, 'the basis of my own activity and my appeal to the writers of the whole world'.[17] It is at the heart of shorter items which he considers to be important, such as 'Live not by lies,' in which he enumerates a programme of passive resistance based on non-cooperation with what is known to be false[18] and the 'Lenten Letter to Patriarch Pimen' in which he criticises the leadership of the Orthodox Church for not taking the road of heroic witness to the truth, even though it might lead to martyrdom, though that in itself would not compare with the martyrdom of early Christians who were thrown to the lions, 'today one can only lose well-being'.[19] This theme also explains the root of the message Solzhenitsyn attempted to transmit in a series of broadcasts and televised interviews in Western Europe and North America in 1975 in which his calls to resist Marxist ideology were understood by some as calls for massive military rearmament. This was far from Solzhenitsyn's mind. In fact he consistently denies the power of weapons. This comes out most clearly in an interview he gave to a French magazine in early 1976. Asked if his prescription of resistance would lead to war he replied:

> I talk of spiritual purpose and you respond with strategy. My friends and I have no atomic bombs, no tanks, no guns – nothing. But at the very instant when our resignation gave way to determination, at the very moment when we risked death, the huge Soviet machine was held in check. No political or military combination will save you. Inner purpose is more important than politics.[20]

The puzzle of explaining how the Russian people deserted honesty and faith in favour of falsehood and deception is central to his historical epic of the revolution which is not yet completed.

Although biographical details of Solzhenitsyn's life are scattered and unreliable it seems likely that this heroic moral stance led him to be converted to Orthodox Christianity in the mid-1960s, though it certainly existed before that conversion. A realisation that it was incompatible with a materialist philosophy would reflect the path 'from Marxism to idealism' taken by the *vekhovtsy* such as Bulgakov, Berdyaev and Struve. What direct influence they may have had on Solzhenitsyn at this point is not known but his admiration for them increased subsequent to it.

Nothing else in Solzhenitsyn's work can be compared in importance to the central theme of moral integrity and it is the recognition of this theme that has led to the admiration which Solzhenitsyn himself evokes even among those who find his analyses to be weak and contradictory and his solutions unacceptable. Nonetheless some lesser themes do invite comparison with *Vekhi*. Solzhenitsyn's insistence on the pre-eminence of moral, spiritual and cultural values above the practical and material, summed up in his statement that 'For the believer his faith is *supremely* precious, more precious than the food he puts in his stomach,'[21] would be echoed by many members of the pre-revolutionary intelligentsia on the Left and Right as well as among the *vekhovtsy*. The great significance of art which Solzhenitsyn expounds in the opening paragraphs of his Nobel Lecture is derived directly from the pre-revolutionary intelligentsia, as references to Dostoevsky and Vladimir Solov'ev indicate. The reinstatement of 'that ancient trinity of Truth, Goodness and Beauty' which is 'not simply an empty, faded formula as we thought in the days of our self-confident, materialistic youth' is his task. Beauty, as Dostoevsky said, will save the world, and Solzhenitsyn interprets this to mean that a work of art which reaches the whole person through his emotions as well as reason has more weight than political or philosophical programmes because artificial concepts cannot stand up to being expressed in images whereas 'those works of art which have scooped up the truth and presented it to us as a living force – they take hold of us, compel us, and nobody ever, not even in ages to come, will appear to refute them'.[22] The tone of Solzhenitsyn's views here is more reminiscent of Frank and Struve's articles on the connection between culture and the development of personal moral and spiritual values than to most contemporary debates.

Arising from this is the view that politics, in the everyday sense, should not be seen as the most important part of life. Political activities might follow on from the development of authentic values but life should dominate politics rather than the other way about. The attack on the politicisation of culture and ideas was a key theme in *Vekhi*. Interestingly enough both *Vekhi* and Solzhenitsyn conclude from this that oppressive political institutions are not necessarily a supreme disaster and one can live a moral life within their confines even though they are not ideal. Both are sceptical of the possibility or desirability of immediate transition to liberal democracy.

There are also many points at which Solzhenitsyn differs from the *vekhovtsy*, in particular his more overt Russian nationalism and the depth of his hatred of Marxist socialism. Some *vekhovtsy* were more prepared to see positive value in certain aspects of Marxism though they were unanimously against the developing Bolshevik tendency but for Solzhenitsyn Marxism is synonymous with Bolshevism.

Solzhenitsyn provides an excellent summary of his views on *Vekhi*, and particularly on its significance in comparison with his own views on the contemporary Russian intelligentsia, in the opening pages of his article 'The Smatterers' in *From Under the Rubble*. For him the pre-revolutionary intelligentsia with its moral absolutism (criticised by *Vekhi*) is infinitely more admirable and heroic than its modern equivalent which expresses its opposition by 'secretly making a gesture of contempt in [its] pocket'. If this is 'inner freedom' what, Solzhenitsyn asks, is 'inner slavery'?[23] The article provides a most interesting commentary on *Vekhi* but is so densely packed in places with observations that a summary would be inadequate and further investigation has to be left to the interested reader to follow up for himself.[24]

The principles of *Vekhi*, as interpreted and brought up to date by Solzhenitsyn, have proved as contentious as when they first appeared. The most acute responses have come from the same direction as they did in 1909, from liberal and socialist thinkers. Many of the criticisms are levelled against specific proposals but some of the underlying principles have been brought into question. From Andrei Sakharov's liberal—technocratic point of view Solzhenitsyn's Russian nationalism, his distorted view of the West and his mistrust of scientific progress and enthusiasm for a labour-intensive, low-technology society (an interesting point of contact between Solzhenitsyn, the Club of Rome and the ecological movement), are all mistaken. Sakharov says little about Solzhenitsyn's religious views but he expresses his opposition to Solzhenitsyn's opinion that Russia must remain under an authoritarian system of government. For Sakharov a democratic system is imperative. The leading dissenter on the Left, Roy Medvedev, echoes some of Sakharov's points but adds others of his own. The core of Medvedev's view is that what Solzhenitsyn criticises is Stalinism, not Marxism, and that, in fact, 'Stalinism in many ways is the denial and bloody destruction of Bolshevism'.[25] While Lenin certainly made great errors and needs to be criticised 'the sum total of Lenin's activities was,' says Medvedev, 'positive'.[26] He is also opposed to Solzhenitsyn's defence of religion and has a fundamentally different conception of the future of Soviet society, expounded in his book *On Socialist Democracy*.[27] For him, Marxism and scientific socialism will outlive the Stalinist distortions so powerfully criticised by Solzhenitsyn, who, Medvedev claims, probably has no conception of Stalinism, a surmise later confirmed by Solzhenitsyn himself when he wrote that 'there never was any such thing as Stalinism'.[28]

Perhaps one of the most surprising grounds for challenge to Solzhenitsyn has come from Sergei Elagin, an associate of Medvedev, who attacks Solzhenitsyn from almost a Vekhist position. For him, Solzhenitsyn and those gathered round him resemble the ivory tower thinkers of Vyacheslav Ivanov's circle or the aesthetes criticised by Blok in *Russia and the Intelligentsia*.[29] The new religious intelligentsia is too introspective and too little concerned with the real practical problems surrounding it. 'Christ taught that man does not live by bread alone', but he never preached this to hungry people.[30] Instead of searching for real solutions they assume that the descent of God 'categorically and peremptorily resolves everything'.[31] Despite being disorganised and repetitive, Elagin's article, heavily influenced by Solov'ev, Tolstoy and· Berdyaev and reinforced with quotes from people as diverse as the Decembrists, Fonvizin and Cardinal Mindszenty, shows the persistence of a school which sees Christianity and socialism as inseparable. A retreat into the world of the spirit is wrong. For Elagin, one of Russia's problems is that already too many people are concerned only with their private lives, which he believes is what Solzhenitsyn advocates.

Finally the debate has been referred to frequently in official Soviet writing. Ever since 1909 *vekhism* has been one of the pegs on which Bolshevik ideologists and their Soviet successors have hung their intellectual opponents. In the 1960s and 1970s, more than sixty years after the original publication of *Vekhi*, the struggle against *vekhism* is still urged as one of the major tasks of Soviet ideological effort. Recent Soviet encyclopaedias have classified several British and American historians of Russia and the Soviet Union as *vekhisti*, for example, Barghoorn, Daniels, Schapiro and Lampert.[32] The sixtieth anniversary of Lenin's article on *Vekhi* was commemorated by an article published in *Oktyabr'* entitled '*Vekhi*, a catechism of treachery'.[33] Shortly after this, an article in *Literaturnaya gazeta* commended the writer of the article in *Oktyabr'* for showing just the right spirit of struggle on ideological lines called for by the celebration of Lenin's centenary in 1970.[34] Another example of this was provided in November 1972 when Aleksandr Solzhenitsyn, with some justification, was referred to as a *vekhist* in an article, also published in *Literaturnaya gazeta*, written by A. Yakovlev of the history faculty of Leningrad State University. 'As is well-known,' Yakovlev wrote,

anti-communism, in its search for new means of struggle against the Marxist—Leninist world view and the socialist system, is trying to breathe new life into the ideology of *Vekhi*, the ideas of

Berdyaev and other reactionary, nationalistic and religious—
idealistic concepts of the past that were routed by V. I. Lenin.[35]

The most substantial recent article on *Vekhi* in a Soviet journal also
professes to see *Vekhi* as a seminal influence on all the most
reactionary, anti-Soviet tendencies in the modern world, including
the Frankfurt school, the European student revolutionaries of 1968
including Daniel Cohn-Bendit, and others who have seldom been
thought of as having an affinity with them, such as Professor
Richard Pipes and Professor Leonard Schapiro. According to the
author *vekhism*

> in the essence of its ideas and opinions anticipated and in many
> ways prepared the path for the theoretical outlook and political
> conceptions of the bourgeoisie and its ideological arms-bearers,
> in the last quarter of the twentieth century.[36]

In these respects, then, the parameters of the *Vekhi* debate are
beginning to re-emerge and it may be true, as Solzhenitsyn writes,
that 'after sixty years the stratum of Russian society able to lend its
support to the book appears to be deepening'.[37]

Conclusion

The task of the intellectual historian has never been an easy one. One of the most talented, Leszek Kolakowski, warned the reader at the outset of one of his own distinguished contributions to the field that setting boundaries to a current of thought was likely to be at least partly arbitrary. The present work has shown many signs of such arbitrariness. Despite this limitation one of the objectives of the intellectual historian is to show that, as Kolakowski again wrote, that 'certain themes, propositions or assertions held the attention of readers, polemicists and adherents over a given period, while others went almost unnoticed'.[1] Hopefully this is what the present work has achieved because the *Vekhi* debate illustrated vividly the divisions and arguments within the intelligentsia on topics closely associated with its traditional vital concerns. As such it was the last great debate the traditional intelligentsia was able to have before it was overwhelmed by the events of the World War, revolution and civil war. It was also the only time the intelligentsia was able, even though there was not a revolution in 1905 so much as a revolutionary situation, to evaluate revolution as an actual experience rather than as an expected salvation.

The debate of this decade had many important features. In the first place the interdependence of the idealist and materialist schools was striking, even by the usual standards of intellectual debate where dialectical relationships of this kind are common. Both wings built up their arguments against each other in a mutual conflict which gained in intensity from the time of the publication of *Problemy idealizma* to the end of the *Vekhi* debate itself. If the idealists put out a collection of essays, the materialists had to follow suit. If the idealists published a journal then so did the materialists. Each side was forced to strength its arguments before embarking on a new round of escalation. It was perhaps ironic that both schools were transformed beyond recognition and that one of the crudest and least philosophically sophisticated of the contributions to the debate, that by Lenin, has, for reasons having nothing to do with intellectual excellence, become the best known survivor of this interchange of opinions. But Lenin's polemic also showed how intimately the ideas of one protagonist were defined by the need to refute the ideas of others. Even here the interdependence was obvious.

A second important feature was that, despite the interdependence, the divisions within educated Russian society were brought out for all to see. In these years at least there was no question of any one group dominating the mind of the intelligentsia. In fact it brings into question the assumption that there was a progressive sequence of dominant ideas, of generations of sons against fathers, in the history of the intelligentsia. According to this view, the 1860s was a decade of nihilism, the 1870s of populism, the 1880s of the great debate between populism and Marxism and the 1890s of Marxism. Yet in the first decade of the twentieth century all these schools had energetic adherents, the populist impulse was still the strongest and the Marxists were severely divided among themselves. Instead of seeing a sequence of generations, a better model of the intellectual history of Russia would be that of a layer cake. Each new layer was put on top of the earlier ones, which were not thereby destroyed but remained to give greater variety to the finished product. The *Vekhi* debate also showed just how different those layers were. Those who opposed *Vekhi*, for example Kizevetter, Ivanov-Razumnik, Lenin and Tolstoy, did so for very different reasons. Those who welcomed it, for example, Archbishop Antony and Belyi, also had very little in common. The debate of these years showed up these divisions very well and they were to become much more significant after the October revolution. This is scarcely surprising since the question of revolution was at the heart of the arguments after 1905. Blok may have been right to say that the divisions between the symbolists over this question dated from this time but many who remained loyal to the revolutionary ideal in 1909 were forced into a painful re-appraisal of that loyalty after 1917. Blok himself seems to have been going through such a crisis when he died and had he lived longer he would perhaps have joined his former friends and colleagues in the *émigré* circles in Paris.

Thus the debate showed, for the last time in the short history of the intelligentsia, that its vitality and energy were far from exhausted and that it was perhaps bringing forth another major school from within itself, that of liberal idealism, as some of the participants in the debate suggested in either hopeful anticipation, like Ivanov-Razumnik, or extreme revulsion, like Trotsky.

The debate is also of interest because it fits into the context of similar developments taking place elsewhere in Europe at the same time and shows that Russian intellectual life was beginning to co-exist more comfortably with that of western Europe. Russia was not only learning from but also teaching the West, not just through her great novelists as previously but to an increasing extent through painters, composers, dancers, poets, actors, singers and stage directors. The debate, then, offers an interesting comparison with the rest of Europe where small, but significant, groups of artists and philosophers were rejecting the materialism and nationalism which had come to dominate the continent by the end of the nineteenth century. This revolt was so successful that almost all original and creative art took up abstract and non-systematic forms. By the 1920s many musicians no longer wrote harmonies, painters and sculptors no longer reproduced natural forms, novelists no longer wrote 'realistic' stories and thinkers no longer constructed elaborate, all-embracing systems and turned instead to philosophies based on the experience of the individual – ' "I" is not particular,' wrote Un-amuno in 1912, 'it is universal.' In this new Europe of Kafka, Joyce and Picasso, many Russians were to play important roles. These men rejected the ordered and rational side of human nature and, often under the prompting of Freud, who was as much a symptom as a cause of this revolution, explored the irrational, emotional and subconscious layers within the human personality. It was this side of life which many of the positivists, materialists and nihilists of the nineteenth century underestimated and their view of human nature was shown to be based on false rational and mechanical assumptions no longer shared by the new thinkers.

One other lingering question remains to be answered. In view of the fact that most of the ideas in *Vekhi* had been in circulation for some years, why did its publication create a sensation which caught even its authors unawares? In the first place it was a powerful attack on the intelligentsia's Ark of the Covenant – its mystique of revolution (to borrow Professor Schapiro's phrase). The intelligent-sia could not be expected to take such an attack without retaliating. Earlier criticism of the revolutionary ideal had provoked less controversy. For example, the volume *Problemy idealizma* of 1902 had been almost unnoticed outside scholarly circles, but *Vekhi* had an extraordinary instantaneous impact. The difference was due partly to the form of *Vekhi*. It was a small book, full of unusual, apparently reactionary ideas and sometimes outrageous provocations, especially in the case of Gershenzon, the aim of which was to stimulate a debate. Then there was the situation of 1909. The prevailing mood was one of apathy and despondency about the social question and the revolutionary movement was under great pressure from the autocracy. The apparent treachery of such outstanding *intelligenty* as this group was 'the most unkindest cut of all'. In addition to playing Brutus to the intelligentsia's Caesar, the emotional elements within *Vekhi* elicited an equally emotional response on the part of many of the intelligentsia. This helps to explain one of the most puzzling features of the debate – the misunderstanding of *Vekhi's* outlook by so many of its critics. *Vekhi* was not a reactionary book nor even a conservative one. It was even revolutionary in the sense that it was attacking what it saw as the ossified outlook of the Russian intelligentsia which had itself taken on many of the characteristics of a dogmatic, backward-looking, unimaginative, conservative establishment. The *vekhovtsy* were opposed to what Struve had paradoxically but correctly termed the conservatism of intelligentsia thought. It was this accusation of conservatism which particularly stung the intelligentsia. Nor was *Vekhi* unaware of the need for revolution in Russia and they were not so much opposed to the idea of revolution as such, as fearful of the consequences which would ensue from the violent overthrow of the regime as envisaged by the intelligentsia. The *vekhovtsy* hoped that a spiritual revolution would avoid these consequences.

Thus, for the *vekhovtsy*, 1905 had been a revelation of the underlying weakness of the revolutionary movement as a whole, a weakness that would doom it to failure even if it were to seize power. For the *vekhovtsy* no revolution would succeed until it gave the individual his proper place and stopped dealing with society as though it were a machine which could be altered and improved by anyone who believed that he possessed a modicum of knowledge of the engineering principles on which it was run. They totally rejected the notion that society was subject to rigid scientific laws. If there were to be a revolution, then it would have to be aimed at people not at institutions. They considered each living individual to be of absolute value and no political gain could justify violence against individuals.

Despite the nobility of these utterances, they did not strike a chord in the hearts of the *intelligenty*. The reason for this was obvious. Such a principle made effective action against the government impossible. It tied the hands of the revolutionaries and meant the continuation of the political *status quo*. These conservative implications of *Vekhi's* stance were another cause of the storm of protest raised against it from all quarters of the intelligentsia.

Thus, the impracticality of their call became apparent from the fact that they did not find the hoped-for response among the intelligentsia which was almost uniformly hostile to them. But it is in the nature of true prophecy to be impractical and untimely and if the attacks showed *Vekhi's* untimeliness, they also demonstrated the accuracy of many of its analyses, in particular of the intelligentsia's dogmatism, the sloppiness of its thinking and its uncritical, emotional adherence to the revolutionary myth. Who could deny, from the evidence of the debate itself, the truth of Berdyaev's assertion that the intelligentsia judged thought by its suitability for the revolutionary cause rather than according to any criteria of truth or falsity? Who could deny that the intelligentsia refused to countenance any criticism of the revolutionary tradition which it worshipped, a characteristic which has become a hallmark of Soviet pseudo-revolutionary conservatism which claims that all the truths have been revealed by Marx, Lenin and others? The intelligentsia's negative attitude towards creativity, which the *vekhovtsy* deplored, had the unfortunate result foreseen by Berdyaev, that the revolution would assume the reversed likeness of its opponent, the autocracy. Existing only for the political struggle against the latter, the intelligentsia took on some of its worst aspects and found that, as Bakunin had said, to make an indestructible state one had to combine Machiavelli and Jesuitism – for the body, violence, for the soul, deception. In this respect Struve was mistaken because instead of being against the state the revolution proved to be its apotheosis.

So *Vekhi* was caught in a vicious circle. If its picture of the intelligentsia's nature and mood were correct, then its proposals could be no more than hopeful but doomed gestures. If the intelligentsia were concerned only with immediate practical issues of revolution-making, then the renewal called for by *Vekhi* would not take root. Those who dismiss *Vekhi* as uninfluential are, in a roundabout way, testifying to its accuracy. It was uninfluential and the reasons why this should be so are all contained in the book itself.

From their point of view, the failure of 1905 was inherent in the revolutionary movement. Indeed it must be admitted, though *Vekhi* itself did not go this far, that the history of the Russian revolutionary movement showed above all the futility of contrived attempts to overthrow even the most shaky political regime. Despite the fact that they were opposed only by one of the least efficient and most antiquated and ramshackle systems in Europe, every attempt at overthrow failed. The 'going to the people', the assassination of the tsar in 1881, the December rising in 1905 were all fiascos. Marx himself might have warned them of this for did he not say that the working class, fully conscious of its historical mission and full of the herioc resolve to act up to it, could afford to smile at 'the didactic patronage of well-wishing bourgeois-doctrinaires, pouring forth their ignorant platitudes and sectarian crotchets in the oracular tone of scientific infallibility'?[2] He would have been horrified to find that his own ideas were being used in this way by certain sections of the Russian intelligentsia. The movements which had the greatest success among the workers and peasants, such as the strikes of the mid-1890s and 1905 and the peasant expropriation movement of 1903–5, owed little to intelligentsia participation, which could provoke resentment as much as enthusiasm. The view that revolutionary activity was instigated in 1905 by intelligentsia activity was more common in right-wing circles anxious to blame agitators, Jews and students for upsetting the normally quiescent peasantry.

Thus the facts themselves pointed to the revolutionary movement's ineffectiveness. The intelligentsia could not have been less effective if its members had followed Struve's most extreme advice and become patriotic liberal imperialists seeking to capture Constantinople for the tsar! *Vekhi* was unpopular because it admitted this and exposed the weakness of the intelligentsia. It pricked the bubble of its self-glorification. As with Cyrano de Bergerac's nose, the least acceptable criticism was that which hit most accurately at one's own feared deformity. *Vekhi* hit the intelligentsia at its most sensitive point by calling it conservative. It revived its fear of irrelevance, which was, after all, where it had started out in the period of 'superfluous men'. *Vekhi's* remedies might have been unsound in some cases and even partaken of characteristics they criticised in others, but there can be little doubt that if there were to have been any hope of building a better future for Russia, the intelligentsia would have needed to be shocked out of its complacent stupor which responded to constant failure only by ordering more of the same type of effort. Perhaps an observer would be justified in tentatively believing that the principles of *Vekhi* might have brought about a different history for Russia but, from hindsight, it is clear that by 1909 it was too late to mould a new

intelligentsia opinion which, to judge from the complacency
revealed in the *Vekhi* debate, would in any case have been an
enormous task. Perhaps *Vekhi's* principles have more chance of
success now and in the future than when they first came to light.

Appendix:
Chronological Table of
Main Sources

BOOKS	PERIODICALS
	Periodicals appearing throughout the period: *Russkaya mysl'* *Russkoe bogatstvo* *Voprosy filosofii i psikhologii.* Periodicals not surviving the period: *Mir iskusstva* (to 1904) *Mir Bozhii* (to July 1906)
1900 Volynsky, *Bor'ba za idealizm*	
1901 Berdyaev, *sub"ektivizm i individualizm*, (preface by Struve).	
1902 *Problemy idealizma.* Volynsky, *Borets za idealizm.*	
1903 Bulgakov, *Ot marksizma k idealizmu.*	*Novyi put'*, (1903-4).
1904 Bogdanov, *Empiriomonizm.* Machajski, *Umstvennyi rabochii.* *Ocherki realisticheskogo mirovozzreniya.* Sokolov, *Ob ideyakh i idealakh russkoi intelligentsii.*	*Pravda*, (1904-6). *Vesy*, (1904-9). *Voprosy zhizni*, (1904-5).
1905 Minsky, *Religiya budushchego.*	*Pol'yarnaya zvezda*, (1905-6).

BOOKS	PERIODICALS
1906 Aksel'rod, *Filosofskie ocherki.*	*Sovremennyi mir*, (from August 1906).
Artsybashev, *Sanin.* Chulkov & Ivanov, *O mischeskom anarkhizme.*	*Zolotoe runo*, (1906–9).
Fakely, vol. 1. *Voprosy religii*, vol. 1.	
1907 Berdyaev, *Novoe religioznoe soznanie i obshchestvennost'.*	*Protiv techeniya*, (February–March 1907).
Fakely, vol. 2. Gorky, *Ispoved'.* Ivanov-Razumnik, *Istoriya russkoi obshchestvennoi mysli.* Merezhkovsky, Gippius & Filosofov, *Le Tsar et la Révolution.* Valentinov *Filosofskie postroeniya marksizma.* Yushkevich, *Materializm i kriticheskii realizm.*	
1908 *Fakely*, vol. 3. *Literaturnyi raspad*, vol. 1. Lunacharsky, *Religiya i sotsializm.* *Ocherki po filosofii marksizma.* Plekhanov, *Osnovnye voprosy marksizma.* *Voprosy religii*, vol. 2.	
1909 Lenin, *Materializm i empiriokrititsizm.* *Literaturnyi raspad*, vol. 2.	*Apollon*, (from October 1909). *Zaprosy zhizni*, (1909–12).
Na rubezhe. *Ocherki filosofii kollektivizma.* Plekhanov, 'O t.n. religioznykh iskaniyakh v Rossii'. *Vekhi.* *Vershiny.* *V zashchitu intelligentsii.*	

BOOKS   PERIODICALS

1910   *Kuda my idem?*
        Intelligentsiya v Rossii.
        Iz istorii noveshei russkoi literatury.
        'Vekhi' kak znamenie vremeni.
1911   Lunacharsky, *Religiya i sotsializm,*
        vol. 2.

Notes

NOTES TO INTRODUCTION

1. Ovsyaniko-Kulikovsky (1908–11), vol. 1 p. v.
2. Ivanov-Razumnik (1907) p. 4.
3. I. Turgenev, *Literary Reminiscences* (trans. D. Magarshack) (London: 1959) p. 110.
4. M. Malia in Pipes (1961) p. 1.
5. H. Seton-Watson, *The Russian Empire* (Oxford: 1967), p. 536.
6. V. Leikina-Svirskaya, *Intelligentsiya v Rossi vo vtoroi polovine XIX veka* (Moscow: 1971), pp. 69–70.
7. *Russkaya periodicheskaya pechat' 1895–1917: spravochnik* (Moscow: 1957).
8. Erman (1966) p. 132.
9. Frank (1956) p. 83.
10. Blok (1960) vol. 7., p. 335. The letter was not sent.

NOTES TO CHAPTER 1

1. Venturi (1960), p. 503, or Zernov (1963) p. 26.
2. Struve in his obituary for Solov'ev in *Mir Bozhii* took the view that Solov'ev's journalism was his most important work, especially that collected in *The National Question, Mir Bozhii* no. 9, September 1900, pp. 13–15.
3. It should not be forgotten, however, that Struve wrote in 1909 that to develop the productive forces of the country was a necessary prerequisite for culture itself. The intelligentsia did not understand this, he said. *Russkaya mysl'* 1909, no. 1, pp. 205–6.
4. *Problemy idealizma*, p. IX.
5. Ibid., p. 214.
6. Ibid., p. 232–3.
7. Ibid., p. 218.
8. Ibid., p. 225.
9. Ibid., p. 231.
10. Ibid., p. VIII.
11. Ibid., p. 196–216.
12. Ibid., p. 212.
13. Struve (1901) pp. VI–VII.
14. *Problemy idealizma*, Introduction pp. VII–VIII.
15. Struve (1901) p. VI.
16. Ibid., p. VII.

17. Berdyaev (1901) (II) pp. 45–6.
18. Ibid., p. 36.
19. Ibid., pp. 35–6.
20. Ibid., p. 36.
21. Ibid., p. 51.
22. Ibid., pp. 80–1.
23. Ibid., p. 92.
24. K. Marx, Preface to *A Contribution to the Critique of Political Economy*.
25. *Problemy idealizma*, p. 51.
26. Ibid., p. 70.
27. Ibid., p. 50–1.
28. Ibid., p. 71.
29. Bulgakov (1903) p. 300.
30. Ibid., p. 316.
31. Ibid., p. 330.
32. Ibid., p. 335.
33. Volynsky (1902) p. 56.
34. Ibid., pp. 39–40.
35. Struve and Frank, p. 171.
36. *Polyarnaya zvezda* 1905 no. 3, pp. 170–1.
37. Ibid., no. 2, pp. 113–14.
38. Ibid., p. 114.
39. Botsyanovskii (1911), pp. 126–9.
40. Pascal (1962), p. 24.
41. Chulkov and Ivanov, p. 69.
42. *Fakely* vol. 1, 'Ot redaktskii'.
43. *Fakely* vol. 2, 'Ot redaktsii'.
44. Ivanov (1906), p. 17.
45. Ibid., p. 18.
46. Ibid.
47. Ivanov (1907), pp. 100–2.
48. *Fakely*, vol. 2, p. 25.
49. Chulkov and Ivanov, p. 40.
50. Ibid., p. 18.
51. This denial of the validity of social institutions in favour of an internal reform of individual consciousness is reminiscent of Gershenzon's preface to *Vekhi*.
52. Chulkov and Ivanov, p. 5.
53. Ibid., p. 43–4.
54. Ibid., p. 40.
55. Ibid., p. 63.
56. Ibid., p. 21.
57. *Fakely*, vol. 2, pp. 20–1.
58. Chulkov and Ivanov, p. 9.
59. Ivanov 1907, p. 100.
60. *Fakely*, vol. 2, p. 22.
61. Ibid.
62. Chulkov and Ivanov, p. 27.
63. Ibid., p. 69.
64. *Vesy* 1907, no. 6, p. 55.

65. *Vesy* 1906, no. 8, pp. 48–51.
66. Ibid., pp. 43–7.
67. *Zolotoe runo* 1906 no. 7, pp. 174–5.
68. Ibid., no. 10, pp. 58–66.
69. Ibid., p. 65.
70. *Smert': al'manakh.*
71. F. Tyutchev, *Silentium* 1836.
72. *Vesy* 1906, no. 5, p. 87.
73. *Zolotoe runo* 1906, no. 1, p. 1.
74. *Apollon* 1909, no. 1, p. 1.
75. Belyi (1908).
76. Ivanov (1910) p. 9.
77. Ibid., p. 11.
78. Blok (1910) p. 21.
79. Bryusov (1910) p. 31.
80. Ibid., p. 33.
81. Ellis (1909) p. 63.
82. Ibid., foreword.
83. Ellis (1910) pp. 44–8.
84. Ellis (1909) pp. 61–3.
85. Ellis (1909) p. 68 and (1910), p. 20.
86. Ellis (1910) p. 31.

NOTES TO CHAPTER 2

1. See bibliography for full reference.
2. *Ocherki realisticheskogo mirovozzreniya*, p. V.
3. Ibid., p. VII.
4. Shulyatikov (1908) pp. 132–50.
5. *Russkaya mysl'* 1909, no. 2, p. 106. Izgoev's intuition was in fact correct. Valentinov recalled in his memoirs that he received a letter from Mach in 1912 requesting information about the disputes over 'Machism' in Russia. Mach said that he found it incomprehensible and quite remarkable that in Russia criticism of his scientific views had been transferred to the political field, of which he knew nothing. N. Valentinov, *Encounters with Lenin* (London: 1968), p. 258.
6. See, for example, Wetter (1958) pp. 92–100.
7. Bogdanov (1903) (II).
8. Bogdanov (1903) (I).
9. Bogdanov (1904) (I), p. 13.
10. Bogdanov (1903) (I) p. 232.
11. Ibid., p. 233.
12. Bogdanov (1904) (I).
13. Bogdanov (1906) p. 10.
14. Bogdanov (1905) (II) pp. 136–68.
15. Bogdanov (1906) p. 5.
16. Lenin (1958–65) vol. 18, p. 10.
17. See below, pp. 54–6.

18. *Ocherki po filosofii marksizma*, pp. 1–2.
19. *Vershiny*, p. 371.
20. Ibid., pp. 389–90.
21. Ibid., p. 390.
22. Ibid., p. 391.
23. *Ocherki po filosofii marksizma*, p. 161.
24. Lenin (1958–65) vol. 18, pp. 10–11.
25. Ibid., pp. 127–8.
26. Ibid., p. 35.
27. Ibid., p. 150.
28. Ibid., p. 148.
29. Ibid., 149.
30. Ibid., p. 147.
31. Ibid., 150.
32. Ibid., p. 19.
33. See, for example, A. L. Korneeva, *Leninskaya kritika makhizma i bor'ba protiv sovremennogo idealizma*, Moscow 1971, who criticises A. J. Ayer, the Vienna circle, Bertrand Russell, neo-Thomists, Nils Bohr, Einstein and many others as though they were all in a real sense descendants of Mach.
34. Bogdanov (1910) (II) p. 155.
35. Ibid., p. 168.
36. Ibid., p. 194.
37. Ibid., p. 218.
38. Ibid., pp. XX–XXII.
39. Maslin (1957) p. 5.
40. Baron, p. 286.
41. Plekhanov (1957) vol. III, p. 128.
42. Ibid., p. 124.
43. Plekhanov, *Sochineniya*, vol. XVI, 2nd ed., 1923–7, p. 294.
44. Plekhanov (1957) vol. III, p. 207.
45. Lenin (1958–65) vol. 28, p. 528.
46. K. Marx and F. Engels, *Sochineniya* (Moscow: 1955) vol. 2, p. 120.
47. Schapiro (1970) p. 112.
48. N. Valentinov, *Encounters with Lenin* (London: 1968) p. 245.
49. *Russkaya mysl'* 1909, no. 2, p. 106.
50. Berdyaev (1949), p. 137. In *Vekhi* Gershenzon referred to positivism as a 'general constitutional derangement of consciousness'. *Vekhi*, p. 82.

NOTES TO CHAPTER 3

1. *Vekhi*, p. 180.
2. Butkevich 1907.
3. Ibid., p. 88.
4. Bulgakov (1946) p. 82.
5. See, for example, the articles collected in Bulgakov (1911).
6. Bulgakov (1911) vol. 1, p. IX.
7. Ibid., p. X.
8. Ibid.

9. Ibid., VII–VIII.
10. Bulgakov (1910).
11. Bulgakov (1911) vol. 2, p. 116.
12. Ibid., pp. 117–18.
13. Ibid., p. 307.
14. Ibid., vol. I, p. 223.
15. Ibid., pp. 232–3.
16. Ibid., vol. 2, p. 119.
17. Ibid., p. 307.
18. Ibid., p. 310.
19. Ibid., p. 309.
20. Ibid. (1946) p. 80.
21. Ibid., p. 79.
22. Ibid., p. 76.
23. Ibid. (1905) pp. 359–360.
24. *Novyi put'*, 1904, No. 10, p. 275.
25. *Voprosy zhizni*, September 1905, p. 339.
26. Ibid., p. 335.
27. Bulgakov (1906) pp. 125–6.
28. *Polyarnaya zvezda*, 1906, no. 13, p. 130.
29. Berdyaev (1949) pp. 165–8.
30. Berdyaev (1935) pp. 10–11.
31. See, for example, Berdyaev (1907) (II).
32. Berdyaev (1907) (I).
33. Ibid. (1907) (II) p. V.
34. Ibid., p. XVII.
35. Ibid.
36. Ibid., p. XVIII.
37. Ibid., p. XXXI.
38. Ibid., p. XLIX.
39. Ibid. (1908) (II) p. 55.
40. Ibid. (1907) (II) p. X.
41. A. Radishchev, *Puteshestvie iz Peterburga v Moskvu*, preface.
42. Berdyaev (1960) p. 22.
43. Ibid. (1949) p. 105.
44. *Voprosy zhizni*, June 1905, p. 180.
45. *Novyi put'*, October 1904, pp. 278–96.
46. Ibid., p. 285.
47. Berdyaev (1910) p. 151. This article was originally published in *Moskovskii ezhenedel'nik*, 12 December 1908, that is, at the time when *Vekhi* was being prepared for publication.
48. *Voprosy zhizni*, April–May 1905, p. 325.
49. Ibid., p. 325.
50. Ibid., p. 327.
51. Ibid., p. 326.
52. Ibid., p. 327.
53. Ibid., p. 333.
54. Berdyaev (1910) pp. 151–2.
55. See above, p. 18.

56. Berdyaev (1901) (I) p. 3.
57. Ibid., p. 2.
58. Ibid.
59. Ibid., p. 3.
60. Ibid., p. 16.
61. Ibid., pp. 10–11.
62. Ibid., p. 12.
63. Ibid., p. 25.
64. Ibid. (1904) p. 699.
65. Ibid. (1906) p. 684.
66. Ibid., p. 686.
67. Ibid., p. 682.
68. Ibid., p. 681.
69. Ibid., p. 683.
70. Ibid.
71. Ibid., p. 684.
72. Ibid., p. 685.
73. Berdyaev (1908) (I) p. 126.
74. Ibid., p. 123.
75. Ibid.
76. Ibid., p. 126.
77. Ibid.
78. Ibid., p. 126.
79. Ibid., p. 138.
80. Berdyaev (1905) p. 148.
81. 'Zametki o meshchanstve' in Gorky (1949–55) vol. 23, pp. 341–67. The article was originally published in *Novaya zhizn'*, nos. 1, 4, 12 and 18 in October and November 1905.
82. Berdyaev (1905) p. 151.
83. Ibid., p. 148.
84. Berdyaev (1908) (I) p. 133.
85. Berdyaev (1905) p. 148.
86. Berdyaev (1928) p. 57.
87. Ibid., p. 45.
88. Berdyaev (1907) (II) pp. XXIX–XXX.
89. Ibid.
90. Ibid., p. XXXVII.
91. Ibid., p. XVIII.
92. Ibid., p. XLIX.
93. Even Dostoevsky, Solov'ev and others sympathetic to the Russian Orthodox Church criticised it as an agent of the autocracy. How could one respect a Church which depended on the policeman for its continued existence, asked Solov'ev?
94. The 1907 London Congress of the Russian Social Democratic Workers' Party was held in a socialist church in Whitechapel. Krupskaya recalled a visit which she and Lenin paid to a Social Democratic church in London in 1902 or 1903. N. Krupskaya, *Memories of Lenin* (London: 1970) p. 67.
95. His main work in this field was J. Dietzgen, *Die Religion der Sozialdemokratie* (Berlin: 1891).

96. See, for example, Andreev (1907) and Yushkevich (1907) (I). Lenin and Engels also thought highly of Dietzgen.
97. Lunacharsky (1908 and 1911). On page 9 of the first volume, he said that he had been interested in religion 'as artistic expression' since his childhood.
98. Lunacharsky (1908) vol. 1, p. 7.
99. Ibid., p. 18.
100. Ibid., p. 31.
101. Ibid., p. 40.
102. Ibid., p. 42.
103. Ibid., p. 33. Dietzgen's words were taken from his *Die Religion der Sozialdemokratie*, p. 1.
104. Ibid., p. 33.
105. Ibid., p. 36.
106. Ibid., p. 37.
107. Ibid., p. 46.
108. Ibid., p. 49.
109. Ibid., pp. 136–7.
110. Ibid., pp. 223–4.
111. Lunacharsky (1911) vol. 2, p. 59.
112. Ibid., pp. 61–3.
113. Ibid., p. 66.
114. Ibid., p. 101.
115. Ibid., p. 115.
116. Ibid., p. 121.
117. Ibid., p. 134.
118. Ibid., p. 138.
119. Ibid., p. 60.
120. Ibid., p. 178.
121. Ibid., p. 326.
122. Ibid.
123. Ibid., p. 371.
124. Ibid., pp. 371–2.
125. Ibid., p. 372.
126. Ibid., p. 385.
127. Gorky (1949–55) vol. 8, p. 323.
128. Ibid., p. 331.
129. Ibid., p. 332.
130. Ibid., p. 344.
131. Ibid., p. 378.
132. Ibid.
133. Letter to Chekhov, October 1900, in Gorky (1949–55) vol. 28, p. 135.
134. Gorky (1949–55) vol. 28, p. 323.
135. Berdyaev (1935) pp. 8–9.
136. Lunacharsky (1908) vol. 1, p. 7.
137. Ibid., p. 7.
138. Bazarov (1910) (II).
139. Bazarov (1909) (I) pp. 362–3.
140. Bazarov (1908) p. 239.
141. Lunacharsky (1908) vol. 1, p. 40.

142. Plekhanov (1909) no. 9, p. 184.
143. Ibid., no. 10, p. 188.
144. Gippius, *Sobranie stikhov* (1899–1903) (Moscow: 1904) p. VI.
145. Plekhanov (1909) no. 12, p. 197.
146. Lenin (1958–65) vol. 18, p. 10.
147. Ibid., vol. 48, p. 226.
148. Ibid., vol. 17, p. 415.
149. Ibid., p. 418.
150. Ibid., p. 422.
151. Ibid., p. 421.
152. Ibid., p. 417.
153. Ibid., p. 416.
154. Ibid.
155. Ibid., p. 419.
156. Ibid.

NOTES TO CHAPTER 4

1. See Machajski (1904–5 and 1906) and Lozinskii (1907). Lozinskii also edited a short-lived Makhaevist newspaper *Protiv techeniya (Against the Current)* in the spring of 1907.
2. See for example Gruppa peterburgskikh svyaschennikov, *K tserkovnomu soboru* (St Petersburg: 1906). This was an appeal by a number of priests from St Petersburg who wanted the projected Church council to be called rather more quickly than the hierarchy planned.
3. N. Struve, *Christians in Contemporary Russia* (London: 1967) p. 22.
4. Aivazov (1910).
5. Ibid., p. 35.
6. Bulatovich (1909) (III).
7. Ibid., no. 143.
8. Ibid., no. 154.
9. Ibid., no. 175.
10. Volkov (1909).
11. Volkov no. 250.
12. Sokolov, p. 6.
13. Ibid., pp. 7–8.
14. Sokolov was referring to H. Fielding-Hall, *The Soul of a People: the Burmese* (London: 1898).
15. Sokolov, p. 45.
16. Ibid., pp. 97–8.
17. Ibid., p. 133.
18. Ibid., pp. 209–11.
19. Ibid., p. 137.
20. Ibid., p. 303.
21. Ibid., p. 304.
22. Ibid., p. 307.
23. Ibid., p. 311.

24. Ibid.
25. Ibid., p. 457.
26. Ibid., p. 386.
27. Ibid.
28. Ibid., p. 387.
29. Ibid., p. 494.
30. Ibid., p. 497.
31. Ibid., p. 395.
32. Ibid., p. 486.
33. Ibid., p. 453.
34. Ibid., p. 488.
35. Ibid., p. 460.
36. Ibid., p. 527.
37. *Vekhi*, introduction.
38. Ibid., p. 22.
39. Ibid., pp. 191–2.
40. Ibid., p. 3.
41. Ibid.
42. Ibid., pp. 93–4 (Gershenzon).
43. Ibid., p. 193 (Frank).
44. S. H. Baron, *Plekhanov* (New York: 1963) p. 242.
45. *Vekhi*, p. 140.
46. Ibid., p. 129.
47. Ibid., p. 130.
48. Ibid., p. 119.
49. Ibid., pp. 122–4.
50. Ibid., p. 43.
51. Ibid., p. 44.
52. Ibid., p. 45.
53. Ibid., p. 46.
54. Ibid., p. 80.
55. Ibid., p. 196 (Frank).
56. Ibid., p. 43.
57. Ibid., p. 54.
58. Ibid., pp. 6–7.
59. Ibid., p. 4.
60. Ibid., p. 8.
61. Ibid.
62. Ibid., p. 9.
63. Ibid., p. 36.
64. Ibid., p. 29. He could have added his own name as a further example.
65. Ibid., p. 30.
66. Ibid., p. 29.
67. Ibid., p. 31.
68. Ibid., p. 192.
69. Ibid., p. 204.
70. Ibid., p. 189.
71. Ibid., p. 193.
72. Ibid., p. 4.

73. Ibid., p. 162 (Struve).
74. Ibid., pp. 5–6.
75. Ibid., p. 170.
76. M. Florinsky, *Russia* 1953, vol. 2, p. 1195.
77. Sir John Maynard in *Russia in Flux* (New York: 1962) p. 99, said that contemporary estimates of executions at this period were as high as 3500.
78. L. Kamenev, *Mezhdu dvumya revolyutsyami* (Moscow: 1923) p. 572.
79. This is an estimate by Trotsky given in L. Schapiro, *The Communist Party of the Soviet Union* (London: 1970) p. 103.
80. *Vekhi*, p. 25.
81. Ibid., pp. 176–7.
82. Ibid., p. 161.
83. Ibid., pp. 170–1.
84. Ibid., p. 174.
85. Ibid., p. 163.
86. Ibid., p. 1.
87. Ibid., pp. 70–1 (Gershenzon).
88. Ibid., p. 47 (Bulgakov).
89. Ibid., pp. 19–20.
90. Ibid., Introduction.
91. N. Valentinov (1969) pp. 204–8. See below, pp. 136–7.
92. *Vekhi*, p. 89.
93. Frank (1956) p. 82.
94. Ibid., pp. 82–3.
95. M. A. Beketova, *Aleksandr Blok* (Petrograd: 1922), pp. 93–4.
96. Gippius (1951) p. 80.
97. Merezhkovsky (1906).
98. Belyi (1909) (I) no. 3., p. 76.
99. Ibid.
100. Rozanov (1910).
101. Ibid., p. IV.
102. Ibid.
103. Ibid., p. 4.
104. Ibid., p. 345.
105. Ibid., p. 28.
106. Ibid., p. 146.
107. Ibid., p. 379.
108. Merezhkovsky (1907) (I) and 1907 (II).
109. Merezhkovsky (1906).
110. Merezhkovsky (1907) (I) pp. 260–2.
111. Ibid., p. 241.
112. Ibid., p. 104.
113. Ibid., p. 36.
114. Ibid., p. 283.
115. The version of this article which appeared in *Russkaya mysl'* was preceded by a warning from Struve and Kizevetter, the editors of the journal. 'The editors consider it their duty . . . to acquaint the readers of the journal with those deep, religious-philosophical currents which at the present time are maturing and taking shape more and more in Russia. The editors maintain a strictly

negative attitude towards the theological content and the mystical character of these tendencies.' *Russkaya mysl'* 1907, no. 2, p. 64.
116. Merezhkovsky (1907) (II), no. 2, p. 65.
117. Ibid., p. 66.
118. Ibid., p. 70.
119. Ibid., pp. 72–85.
120. Ibid., p. 81.
121. Ibid., p. 84.
122. Ibid., pp. 84–5.
123. Ibid., p. 85.
124. Ibid. (1906) p. 90.
125. Ibid. (1907) (I) pp. 232–3.
126. Ibid. (1907) (II) no. 2, p. 26.
127. Minsky (1909) (II) p. 110.
128. Ibid. (1909) (I) p. 238.
129. Ibid., p. 206.
130. Ibid., p. 238.
131. Ibid., p. 239.
132. See above, p. 32.
133. Minsky (1907) vol. 1, pp. 13–15.
134. Ibid., p. 19.
135. Ibid., p. 20.
136. Ibid., vol. 3, p. 18.
137. Ibid., vol. 2, pp. 43–4.
138. Ibid., vol. 3, p. 24.
139. Ibid., p. 25.
140. Minsky (1909) (I) p. 72.
141. Ibid.
142. Ibid., pp. 72–3.
143. Ibid. (1907) vol. 3, p. 27.
144. Reprinted in Minsky (1909) (I) pp. 193–9. Minsky came to be in this position because he had been given permission to edit a journal. Lenin persuaded him to surrender effective control of it to the Bolsheviks, while remaining as editor. The paper was closed down by the government in December after 27 issues had been published. *Russkaya periodicheskaya pechat' (1895 – Oktyabr' 1917) Spravochnik* (Moscow: 1957) pp. 76–9.
145. Minsky (1909) (I) p. 199.
146. Ibid. (1909) (II).
147. Block (1908) p. 57.
148. Ibid., p. 58.
149. Ibid., p. 59.
150. Blok (1971) p. 260.
151. Ibid. (1907) p. 92.
152. See above, p. 121.
153. M. A. Beketova, *Aleksandr Blok i ego mat': vospominaniya i zametki* (Leningrad-Moscow: 1925), p. 145.
154. Ibid., p. 147.
155. M. A. Beketova, *Aleksandr Blok*, Petersburg 1922, p. 97.
156. Blok (1960–3) vol. 8, p. 141.

157. Ibid., vol. 2, pp. 172–4.
158. Ibid., vol. 8, p. 144.
159. Ibid., p. 269.
160. Blok (1971) p. 264.
161. Ibid., p. 268.
162. Ibid. (1960–63) vol. 8, p. 281.
163. Ibid., p. 289.
164. Valentinov (1969) pp. 205–8.
165. Belyi (1909) (II).
166. Ibid., p. 67.
167. Ibid., p. 66.
168. Ibid., p. 68.
169. Ibid., p. 67.
170. Ibid., p. 68.
171. Ibid., p. 66.
172. Ibid.
173. Ibid.
174. Merezhkovsky (1906) p. 90.
175. V. N. Il'in in *Vestnik Russkogo studencheskogo Khristianskogo dvizheniya* 1971, nos.
   3–4, p. 63.

NOTES TO CHAPTER 5

1. *Intelligentsiya v Rossii*, p. iv.
2. Ibid., p. 238.
3. Ibid., p. 18.
4. Ivanov-Razumnik (1907) vol. 1. pp. 25–6.
5. Ibid., p. 254.
6. Ibid., (1910) (I) p. 200.
7. Friche (1910).
8. *Literaturny raspad*, vol. 1, p. 41.
9. *Intelligentsiya v Rossii*, p. 15.
10. Nikolaev (1906) pp. 12–13.
11. Ibid., p. 13.
12. Petrov (1910).
13. *Intelligentsiya v Rossii*, p. 94.
14. Ibid., pp. 13–14.
15. Ibid., p. 249.
16. Ivanov-Razumnik (1910) (I) p. 200.
17. Zasulich (1921). Originally published in *Sotsial demokrat*, no. 1, 1890 and reprinted as a pamphlet in November 1906.
18. Gorky, letter to Pyatnitsky 7–11 (20–24) January 1902. In Gorky (1949–55) vol. 28, pp. 223–7.
19. Izgoev (1904).
20. Tugan-Baranovsky (1904).
21. Vorovsky, 'Predstavlyaet-li intelligentsiya obshchestvennyi klass' reprinted in Vorovsky (1923).
22. Trotsky (1906) pp. 69–70.

23. Ibid., p. 70.
24. See Section A of bibliography for full references.
25. Aksel'rod, 'Zarozhdenie u nas burzhuaznoi demokratii kak samostoyatel'noi revoliutsionnoi sily' in Aksel'rod (1907) pp. 1–32. This article was first published in 1902.
26. Ibid., pp. 19–20.
27. Martov (1925) pp. 117–9.
28. Ibid., p. 118.
29. Lenin (1958–65) vol. 19, p. 168.
30. Ibid., p. 175.
31. Ibid., vol. 22, pp. 92–3. In a letter to Gorky of August 1912 Lenin referred to the argument between the *vekhovtsy* and the Kadets as a 'quasi-polemic', Ibid., vol. 48, p. 80.
32. Martov (1925) pp. 118–19.
33. For references to these publications see bibliography. The appendix illustrates the chronological relationship between these works.
34. Gorky, letter to Pyatnitsky of 7–11 (20–24) January 1902, in Gorky (1949–55) vol. 28, p. 225.
35. Ibid.
36. See N. N. Sukhanov, *The Russian Revolution 1917*, vol..1 (New York: 1962) pp. 208–9. Sukhanov gives the text of an appeal drawn up by Gorky and other artists of Petrograd which Gorky brought to the soviet for publication. Part of it read, 'Citizens! . . . take care of the pictures, the statues, the buildings – they are the embodiment of the spiritual power of yourselves and your forefathers. Art is the beauty which talented people were able to create even under despotic oppression and which bears witness to the power and beauty of the human soul.'
37. *Literaturnyi raspad*, vol. 2., p. 159.
38. Vorovsky (1908).
39. Vorovsky defended the bourgeoisie proper in this article, because, he said, 'it is possible to be bourgeois and progressive at one and the same time' whereas these latter day descendants of the *raznochintsy* were only reactionary. Ibid.
40. See bibliography for names of contributors.
41. Byalik (1972), p. 417.
42. *Literaturnyi raspad*, vol. 1, p. 311.
43. See above, pp. 85–8.
44. *Literaturnyi raspad*, vol. 1.
45. Ibid., p. 9.
46. Ibid., p. 296.
47. Ibid., vol. 2 p. 66.
48. Ibid., p. 39.
49. Ibid., vol. 1 p. 6.
50. Ibid., p. 8.
51. Ibid., p. 9.
52. Ibid., pp. 10–11.
53. Ibid., pp. 109–10.
54. Ibid., vol. 2 pp. 264–6.
55. Ibid., p. 276.
56. Ibid., p. 277.

57. Ibid., p. 279.
58. *Ocherki filosofii kollektivizma*, p. 5.
59. Ibid., p. 6.
60. Ivanov-Razumnik (1907) vol. 1, p. XV.
61. Ibid., p. 2.
62. Ibid., vol. 2 p. 432.
63. Ibid., p. 430.
64. Ibid., pp. 433–4.
65. Ibid., pp. 443–4.
66. Ibid., p. 468.
67. Ibid., p. 493.
68. *Russkoe bogatstvo* 1907, no. 1, pp. 246–66, and no. 2, 135–69.
69. Ivanov-Razumnik (1910) (II) p. 44.
70. Ibid., pp. 45–6.
71. Ibid., 1910 (I) p. 159.
72. Ibid., p. 145.
73. Ibid., pp. 79–80.

NOTES TO CHAPTER 6

1. *Vekhi*, p. 18.
2. *Alger-Republic* 25 June 1939, p. 3.
3. *Dve press-Konferentsii. K sborniku Iz pod glyb* (Paris: 1975) p. 65.
4. *Kontinent: The Alternative Voice of Russia and Eastern Europe* (London: Coronet Books 1976).
5. Ibid., p. 8.
6. M. Browne (ed.), *Ferment in the Ukraine* (London: 1971) p. 129.
7. G. Sanders (ed.), *Samizdat: Voices of the Soviet Opposition* (New York: 1974) p. 271.
8. Ibid., p. 404.
9. See, for example, V. Chornovil, *The Chornovil Papers* (Toronto: 1968) p. 13.
10. R. Medvedev, *On Socialist Democracy*, 2nd ed. (London: 1977) pp. 32–3.
11. *Veche* no. 2 19 May 1971, quoted in *Religion in Communist Lands* vol. 4 no. 3. Autumn 1976, p. 27.
12. P. Reddaway (ed.), *Uncensored Russia* (London: 1972) p. 431.
13. See D. Pospielovsky 'The Resurgence of Russian Nationalism in Samizdat', *Survey* no. 86 Winter 1973, p. 63.
14. A. Solzhenitsyn, *From Under the Rubble*, 2nd ed. (London: 1976) p. 249.
15. A. Solzhenitsyn, *Letter to Soviet Leaders* (London: 1974) p. 43.
16. Ibid., p.46.
17. L. Labedz (ed.), *Solzhenitsyn: A Documentary Record*, 2nd ed. (Harmondsworth: 1974) p. 322.
18. Ibid., pp. 375–99.
19. Ibid., pp. 296–8.
20. *Daily Express* 23 March 1976, p. 8.
21. *Letter to Soviet Leaders*, p. 44.
22. Labedz, pp. 307–8.
23. *From Under the Rubble*, p. 255.

24. See Ibid., p. 229-78.
25. J. Dunlop, R. Haugh, A. Klimoff (eds.), *Aleksandr Solzhenitsyn: Critical Essays and Documentary Materials*, 2nd ed., (New York and London: 1975) p. 468.
26. Ibid., p. 470-1.
27. See footnote 10 above.
28. Dunlop, p. 468, and *From Under the Rubble* p. 12.
29. R. Medvedev (ed.), *The Samizdat Register* (London: 1977) p. 244.
30. Ibid., p. 255.
31. Ibid., p. 245.
32. See, for example, articles on 'Vekhovstvo' in *Filosofskaya entsiklopediya* (Moscow: 1960) vol. 1, p. 248, and on '*Vekhi*' in *Sovetskaya istoricheskaya entsiklopediya* (Moscow: 1963) vol. 3, p. 409.
33. Solov'ev, 1969.
34. *Literaturnaya gazeta*, 1970, no. 8, p. 5.
35. Yakovlev, pp. 4-5.
36. M. Gus, '"Vekhi" reaktsionnoi ideologii', *Voprosy literatury* 1977, p. 141.
37. *From Under the Rubble*, pp. 229-30.

NOTES TO CONCLUSION

1. L. Kolakowski, *Positivist Philosophy* (London: 1972) pp. 9-10.
2. K. Marx, *The Civil War in France*, section 3, in Marx and Engels, *Selected Works* (Moscow and New York: 1968) p. 295.

Bibliography

Dates of publication appear at the end of each item in order to facilitate cross reference to footnotes. Journals and newspapers included in Section A were published throughout the period from 1900–12 unless otherwise stated.

A. WORKS IN RUSSIAN.

A., (Meshchersky D., Kn.), 'Dnevniki', Grazhdanin, nos. 51 & 52 (1909).

A. B., 'Kriticheskie zametki. Problemy idealizma. Sbornik statei', Mir Bozhii, no. 2, pp. 1–12 (1903).

Aikhenval'd Yu. I., 'Obzor knig. Problemy idealizma', Voprosy filosofii i psikhologii, no. 2, pp. 333–56 (1903).

Aivazov I. G., Religioznoe obnovlenie nashikh dnei (Novoputeitsy, 'Vekhi'), 3rd ed. (Moscow: 1910).

Aksel'rod L., (Ortodoks), Filosofskie ocherki. Otvet filosofskim kritikam istoricheskogo materializma (Petersburg: 1906).

——, O 'Problemakh idealizma' (Odessa: 1905).

Aksel'rod P., Bor'ba sotsialisticheskikh i burzhuaznykh tendentsii v russkom revolyutsionnom dvizhenii, 2nd ed. (Petersburg: 1907).

Aleksandrovich Yu., 'Novyi pokhod protiv obshchestvennosti', Rul', 31 March 1909.

Andreev N., 'Dialekticheskii materializm i filosofiya Iosifa Ditzgena', Sovremennyi mir, no. 11, pp. 1–36 (1907).

Antony of Volhynia, Archbishop, 'Otkrytoe pis'mo avtoram sbornika Vekhi', Slovo, no. 791, 10 May 1909 (I).

——, 'Otvetnoe pis'mo arkhiepiskopa Antoniya N. A. Berdyaevu o Vekhakh, o Tserkvi i dukhovenstve', Kolokol, nos. 1045 & 1049, 3 and 4 September, 1909 (II).

A. P., 'Intelligentsiya. Lektsiya K. I. Arabazhina', Russkoe slovo, 4 February 1910.

Apollon (Petersburg) (from October 1909).

Arsen'ev K., 'Prizyv k pokayaniyu', *Vestnik Evropy*, no. 5, pp. 299–310 (1909).

Artsybashev M., *Sanin* (Petersburg: 1906).

Balakina I. F., 'O tak nazyvaemom russkom eksistentsializme', *Vestnik Moskovskogo Universiteta*, 18, Series VII, ekonomika, filosofiya, no. 6, pp. 88–96 (Moscow: November–December 1963).

Bazarov V., *Anarkhicheskii kommunizm i marksizm* (Petersburg: 1906).

——, 'Bogoiskatel'stvo i bogostroitel'stvo', *Vershiny, Literaturno-kriticheskii i filosofsko–publitsisticheskii sbornik*, pp. 331–64 (Petersburg: 1909) (I).

——, 'Khristiane Tret'ego Zaveta i stroiteli bashni vavilonskoi', *Na dva fronta*, pp. 167–211 (Petersburg: 1910) (I).

——, 'Lichnost' i lyubov' v svete "novogo religioznogo soznaniya"', *Literaturnyi raspad. Kriticheskii sbornik*, vol. 1, pp. 221–40 (Petersburg: 1908).

——, *Na dva fronta* (Petersburg: 1910) (II).

——, 'O tom pochemu vazhnye veshchi kazhutsya inogda pustyakami', *Nash zarya*, no. 4, pp. 80–9 (1910) (III).

Bebel' A., (Bebel, A.) *Intelligentsiya i sotsializm* (Petersburg: 1906).

Belyi A., 'Nastoyashchee i budushchee russkoi literatury', *Vesy*, no. 2, pp. 59–68, and no. 3, pp. 71–82 (1909) (I).

——, 'Pravda o russkoi intelligentsii. Po povodu sbornika *Vekhi*', *Vesy*, no. 5, pp. 65–8 (1909) (II).

—— 'Simvolizm i russkoe iskusstvo', *Vesy*, no. 10, pp. 38–48 (1908).

Benua A., 'V ozhidanii gimna Apollonu', *Apollon*, no. 1, pp. 5–11 (1909).

Beranzhe A., (Beranger H.), *Intelligentnyi proletariat vo frantsii*, (Petersburg: 1902).

Berdyaev, N. A., 'Bor'ba za idealizm', *Mir Bozhii*, no. 6, pp. 1–26 (1901) (I).

—— 'Dekadentstvo i misticheskii realizm', *Russkaya mysl'*, no. 6, pp. 114–23 (1907) (I).

—— *Dukhovnyi krizis intelligentsii. Stat'i po obshchestvennoi i religioznoi psikhologii (1907–09g)* (Petersburg: 1910).

—— 'K'istorii i psikhologii russkogo marksizma', *Polyarnaya zvezda*, no. 10, pp. 678–86 (1906).

—— 'K psikhologii revolyutsii', *Russkaya mysl'*, no. 7, pp. 122–38 (1908) (I).

—— 'Kritika istoricheskogo materializma', *Mir Bozhii*, no. 10 (1903).

—— *Novoe religioznoe soznanie i obshchestvennost* (Petersburg: 1907) (II).

—— 'O kharakhtere russkoi religioznoi mysli XIX-go v.', *Sovremennye zapiski* (1930).

—— 'Otkrytoe pis'mo arkhiepiskopu Antoniyu', *Moskovskii ezhenedel'nik*, no. 32, 15 August 1909.

—— 'O novom russkom idealizme' *Voprosy filosofii i psikhologii*, no. 75, pp. 683–725 (November–December 1904).

—— 'Problemy novogo religioznogo soznaniya', *Russkaya mysl'*, no. 1, pp. 33–55 (1908) (II).

—— 'Revolyutsiya i kul'tura', *Polyarnaya zvezda*, no. 2, pp. 146–55 (1905).

—— 'Russkaya religioznaya mysl' i revolyutsiya', *Versty*, no. 3, pp. 40–62 (1928).

—— 'Russkii dukhovnyi renessans nachala XX-go v. i zhurnal *Put'* (k desyatiletiyu *Puti*)', *Put'*, no. 49, pp. 3–23 (Paris: 1935).

—— *Samopoznanie. Opyt filosofskoi avtobiografii* (Paris: 1949).

—— *Sub"ektivizm i individualizm v obshchestvennoi filosofii, Kriticheskii etyud o N. K. Mikhailovskom. S predisloviem Petra Struve* (Petersburg: 1901) (II).

—— *Sub specie aeternitatis. Opyty filosofskye, sotsial'nye i literaturnye (1900–1906gg)* (Petersburg: 1907) (III).

Berman Ya. A., *Dialektika v svete sovremennoi teorii poznaniya* (Petersburg: 1907).

'Beseda ob intelligentsii', *Russkie vedomosti*, 4 February 1910.

B—ich A. (Butkevich), *Ortodoksal'nyi marksizm i pravoslavie. Ocherk partiinoi psikhologii* (Moscow: 1907).

Blok A. A., 'Literaturnye itogi 1907 goda', *Zolotoe runo*, nos. 11–12, pp. 90–8 (1907).

—— 'Narod i Intelligentsiya', *Sobranie sochinenii v shesti tomakh*, vol. 5, pp. 259–68 (Moscow: 1971).

—— 'O sovremennom sostoyanii russkogo simvolizma. Po povodu doklada V. I. Ivanova', *Apollon*, no. 8, pp. 21–30 (1910).

—— *Rossiya i intelligentsiya* (Berlin: 1920).

—— *Sobranie sochinenii v vos'mi tomakh* (Moscow–Leningrad: 1960–3).

—— 'Tri voprosa', *Zolotoe runo*, no. 2, pp. 55–9 (1908).

Boborykin P., 'Oblichiteli intelligentsii (otryvok iz zlobodnevnogo dialoga)', *Russkoe slovo* (17 April 1909).

Boborykin P., 'Podgnivshiya Vekhi', *Russkoe slovo* (17 May 1909).
Bogdanov A. A., 'Avtoritarnoe myshlenie', *Iz psikhologii obshchestva. (Stat'i 1901–04gg)* pp. 95–156 (Petersburg: 1904) (I).
—— *Empiriomonizm. Stat'i po filosofii,* 3 vols. 2nd ed. (Petersburg: 1905) (I).
—— 'Ideal poznaniya (Empiriokrititsizm i empiriomonizm)', *Voprosy filosofii i psikhologii,* no. 2, pp. 186–234 (1903) (I).
—— *Iz psikhologii obshchestva. Stat'i 1901–04* (Petersburg: 1904)(II).
—— *Novyi mir. Stat'i 1904–05g* (Moscow: 1905) (II).
—— *Padenie velikogo fetishizma. Sovremennyi krizis ideologii* (Moscow: 1910) (I).
—— 'Proklyatye voprosy filosofii', *Pravda,* no. 12 (1904) (III).
—— *Revolyutsiya i filosofiya* (Petersburg: 1906).
—— *Vera i nauka. O knige V. Il'ina 'Materializm i empiriokrititsizm'* (Moscow: 1910) (II).
—— 'Zhizn' i psikhika. Empiriomonoizm v uchenii o zhizni', *Voprosy filosofii i psikhologii,* no. 4, pp. 682–708, and no. 5, pp. 822–66 (1903) (II).
Borovoi A. A., *Obshchestvennye idealy sovremennogo chelovechestva. Liberalizm, sotsializm, anarkhizm* (Moscow: 1906).
—— *Revolyutsionnoe mirosozertsanie* (Moscow: 1907).
Botsyanovskii V. F., *Bogoiskateli* (Petersburg–Moscow: 1911).
—— 'Nechto o truslivom intelligente', *Novaya rus',* 8 May 1909.
Bryusov V., 'O "rechi rabskoi" v zashchitu poezii', *Apollon,* no. 9, pp. 31–5 (1910).
Bulatovich D., 'Ubelennye sedinami', *Russkoe znamya,* 21 October 1909 (I).
—— '*Vekhi* ili dymayashchiyasya goloveshki. Kriticheskii razbor sbornika *Vekhi*', *Russkoe znamya,* nos. 143, 145, 149, 154, 157, 165, 169, 171 & 175, 1909 (III).
—— 'Vekhi i Novovremenskii vestovoi', *Russkoe znamya,* 5 May 1909 (II).
Bulgakov S., 'Apokaliptika i sotsializm', *Russkaya mysl',* nos. 6 & 7 (reprinted in *Dva grada,* vol. 2) pp. 51–127, 1910.
—— *Avtobiograficheskie zametki* (Paris: 1946).
—— *'Dva grada. Issledovaniya o prirode obshchestvennykh idealov* (Moscow: 1911).
—— 'Idealizm i obshchestvennye programmy', *Novyi put',* no. 10, pp. 260–77, no. 11, pp. 342–60; and no. 12, pp. 302–21, 1904.
—— *Intelligentsiya i religiya. O protivorechivosti sovremennogo bezreligioznogo mirovozzreniya* (Moscow: 1908).

—— 'Neotlozhnaya zadacha', *Voprosy zhizni*, pp. 332–60, September 1905.

—— *Ot marksizma k idealizmu. Sbornik statei 1896–1903* (Petersburg: 1903).

—— 'Religiya i politika', *Polyarnaya zvezda*, no. 13, pp. 118–27, 1906.

Bunin Yu., *'Vekhi'*, *Vestnik vospitaniya*, no. 10, pp. 1–26 (1909).

Butkevich, See B—ich A.

Byalik B. A., (ed.) *Russkaya literatura kontsa XIX-go nachale XX-go v., 1908–1917* (Moscow: 1972).

Chermenskii E. D., *Burzhuaziya i tsarizm v pervoi russkoi revolyutsii*, 2nd ed. (Moscow: 1970).

Chernov V. (Ya. Vechev, pseud.), 'Dela i dni. "Umerennye" i "krainie"', *Zavety*, no. 1, pp. 117–51 (1912).

—— 'Sub"ektivnyi metod v sotsiologii', *Russkoe bogatstvo*, vols. 7–12 (1901).

Chernyi L., *Novoe napravlenie v anarkhizme. Assotsiatsionnyi anarkhizm* (Moscow: 1907).

Chulkov G., 'Ob utverzhdenii lichnosti', *Fakely*, vol. 2, pp. 20–1 (Petersburg: 1907).

—— and Ivanov V., *O misticheskom anarkhizme* (Petersburg: 1906).

Dan D., 'Rukovodstvo i kurovodstvo', *Vozrozhdenie*, nos. 9–12, pp. 79–90 (Moscow: 1909).

Davydov I., *Istoricheskii materializm i kriticheskaya filosofiya* (Petersburg: 1905).

'Disput o russkoi intelligentsii', *Russkoe slovo*, 3 November 1909.

Ellis (Kobylinsky L. L.), 'Itogi simvolizma', *Vesy*, no. 7, pp. 55–74 (1909).

—— *Russkie simvolisty* (Moscow: 1910).

Erman L. K., *Intelligentsiya v pervoi russkoi revolyutsii* (Moscow: 1966).

Fakely, vol. 1 (1906); vol. 2 (1907); vol. 3 (1908) (Petersburg). (Contributors include: G. Chulkov, I. Davydov, A. Meier, L. Shestov, A. Vetrov, S. Gorodetsky, F. Sologub, V. Bruysov, A. Blok, A. Belyi, I. Bunin, Vyacheslav Ivanov, L. Andreev).

Filevskii, Ioann, svyashch, 'Povorot v nashei intelligentsii', *Tserkovnyi vestnik*, no. 26, pp. 804–5; no. 29, pp. 899–900; no. 31, pp. 969–70; and no. 32, pp. 994–6 (1909).

Filosofov D., 'Druz'ya ili vragi? Bogoiskateli i bogostroiteli', *Russkaya mysl'.*, no. 8, pp. 120–47 (1909).

—— *Slova i zhizn'. Literaturnye spory noveishego vremeni 1901–1908* (II) (Petersburg: 1909).

Filosofov D., 'Spor vokrug *Vekh*', *Russkoe slovo*, 17 May 1909.

Frank S. L., *Biografiya Struve* (New York: 1956).

—— 'D. M. Merezhkovskii o *Vekhakh*', *Slovo*, 28 April 1909.

—— *Filosofiya i zhizn'. Etyudy i nabroski po filosofii kul'tury* (I) (Petersburg: 1910).

—— 'Filosofskie otkliki. Filosofskaya rasprya v marksizme', *Russkaya mysl'*, no. 4, pp. 141–5 (1910) (II).

—— 'Intelligentsiya i osvoboditel'noe dvizhenie', *Polyarnaya zvezda*, no. 9, pp. 643–55 (1906).

—— 'Kul'tura i religiya. Po povodu stat'i o *Vekhakh* S. V. Lur'e', *Russkaya mysl'*, no. 7, pp. 147–61 (1909).

—— 'Politika i idei. O programme *Polyarnoi zvezdy*', *Polyarnaya zvezda*, no. 1, pp. 18–31 (1905).

—— '*Vekhi* i ikh kritiki', *Slovo*, 1 April 1909.

Friche V. M., *Ot Chernyshevskogo k 'Vekham'* (Moscow: 1910).

Gippius Z., *Dmitrii Merezhkovskii* (Paris: 1951).

—— (Krainii A., pseud.), 'Dobryi khaos', *Obrazovanie*, no. 7, pp. 12–18.

—— *Literaturnyi dnevnik 1899–1908* (Petersburg: 1909).

Gorev B. I., 'Apoliticheskie i antiparlamentskie gruppy—anarkhisty, maksimalisty, makhaevtsy', in L. Martov, A. Maslov & A. Potresov (eds.), vol. 3, pp. 473–534.

Gorky, M., *Ispoved'* (Petersburg: 1907).

—— 'Razrushenie lichnosti', *Ocherki filosofii kollektivizma* (Petersburg: 1909).

—— *Sobranie sochinenii v tridtsati tomakh* (Moscow: 1949–55).

Gorn, V., Mech V., Cherevanin N., *Bor'ba obshchestvennkh sil v russkoi revolyutsii* (Moscow: 1907).

Gornyi S., 'Istoriya odnogo puteshestviya. Posvyashchaetsya P. B. Struve', *Russkoe slovo*, 7 May 1909.

Grazhdanin, Petersburg.

Gredeskul N., *Marksizm i idealizm* (Kharkov: 1905).

Groman V., 'O ponimanii sovremennogo momenta', *Voprosy momenta. Sbornik statei* (Moscow: 1906).

—— See also Gorn V.

Grosman I., 'Makhaevtsy sverkhu i makhaevtsy snizu', *Kievskie vesti*, 28 May 1909.

Grot, N. Ya., *Filosofiya i ee obshchie zadachi. Sbornik statei* (Petersburg: 1904).

Idealist, 'Tsusima literaturnogo aferizma i fariseistva', *Novyi vecher*, 15 October, 1909.

Intelligent, 'A sud'i kto? Pis'mo k sovremennym intelligentam', *Russkoe znamya*, 16 July 1909.

'Intelligentsiya i natsionalizm', *Russkie vedemosti*, 25 April 1909.

Intelligentsiya v Rossii. *Sbornik statei* (Petersburg: 1910). (Contributors: K. K. Arsen'év, N. A. Gredeskul, M. M. Kovalevsky, D. N. Ovsyaniko-Kulikovsky, P. Milyukov, I. I. Petrunkevich, M. I. Tugan-Baranovsky, M. A. Slavinsky).

Iordanskii N., 'Bezplodnyi pessimizm', *Sovremennyi mir*, no. 11, pp. 137–42 (1909) (I).

—— 'Krizis intelligentsii', *Sovremennyi mir*, no. 2, pp. 84–96 (1908).

—— 'Tvortsy novogo shuma', *Sovremennyi mir*, no. 5, pp. 128–37 (1909) (II).

—— *Zemskii liberalizm*, 2nd ed. (Petersburg: 1906).

I. P., 'O nashei intelligentsii', *Tifliskii listok*, 26 April 1909.

Isaev A., *Individual'nost' i sotsializm* (Petersburg: 1907).

Ivanov, Vyacheslav, 'Zavety simvolizma', *Apollon*, no. 8, pp. 5–20 (1910).

—— 'Ideya nepriyatie mira i misticheskii anarkhizm. Vstupitel'naya stat'ya', in Chulkov and Ivanov, pp. 5–26.

—— 'Ty esi', *Zolotoe runo*, nos. 7–9, pp. 100–2 (1907).

Ivanov-Razumnik R. V., *Istoriya russkoi obshchestvennoi mysli*, 2 vols. (Petersburg: 1907).

—— *Ob intelligentsii. Chto takoe makhaevshchina? Kayushchiesya raznochintsy*, 2nd ed. (Petersburg: 1910) (I).

—— *Literatura i obshchestvennost'*. *Sbornik statei* (Petersburg: 1910) (II).

Iz glubiny. *Sbornik statei o russkoi revolyutsii* (Moscow–Petrograd: 1918); 2nd ed. (Paris: 1967). (Contributors: S. A. Askol'dov, N. Berdyaev, S. Bulgakov, V. Ivanov, A. S. Izgoev, S. A. Kotlyarevskii, V. Murav'ev, P. Novgorodtsev, I. Pokrovskii, P. Struve, S. L. Frank).

Izgoev A. S., 'Intelligentsiya kak sotsial'naya gruppa', *Obrazovanie*, no. 1, pp. 72–94 (1904).

—— 'Na perevale. Makhomakhiya v lagere marksistov', *Russkaya mysl'*, no. 2, pp. 106–14 (1910) (I).

—— 'Na perevale. *Vekhist* sredi marksistov', *Russkaya mysl'*, no. 8, pp. 63–72 (1910) (II).

—— *Russkoe obshchestvo i revolyutsiya*. *Sbornik statei* (Moscow: 1910) (III).

—— 'Sol' zemli', *Moskovskii ezhenedel'nik*, no. 46, 21 November 1909.

Izgoev A. S., '*Vekhi i Smena vekh*', *Russkaya mysl'*, no. 3, pp. 176–8 (Prague: 1922).

Iz istorii noveishei russkoi literatury (Moscow: 1910). (Contributors: P. Orlovsky (V. V. Vorovsky), V. Friche, V. Bazarov, V. Shulyatikov).

Iz-pod glyb. Sbornik statei (Moscow: 1974). (Contributors: M. S. Agursky, E. V. Barabanov, B. M. Borisov, A. B., F. Korsakov, A. I. Solzhenitsyn, I. R. Shafarevich).

Kara-Murza P., 'Bor'ba idei', *Kaspii*, 12 April 1909.

—— 'Kniga o gor'koi pravde', *Kaspii*, 5 July 1909.

—— '*Kritiki Vekh*', *Kaspii*, 12 July 1909.

Kaspii, Baku.

Kautsky K., *Intelligentsiya i proletariat* (Odessa: 1905).

—— *Intelligentsiya i sotsial-demokratiya* (Petersburg: 1906).

Khristianka, *Usloviya vozrozhdeniya Rossii. Ovtet avtoram knigi 'Vekhi'* (Moscow: 1909).

Kievskaya mysl' (from 1906) (Kiev).

Kievskie vesti (Kiev).

Kizevetter A., *Na rubezhe dvukh stoletii* (Prague: 1929).

—— 'O sbornike *Vekhi*', *Russkaya mysl'*, no. 5, pp. 127–37 (1909).

—— 'Postscriptum k stat'e gospodina Berdyaeva', *Russkaya mysl'*, no. 7, pp. 139–44 (1908).

Korobka N., '*Vekhi* na puti k reaktsionnomu kvietizmu', *Pravda zhizni*, 20 April 1909.

Kovalevsky M., ' "Grekhi" intelligentsii', *Zaprosy zhizni*, no. 1, 18, pp. 3–10, October 1909.

Krainii A.: See under Gippius Z.

Krylenko I., 'Istoricheskii moment. Etyud po istorii russkoi intelligentsii', *Obrazovanie*, no. 7, pp. 243–62 and no. 8, pp. 119–36 (1906).

Kuda my idem? Nastoyashchee i budushchee russkoi intelligentsii, literatury, teatra i iskusstv (Moscow: 1910). (Contributors include: A. A. Kizevetter, M. M. Kovalevsky, A. Belyi, N. Valentinov, Archbishop Antony of Volhynia, A. S. Izgoev, V. Meierkhol'd, A. Remizov, D. Filosofov, P. Novgorodtsev).

Lafarg P. (Lafargue P.), *Sotsializm i intelligentsiya* (Odessa: 1906).

Lagardelle H., See Lyagardell' G.

Lenin, V. I., *Materializm i empiriokrititsizm. Kriticheskie zametki ob odnoi reaktsionnoi filosofii* (Moscow: 1909) (in Lenin 1958–65).

—— *Polnoe sobranie sochinenii,* 55 vols., 5th ed. (Moscow: 1958–65).

Literaturnyi raspad. Kriticheskii sbornik, vol. 1 (Petersburg: 1908). (Contributors: Yu Steklov, P. Yushkevich, St. Ivanovich, A. Lunacharsky, L. Voitolovsky, V. Bazarov, M. Morozov, M. Gorky, L. Trotsky).

—— Vol. 2 (Petersburg: 1909). (Contributors: V. Bazarov, L. Voitolovsky, A. Lunacharsky, M. Morozov, P. Orlovsky, Yu. M. Steklov, V. Friche, V. Shulyatikov, P. Yushkevich, L. Kamenev).

L—n N., '*Vekhi*', *Khar'kovskie vedemosti,* 15 May 1909.

Louis P.: See Lui P.

Lozinskii E. Yu., *Chto zhe takoe, nakonets, intelligentsiya* (Petersburg: 1907).

—— 'Neo-kantianskoe techenie v marksizme. K. istorii sovremennykh eticheskikh iskanii', *Zhizn'*, no. 12, pp. 132–54 (1900).

Lui P. (Louis P.), *Intelligentsiya i sotsializm. Vseobshchaya stachka i sotsializm* (Petersburg: 1906).

Lunacharsky A., 'Budushchee religii', *Obrazovanie,* no. 10, pp. 1–25, and no. 11, pp. 30–67 (1907).

—— '*O Problemakh idealizma*', *Etyudy kriticheskie i polemicheskie,* pp. 214–55 (Moscow: 1905).

—— *Religiya i sotsializm,* 2 vols, vol. 1 (Petersburg: 1908); vol. 2. (Petersburg: 1911).

Lur'e S., 'O sbornike *Vekhi*', *Russkaya mysl'*, no. 5, pp. 137–46 (1909) (I).

—— 'Religioznye iskaniya v sovremennoi literature', *Russkaya mysl'*, no. 10, pp. 44–67 (1909) (II).

—— 'Zhizn' i idei. Otvet S. L. Franku', *Russkaya mysl'*, no. 7, pp. 162–9 (1909) (III).

'L'vov-Rogachevsky V., 'Byt' ili ne byt' russkomu simvolizmu?', *Sovremennyi mir,* no. 10, pp. 76–86 (1910).

—— 'Novaya vera', *Obrazovanie,* no. 7, pp. 19–38 (1908).

Lyagardell' G. (Lagardelle H.), *Intelligentsiya i sindikalizm* (Petersburg: 1906).

Machajski J. W. (Vol'skii A., pseud.), *Burzhuaznaya revolyutsiya i rabochee delo* (Petersburg: 1906).

—— *Umstvennyi rabochii,* 3 vols. (Geneva: 1904–5).

Malinovskii I., 'Nachal'naya stranitsa iz istorii russkoi intelligentsii', *Sibirskaya zhizn'*, nos. 254, 255 & 256 (1909).

Markelov G., 'Idealizm i marksizm', *Mir Bozhii,* no. 5 (1902).

Martov L., *Obshchestvennye i umstvennye techeniya v Rossii 1870–1905*, (Leningrad—Moscow: 1925).

—— Potresov A. N., and Maslov P. P., (eds.), *Obshchestvennoe dvizhenie v Rossii v nachale XX-go v.*, 4 vols (Petersburg: 1909–14).

Maslin A. N., 'Kritika G. B. Plekhanovym idealizma i zashchita im idei marksistskoi filosofii v trudakh 1904–1913', in Plekhanov, vol. 3 (1957).

Massarik T. (Masaryk T.), *Filosofskie i sotsiologicheskie osnovaniya marksizma* (Moscow: 1900).

Mauernbrekher M. (Mauernbrecher M.), *Intelligentsiya i sotsialdemokratiya* (Petersburg: 1906).

Mech V., *Liberal'naya i demokraticheskaya burzhuaziya* (Moscow: 1907).

Meier A., *Religiya i kul'tura. Po povodu sovremennykh religioznykh iskanii* (Petersburg: 1909).

Meilakh B., *Lenin i problemy russkoi literatury kontsa XIX-go-nachala XX-go v.*, 2nd ed. (Moscow – Leningrad: 1951).

Merezhkovsky D. S., *Polnoe sobranie sochinenii*, vols. 10 & 11 (Petersburg – Moscow: 1911–13).

—— 'Revolyutsiya i religiya', *Russkaya mysl'*, no. 2, pp. 64–85, and no. 3, pp. 17–34 (1907) (II).

—— 'Sem' smirennikh', *Rech'*, 9 May 1909.

—— 'Vse protiv vsekh', *Zolotoe runo*, no. 1, pp. 90–96 (1906).

—— 1907 (I), see Section B of bibliography.

Milyukov P., 'Intelligentsiya i istoricheskaya traditsiya', *Intelligentsiya v Rossii. Sbornik statei*, pp. 88–191 (Petersburg: 1910).

Miloradovich K. M., '*Vekhi*', *Zhurnal Ministerstva narodnogo prosveshcheniya*, no. 8, pp. 423–34 (1909).

Minsky N. M., (Vilenkin N. M.), 'Ideya russkoi revolyutsii', *Pereval*, vol. 1, pp. 11–22; vol. 2, pp. 34–47; and vol. 3, pp. 12–26 (1907).

—— 'Intelligentsiya i meshchanstvo', *Na obshchestvennye temy*, pp. 200–5 (Petersburg: 1909).

—— *Na obshchestvennye temy* (Petersburg: 1909) (I).

—— 'Narod i intelligentsiya', *Russkaya mysl'*, no. 9, pp. 99–110 (1909) (II).

—— *Religiya budushchego. Filosofskie razgovory* (Petersburg: 1905).

Mir Bozhii, (to July 1906 and then *Sovremennyi mir*) (Petersburg).

Moskovskie vedemosti (Moscow).

Moskovskii ezhenedel'nik, (1906–10) (Moscow).

Na rubezhe. K kharakteristike sovremmenykh iskanii. Kriticheskii sbornik (Petersburg: 1909).

    (Contributors: L. M—v, A. Deborin, F. D—n, P. Maslov, V. L'vov, D. Kol'tsov, A. Martynov, L. Ortodoks, M. Nevedomsky, A. Potresov).

N. F., '*Vekhi*', *Poltavskie vedemosti*, 6 August 1909.

N. G., 'Literaturnyi dnevik. *Vekhi*', *Odesskie novosti*, 9 and 12 April 1909.

Nich, 'Spor ob intelligentsii', *Golos Moskvy*, 4 February 1910.

Nikolaev, A. A., *Intelligentsiya i narod* (Moscow: 1906).

Niks, 'Da budet ei triumf. Lektsiya K. I. Arabazhina', *Utro Rossii*, 4 February 1910.

Novomirskii D. I., *Chto takoe anarkhizm?* n.p. (1907).

'Novye puti', *Varshavskii dnevnik*, 9 August 1909.

Novyi put', (1903–4 and then *Voprosy zhizni*) (Petersburg).

Obrazovanie (to 1909) (Petersburg).

Ocherki filosofii kollektivizma (Petersburg: 1909).

    (Contributors include: N. Verner, A. Bogdanov, V. Bazarov, A. Lunacharsky, M. Gorky).

Ocherki po filosofii marksizma. Filosofskii sbornik (Petersburg: 1908).

    (Contributors: V. Bazarov, A. Berman, A. Bogdanov, I. Gel'fond, A. Lunacharsky, S. Suvorov, P. Yushkevich).

Ocherki realisticheskogo mirovozzreniya. Sbornik statei po filosofii, obshchestvennoi nauke i zhizni (Petersburg: 1904).

    (Contributors: S. Suvorov, A. Lunacharsky, V. Bazarov, A. Bogdanov, A. Finn, P. Maslov, P. Rumyantsev, N. Korsak, V. Shulyatikov, V. Friche).

Olenin R., 'Krest'yane i intelligentsiya. K kharakhteristike osvoboditel'nogo dvizheniya v Malorosii', *Russkoe bogatstvo*, nos. 1 and 2 (1907).

Olenov M., *Ideologiya russkogo burzhua. O starom i novom idealizme* (Petersburg: 1906).

—— *Tak nazyvaemyi 'krizis marksizma'* (Petersburg: 1906).

Om—Ber, *K 'Vekham'. Iz sovremmenykh nastroenii v oblastii filosofii istorii* (Kiev: 1910).

Oniani V., *Bol'shevistskaya partiya i intelligentsiya v pervoi russkoi revolyutsii* (Tbilisi: 1970).

Or O. L. d', 'Sud nad intelligentsiei. Tyazhelaya drama v 1 deistvii', *Pridneprovskii krai*, 12 May 1909.

O—v N., 'Pyatidesyatiletie *Vekh*', *Mosty*, vol. 3, pp. 279–4 (Munich: 1959).

Ovsyaniko-Kulikovsky D. N., *Istoriya russkoi intelligentsii*, 3 vols. (Petersburg: 1908–11).

—— (ed.), *Istoriya russkoi literatury XIX-go v.*, 5 vols. (Petersburg: 1909).

Pantin I., and Polyakov A., 'O *Vekhakh* i vekhovstve', *Nauka i religiya*, no. 5 (1970).

'Peredovaya stat′ya', *Vilenskii vestnik*, 2 May 1909.

Peshekhonov A., *K voprosu ob intelligentsii* (Petersburg: 1906).

—— 'Novy pokhod protiv intelligentsii', *Russkoe bogatstvo*, no. 4, pp. 100–26 (1909) (I).

—— 'Svobodnaya kooperatsiya', *Kievskie vesti*, 30 April 1909 (II).

—— *V temnuyu noch. Sbornik statei* (III) (Petersburg: 1909).

Petrov G., 'Knutom po pristyazhnoi', *Yuzhnyi krai*, Khar′kov, 9 February 1910.

—— 'Obvinennye sud′i' *Russkoe slovo*, 17 May 1909.

Plekhanov G. V., *Izbrannye filosofskie proizvedeniya v pyati tomakh*, vol. 3 (Moscow: 1957).

—— *Osnovnye voprosy marksizma* (Petersburg: 1908).

—— 'O tak nazyvaemykh religioznykh iskaniyakh v Rossii', *Sovremennyi mir*, no. 9, pp. 182–216; no. 10, pp. 164–200 and no. 12, pp. 167–201 (1909).

—— *Ot oborony k napadeniyu* (Moscow: 1910).

Poltoratzky N., '*Vekhi* i russkaya intelligentsiya', *Mosty*, vol. 10, pp. 292–304 (Munich: 1963).

Polyarnaya zvezda, (Petersburg: 1905–6).

Potresov A. N., *Etyudy o russkoi intelligentsii. Sbornik statei* (Petersburg: 1906).

Pravda (Moscow: 1904–6).

Problemy idealizma. Sbornik statei (Moscow: 1902).
    (Contributors: S. N. Bulgakov, Kn. E. N. Trubetskoi, P. G. (P. Struve), N. A. Berdyaev, S. L. Frank, S. A. Askol′dov, Kn. S. N. Trubetskoi, P. I. Novgorodtsev, B. A. Kistyakovsky, A. S. Lappo-Danilevsky, S. Ol′denburg, D. E. Zhukovsky).

Protiv techeniya (Moscow: February to May 1907 only).

'Referat o *Vekhakh*', *Kaspii*, 22 September 1909.

Rozanov V. V., *Kogda nachal′stvo ushlo 1905–1906* (Petersburg: 1910).

—— 'Merezhkovskii protiv *Vekh*', *Novoe vremya*, 27 April 1909.

—— 'Mezhdu Azefom i *Vekhami*', *Novoe vremya*, 20 August 1909.

Rozhkov N., 'Znachenie i sud′by noveishogo idealizma v Rossii. Po povodu knigi *Problemy idealizma*', *Voprosy filosofii i psikhologii*, no. 2, pp. 314–32 (1903).

Rul', Moscow.

Rum—Vum, 'Chernosotennye *Vekhi*', *Russkoe znamya*, 27 June 1909.

Russkaya mysl' (Moscow).

Russkie vedemosti (Moscow).

Russkoe bogatstvo (Petersburg).

Russkoe slovo (Moscow).

Russkoe znamya (Petersburg: from 1905).

'Sbornik *Vekhi*', *Russkoe slovo*, 15 April 1909.

Severnyi S., '*Vekhi* i Chekhov', *Slovo*, 13 June 1909.

Sh. P., 'Moskva', *Kievskaya mysl'*, 7 February 1910.

Shakovskoi D., Kn., 'Slepye vozhdi slepykh', *Golos*, Yaroslavl', 3 April 1909.

Shchepetev A., 'Kritika marksizma sleva', *Russkaya mysl'*, no. 2, pp. 114–34 (1909).

—— 'Sovremennyi anarkhizm i klassovaya tochka zreniya', *Russkoe bogatstvo*, no. 1, pp. 114–48 (1907).

Shchipanov I. Ya., 'Kritika V. I. Leninim ideologii *Vekh* i sovremennost'', *Vestnik Moskovskogo Universiteta*, filosofiya, no. 2 (Moscow: 1970).

Sh—g L., 'Starye i novye bogoiskateli', *Zaprosy zhizni*, no. 4, pp. 12–16 (1909).

Shtampfer F., 'Religiya-chastnoe delo', in Shtampfer F. and Vandervelde E., *Sotsial-demokratiya i religiya* (Moscow: 1907).

Shulyatikov V., *Opravdanie kapitalizma v zapadno-evropeiskoi filosofii. Ot Dekarta do Makha* (Moscow: 1908).

Skhimnik, 'Geroizm i podviznichestvo', *Sibir'*, Irkutsk, 6 January 1910.

Slovo (Petersburg: 1904–9).

Smena vekh. Sbornik statei (Prague: 1921) (2nd ed., 1922). (Contributors: Yu. V. Klyuchnikov, N. V. Ustryalov, S. S. Luk'yanov, A. V. Bobrishchev-Pushkin, S. S. Chakhotin, Yu. N. Potekhin).

Smert'. *Al'manakh* (Petersburg: 1910). (Contributors include: V. Ivanov, S. Gorodetsky, V. Rozanov, I. Repin).

Sokolov N. M., *Ob ideyakh i idealakh russkoi intelligentsii* (Petersburg: 1904).

Solov'ev B., 'Vekhi ili katekhizis predatel'stva', *Oktyabr'*, no. 12 (1969).

Solzhenitsyn A. I., 'Obrazovanshchina', *Iz-pod glyb. Sbornik statei*, pp. 217–59 (Moscow: 1974).

Sovremennyi mir (from August 1906, formerly *Mir Bozhii*) (Petersburg).

Stolypin A., 'Eshche o *Vekhakh*', *Novoe vremya*, 28 April 1909.

—— 'Intelligenty ob intelligentakh', *Novoe vremya*, 23 April 1909.

Struve P. B., *Idei i politika v sovremennoi Rossii* (Moscow: 1907).

—— 'Istoricheskii smysl russkoi revolyutsii i natsional'nye zadachi', *Iz glubiny*, pp. 285–306 (Paris: 1967).

—— 'K kharakteristike nashego filosofskogo razvitiya', *Problemy idealizma*, pp. 72–90 (Moscow: 1902).

—— 'Konservatizm intelligentskoi mysli. Iz razmyshlenii o russkoi revoluytsii', *Russkaya mysl'*, no. 7, pp. 172–8 (1907).

—— 'Liberalizm i tak nazyvaemye "revolyutsionnye napravleniya", *Osvobozhdenie*, no. 7, pp. 104–5 (1902).

—— 'Otvet arkhiepiskopy Antoniyu', *Slovo*, 10 May 1909 (I).

—— Preface to N. A. Berdyaev, *Sub"ektivizm i individualizm* (1901), Berdyaev (1901) (II).

—— 'Religiya i sotsializm', *Russkaya mysl'*, no. 8, pp. 148–56 (1909) (II).

—— and Frank S. L., 'Ocherki filosofii kul'tury', *Polyarnaya zvezda*, no. 2, pp. 104–17, and no. 3, pp. 170–84 (1905).

Syrkin L. N., *Makhaevshchina* (Moscow–Leningrad: 1931).

T—n S., 'Intelligentsiya i *Vekhi*', *Kievskie vesti*, 12 December 1909.

Tolstoy L. N. See 'L. N. Tolstoy o sbornike *Vekhi*', and 'L. N. Tolstoy o *Vekhakh*', *Russkoe slovo*, 12 and 21 May 1909.

—— 'O *Vekhakh*', *Polnoe sobranie sochinenii*, vol. 38 pp. 285–90 (Moscow: 1936).

Trotsky L. (Takhotsky L., pseud.), *Gospodin Petr Struve v politike* (Petersburg: 1906).

Trubetskoi E. N., Kn., '*Vekhi* i ikh kritiki', *Moskovskii ezhenedel'nik*, no. 23, pp. 1–18, 13 June 1909.

Tugan-Baranovsky M. I., 'Chto takoe obshchestvennyi klass?', *Mir Bozhii*, no. 1, pp. 64–72 (1904).

Valentinov N., *Dva goda s simvolistami* (Stanford, California: 1969).

—— *Filosofskie postroeniya marksizma. Dialekticheskii materializm, empiriomonizm, i empiriokriticheskaya filosofiya* (Moscow: 1907).

—— 'Eshche o *Vekhakh*', *Kievskaya mysl'*, 14 May 1909 (I).

—— '*Vekhi*', *Kievskaya mysl'*, 19 and 22 April 1909 (II).

Vandervelde E., *Idealizm v marksizme. S predisloviem V. Chernova* (Nizhnii Novgorod: 1905).

Vekhi. Sbornik statei o russkoi intelligentsii 2nd ed. (Moscow: 1909).
(Contributors: N. A. Berdyaev, S. N. Bulgakov, M. O. Gershenzon (ed.), A. S. Izgoev, V. A. Kistyakovsky, P. B. Struve, S. I. Frank).

'Vekhi' kak znamenie vremeni (Moscow: 1910).
(Contributors: V. Chernov, A. Ayksent'ev, I. Brusilovsky, L. Shishko, N. Rakitnikov, M. Ratner).

Vengerov S., 'Literaturnoe nastroenie v 1909', *Russkie vedemosti*, 1 January 1910.

Vershiny, Literaturno-kriticheskii i filosofsko-publitsisticheskii sbornik (Petersburg: 1909).
(Contributors include: I. Bunin, A. Lunacharsky, M. Morozov, P. Berlin, St. Ivanovich, L. Martov, V. Bazarov, P. Yushkevich, M. Nevedomskii).

Vesy (Moscow: 1904–9).

Volkov L., 'Novaya religioznost' i neo-natsionalizm', *Moskovskie vedemosti*, nos. 249 and 250, 30 and 31 October 1909.

Vol'nyi, 'Grekh intelligentsii', *Grazhdanin*, nos. 51 and 52 (1909).

Vol'skii A.: See under Machajski J. W.

Volynsky A. (Flekser A. L.), *Bor'ba za idealizm* (Petersburg: 1900).

—— *Borets za idealizm* (Riga: 1902).

Voprosy filosofii i psikhologii (Moscow).

Voprosy religii. Sbornik, vol. 1 (Moscow: 1906); vol. 2 (Moscow: 1908).
(Contributors include: S. N. Bulgakov, N. A. Berdyaev, V. P. Sventsitsky, V. Ern, P. Florensky, A. Askol'dov).

Voprosy zhizni, (formerly *Novyi put'* (Petersburg) (1904–5).

Vorovsky V., *Literaturno-kriticheskie stat'i* (Moscow: 1956).

—— 'O burzhuaznosti modernistov', *Odesskoe obozrenie*, 10–11 May 1908.

—— *Russkaya intelligentsiya i russkaya literatura* (Khar'kov: 1923).

Vozrozhdenie (Moscow) (1908–10).

V zashchitu intelligentsii. Sbornik statei (Petersburg: 1909).
(Contributors: F. Muskatblit, K. Arsen'ev, N. Iordanskii, M. Bikerman, D. Levin, I. Ignotov, N. Valentinov, G. Petrov, P. Boborykin, N. Gekker, V. Botsyanovskii).

Yakovlev A., 'Protiv antiistoritsizma', *Literaturnaya gazeta*, no. 46, pp. 4–5, 15 November 1972.

Yushkevich P., 'I. Ditsgen', *Obrazovanie*, no. 9, pp. 69–89 (1907) (I).

—— *Materializm i kriticheskii realizm. O filosofskikh napravleniyakh v marksizme* (Petersburg: 1908).

Yushkevich P., *O materialisticheskom ponimanii istorii* (Moscow: 1907) (II).

Yuzhnyi I., 'Doklad Yu. V. Portugalova', *Orenburgskii krai*, 13 December 1909.

Zaitsev D., 'Marksizm i makhaevshchina', *Obrazovanie*, no. 3, pp. 35–71 (1908).

Zakrzhevsky A., *Religiya. Psikhologicheskie paralleli* (Kiev: 1913).

Zaprosy zhizni (Petersburg) (1909–12).

Zasulich V., *Elementy idealizma v sotsializme* (Petersburg: 1906).

—— *Revolyutsionery iz burzhuaznoi sredy* (Petrograd: 1921).

Zetkin K., *Intelligentnyi proletariat, zhenskii vopros i sotsializm* (Odessa: 1906).

Zhurnal Ministerstva narodnogo prosveshcheniya (Petersburg).

Zolotoe runo (Moscow) (1906–9).

B. WORKS IN OTHER LANGUAGES.

Agostino, A. D., 'Intelligentsia Socialism and the Workers' Revolution: the views of J. W. Machajski', *International Review of Social History*, vol. XIV (1969).

Baron, S. H., *Plekhanov: the father of Russian Marxism* (London: 1963).

Bedford, C. H., 'Dmitri Merzhkovsky, the Intelligentsia and the Revolution of 1905', *Canadian Slavonic Papers*, vol. III, pp. 27–42 (1958).

—— 'Dmitri Merezhkovsky, the Third Testament and the Third Humanity', *Slavonic and East European Review*, vol. XLII, no. 98, pp. 144–60 (December 1963).

Berdyaev, N., *The Origin of Russian Communism* (Ann Arbor, Michigan: 1960).

Billington, J. H., *The Icon and the Axe: an Interpretive History of Russian Culture* (London: 1966).

Brooks, J., ' "Vekhi" and the Vekhi Dispute', *Survey*, vol. 19, no. 1, (89), pp. 21–50 (1971).

Dahm, H., 'Die russische philosophie von Solovev bis Sestov: Zur revision eines sowjetischen Tabus', *Berichte*, no. 46 (Köln: 1969).

Fischer, G., *Russian Liberalism: from Gentry to Intelligentsia* (Cambridge, Mass.: 1958).

—— 'The Intelligentsia and Russia', in C. E. Black, (ed.), *The Transformation of Russian Society: Aspects of Social Change since*

1861, pp. 253–74 (Cambridge, Mass.: 1960).

—— 'The Russian Intelligentsia', *Harvard Slavonic Studies*, vol. IV, pp. 317–36 (1957).

Florovsky G., 'Michael Gerschensohn', *Slavonic and East European Review*, vol. V., no. 14, pp. 315–31 (December 1926).

Frank S. L., 'Contemporary Russian Philosophy', *The Monist*, vol. 37, no. 1, pp. 1–25 (Chicago: January 1927).

Grover S. R., 'The World of Art Movement in Russia', *Russian Review*, vol. 32, no. 1, pp. 28–46, January 1973.

Haimson L., *The Russian Marxists and the Origins of Bolshevism* (Cambridge, Mass.: 1955).

Kelly A., *Attitudes to the Individual in Russian Thought and Literature with Special Reference to the 'Vekhi' Controversy*, unpublished. D.Phil. thesis, Oxford, 1970.

Kline G. L., ' "Nietzschean Marxism" in Russia', *Boston College Studies in Philosophy*, vol. II, pp. 113–56 (The Hague: 1969).

—— *Religious and Anti-Religious Thought in Russia* (Chicago: 1968).

Levin A., 'M. O. Gershenzon and Vekhi', *Canadian Slavic Studies*, vol. 4, no. 1, pp. 60–75 (1970).

Lossky N., *History of Russian Philosophy* (London: 1952).

Lowrie D. A., *Rebellious Prophet: a Life of Nicolai Berdyayev* (London: 1960).

Maximoff G. P. (ed.), *The Political Philosophy of Bakunun. Scientific Anarchism* (New York: 1953).

Merezhkovsky D., Gippuis Z. and Filosofov D., *Le Tsar et la Revolution* (Paris: 1907) (I).

Moser C., *Antinihilism in the Russian Novel of the 1860s* (The Hague: 1964).

Oberlander G., *Die Vechi-Diskussion (1909–1912)* (Köln: 1965).

Pascal P., 'Les Grands Courants de la Pensée Russe Contemporaine', *Cahiers du Monde Russe et Soviètique*, vol. 3 (Paris: 1962).

Pipes R. (ed.), *The Russian Intelligentsia* (New York: 1961).

—— *Struve: Liberal on the Left* (Cambridge, Mass.: 1970).

Pollard A. P., 'The Russian Intelligentsia. The Mind of Russia', *California Slavic Studies*, vol. III, pp. 1–33 (Berkeley, Los Angeles: 1964).

Poltoratzky N., 'Lev Tolstoy and Vekhi', *Slavonic and East European Review*, vol. XLII, no. 99, pp. 332–5 (June 1964).

—— 'The *Vekhi* Dispute and the Significance of *Vekhi*', *Canadian Slavonic Papers*, vol. IX, no. 1, pp. 86–106 (1967).

Putnam G., 'P. B. Struve's View of the Russian Revolution of 1905', *Slavonic and East European Review*, vol. XLV, no. 105, pp. 451–73 (July 1967).

Scanlan J. P., 'The New Religious Consciousness. Merezhkovskii and Berdiaev', *Canadian Slavic Studies*, vol. 4, no. 1, pp. 17–35 (Spring 1970).

Schapiro L. B., *The Communist Party of the Soviet Union*, 2nd ed. (London: 1970).

—— 'The *Vekhi* Group and the Mystique of Revolution', *Slavonic and East European Review*, vol. XXXIV, no. 82, pp. 56–76 (December 1955).

Seliber N., 'La Philosophie Russe Contemporaine', *Revue Philosophique*, no. 74, pp. 27–64 and 243–75 (Paris: 1912).

Shatz M. S., 'The Makhaevists and the Russian Revolutionary Movement', *International Review of Social History*, vol. XV (1970).

Struve N., *Christians in Contemporary Russia* (London: 1967).

Tompkins, S. R., *The Russian Intelligentsia* (Norman, Oklahoma: 1957).

—— '*Vekhi* and the Russian Intelligentsia', *Canadian Slavonic Papers*, vol. II, pp. 11–25 (1957).

Valentinov N., *Encounters with Lenin* (London: 1968).

Venturi F., *Roots of Revolution: a History of the Populist and Socialist Movements in Nineteenth Century Russia* (London: 1960).

West J., *Russian Symbolism: a Study of Vyacheslav Ivanov and the Russian Symbolist Aesthetic* (London: 1970).

Wetter G., *Dialectical Materialism* (London: 1958).

White J. D., 'The First *Pravda* and the Russian Marxist Tradition', *Soviet Studies*, vol. XXVI, no. 2, pp. 181–204 (April 1974).

Zenkovsky V. V., *History of Russian Philosophy*, 2 vols. (London: 1953).

Zernov N., *The Russian Religious Renaissance of the Twentieth Century* (London: 1963).

Index

217

Volynsky A. L., see Flekser
Voprosy kultury (Problems of Culture), 22
Voprosy zhizni (Problems of Life), 22, 31, 34, 63, 68, 122, 135
  editors of, 65
Vorovsky V. V., 145, 152–4

Yakovlev A., 172–3

Yushkevich P., 47–8, 155–6
Materializm i kriticheskii realizm (Materialism and Critical Realism), 41

Znanie (Knowledge), 35, 87
Zolotoe runo (Golden Fleece), 30, 33, 34–5
  circulation of, 7